8 ,+2'

ch 4

175-176

THE LAW OF
HABEAS CORPUS

The Law of
Habeas Corpus

Second Edition

R. J. SHARPE

CLARENDON PRESS · OXFORD
1989

Oxford University Press, Walton Street, Oxford OX2 6DP
Oxford New York Toronto
Delhi Bombay Calcutta Madras Karachi
Petaling Jaya Singapore Hong Kong Tokyo
Nairobi Dar es Salaam Cape Town
Melbourne Auckland
and associated companies in
Berlin Ibadan

Oxford is a trade mark of Oxford University Press

Published in the United States
by Oxford University Press, New York

© R. J. Sharpe 1989

British Library Cataloguing in Publication Data
Sharpe, R. J. (Robert)
The law of habeas corpus. – 2nd. ed.
1. England. Habeas corpus. Law
I. Title
344.205'56
ISBN 0–19–825404–0

Library of Congress Cataloging in Publication Data
Sharpe, R. J. (Robert J.)
The law of habeas corpus / R. J. Sharpe.—2nd ed.
Includes bibliographical references and index.
1. Habeas corpus—Great Britain. I. Title.
KD7612.S45   1989   345.41'056—dc20   [344.105 56]   89–33978
ISBN 0–19–825404–0

Typeset by Footnote Graphics, Warminster, Wilts

Printed and bound in
Great Britain by Biddles Ltd,
Guildford and King's Lynn

Note to Second Edition

I have attempted to canvas all recent developments in relation to the law of habeas corpus while maintaining the structure and organization of the first edition. The most significant changes occur in chapter 3, dealing with the review of questions of fact; chapter 4, considering the review of executive powers; chapter 5, discussing the role of habeas corpus in the criminal law, and chapter 6, examining the review of commitments for compulsory treatment.

In recent years, habeas corpus has been frequently used in immigration cases. While a series of disappointing decisions drastically curtailed the powers of review on habeas corpus, the decision of the House of Lords in *Khawaja* v. *Secretary of State for the Home Department* [1984] A.C. 74 fully and properly restores the remedy as an important guarantee of personal liberty. This positive approach has been paralleled on various aspects of the writ by a number of decisions in Canada where habeas corpus is now firmly entrenched in the Charter of Rights and Freedoms. Having assessed these recent developments, I restate with increased assurance my conclusion from the first edition, namely, that habeas corpus is a versatile and flexible remedy, properly seen as a fundamental constitutional guarantee and a cornerstone of the rule of law.

Preface

This book is an attempt to present a comprehensive and critical account of the law of habeas corpus. It may be divided into three parts. The first, one chapter in length, provides an historical introduction, briefly tracing the development of the writ from its origins to the seventeenth century when it took its modern form. The next five chapters all deal with various aspects of the nature of review which is available on habeas corpus. They aim to rationalize and to explain the various historical, constitutional, and sometimes accidental factors which define the possibilities for review. The final four chapters deal with certain rather more technical and procedural considerations peculiar to habeas corpus. In the pages that follow, I conclude that habeas corpus is a versatile and flexible remedy. The writ still has significant day-to-day uses, and is properly seen as a fundamental constitutional guarantee and a cornerstone of the rule of law.

While the book focuses on the law of England, there are extensive references to Australian, Canadian and New Zealand authorities. Only a few American authorities are discussed. The American use of the writ as a post-conviction remedy contrasts markedly with the English practice. Consequently, the principles of review and even the more technical aspects of the writ in the United States are moulded by quite different considerations than those operating in England and the Commonwealth.

The book is a somewhat revised version of my thesis submitted for the D.Phil. degree at Oxford University in 1973. I wish to express my thanks to Professor H. W. R. Wade, Q.C. who suggested habeas corpus as my thesis topic and who acted as my supervisor for one term. I am especially grateful to Dr. Ian Brownlie, my supervisor for the balance of my time at Oxford, who provided me with the guidance and encouragement I needed to see the project through. I am also indebted to David A. Lawson, a fellow doctoral student, who read various drafts of the thesis and gave me many valuable suggestions. I am grateful for the assistance given by the Carswell-Sweet & Maxwell Scholarship and by the Canada Council during my time at Oxford.

ROBERT J. SHARPE
Toronto
March, 1976

Contents

1

Historical Aspects of Habeas Corpus

1. INTRODUCTION

This chapter represents an attempt briefly to trace the historical development of the writ of habeas corpus.[1] Dealing with any aspect of habeas corpus almost inevitably involves the history of the writ. One is very often sent to the early reports to explain the law on any given point and consequently, bits of legal history are found throughout the book. The purpose of this first chapter is merely to trace the broad lines of development through the medieval period to the seventeenth century when the writ took its modern form.

In the discussion which follows, emphasis has been placed on the use of habeas corpus to combat executive committals in the sixteenth and seventeenth centuries. The lessons of this period continue to have great constitutional significance to the present day. It was then that the writ took its modern form, and then that it gained its place as a fundamental part of the British constitution.

2. MEDIEVAL PERIOD

(a) *Origins of the Writ*

By the early part of the thirteenth century, the words 'habeas corpus' were a familiar formula in the language of civil procedure,[2] and it is

---

[1] There are several accounts of the early history of habeas corpus. Hereafter, they are cited by author: Cohen, 'Some Considerations on the Origins of Habeas Corpus' (1938) 16 Can. Bar Rev. 93; Cohen, 'Habeas Corpus Cum Causa—The Emergence of the Modern Writ' (1940) 18 Can. Bar Rev. 10, 172; Fox, 'The Process of Imprisonment at Common Law' (1923) 39 L.Q.R. 46; 6, 9 Holdsworth, *A History of English Law* (7th ed. 1956), 108–25; Jenks, 'The Story of Habeas Corpus' vol. ii, *Select Essays in Anglo–American Legal History*, 531 (reprinted from (1902) 18 L.Q.R. 64); Relf, *The Petition of Right* (1917); Walker, *The Constitutional and Legal Development of Habeas Corpus as the Writ of Liberty* (1960); Duker, 'The English Origins of the Writ of Habeas Corpus: A Peculiar Path to Fame' (1978) 53 N.Y.U.L.R. 983; Duker, *A Constitutional History of Habeas Corpus* (1980).

[2] There are examples from 1214; *Select Pleas of the Crown* (Selden Soc., vol. 1), 67; and 1220: VIII *Curia Regis Rolls* 308.

likely that the phrase first appeared much earlier. The words simply represented a command, issued as a means or interlocutory process, to have the defendant to an action brought physically before the court.[3] The idea of producing the body with the cause of the detention was not present. In fact, there usually had been no detention at all,[4] and the purpose of the process was to order an officer to bring in the defendant, and not at all to subject the cause of a detention to the court's scrutiny. It has even been said that the early use of habeas corpus was to put people in gaol rather than to get them out,[5] but this seems to have been a mistaken impression. Habeas corpus was used not to arrest and imprison, but to ensure the physical presence of a person in court on a certain day.[6]

There is some indication that 'habeas corpus' was also used to signify a command to the sheriff to bring a person accused of crime before the court.[7] Again, this seems to have been merely one way to have the party physically brought in to face the charges where other methods had failed.[8]

The words 'habeas corpus' at this early stage were not connected with the idea of liberty, and the process involved an element of the

---

[3] The law required that short of outlawry the defendant had to be actually present in court before a final determination in a personal action could be made: II Pollock & Maitland, 591–4. Habeas corpus was one of the methods described by Bracton in his discussion of the normal process of compulsion available to bring the defendant before the court: ibid. 593, citing Bracton, *De Legibus et Consuetudinibus Angliae*, fols. 439–41. For a thirteenth-century example, see *Select Cases in the Exchequer of Pleas* (Selden Soc., vol. 48), xlvi, xxxiii, lvii. The focus in this chapter is on the cum causa form of the writ which came to be known as habeas corpus ad subjiciendum. Other forms of habeas corpus also developed (ad respondendum, ad satisfaciendum, ad prosequendum, ad testificandum, ad deliberandum, ad faciendum et recipiendum), but these are not significant in modern times, although cf. the attempt to use habeas corpus ad respondendum in *R.* v. *Governor of Brixton Prison, ex p. Walsh* [1985] A.C. 154. For discussion of these forms of the writ see 3 Blackstone, *Commentaries on the Laws of England*, at 129–30.

[4] II Pollock & Maitland, *The History of English Law* (2nd ed. 1952), 593. For an example of its use in this context where the prisoner was in custody, see (1388) Y.B. 2 Rich. II (*Ames Foundation*) 244.

[5] Jenks.

[6] Fox pointed out, correctly it would seem, that Jenks was wrong in thinking that habeas corpus served the same function as capias. Habeas corpus was used only in suits where force was not alleged; capias was used in others at the same stage of the proceedings. Jenks was apparently unaware of this, and when he failed to find examples of habeas corpus during the fourteenth century, but continued to find capias, he concluded that the two were interchangeable.

[7] *Tyrell* (1214) *Select Pleas of the Crown* (Selden Soc., vol. 1), 67; (1328) *Select Cases in the Court of King's Bench, Edw. III*, vol. v (Selden Soc., vol. 76), 24–5.

[8] Cohen, 16 Can. Bar Rev., 109–10.

concept of due process of law only in so far as it mirrored the refusal of the courts to decide a matter without having the defendant present.[9]

The earliest traces of habeas corpus, then, appear to be its use as an interlocutory process rather than an originating proceeding, really little more than an expression which appears from time to time in other proceedings. It was undoubtedly a significant indication of the authority and respect gained by the King's judges that a person could be brought in to justice on their command, but for the association of these words with liberty, further development was required.

(b) *Other Medieval Remedies*[10]

There were three medieval writs which were more closely associated with the idea of liberty than these early forms of habeas corpus: *de homine replegiando*,[11] mainprize,[12] and *de odio et atia*.[13] The first two writs issued out of Chancery and were used to secure release on bail or mainprize pending trial for those prisoners so entitled. The last mentioned writ was available only in certain circumstances to obtain pre-trial release for a prisoner charged with homicide. These writs were all in desuetude by the seventeenth century,[14] and habeas corpus developed quite independently of them.

These medieval writs really differed in a fundamental way from habeas corpus. They were not remedies of general application but special procedures for special situations. While they enabled prisoners

---

[9] Walker, 16.

[10] Useful accounts of these remedies are: 9 Holdsworth, 105–8; II Pollock & Maitland, op. cit. 585–9, I Stephen, *A History of the Criminal Law of England* (1883), 239–42; 3 Bl. *Comm.*, 128–9; II Hale *P.C.*, 141–3, 147; Cohen, 16 Can. Bar Rev., 95–102. There were also writs relating to the liberty of villains. The writ of *de nativo habendo* allowed a lord to assert his right of possession. The villain could forestall proceedings by suing out a writ of *de libertate probanda*, preventing his arrest until the Eyre of the Justices: Fitzherbert, *N.B.*, 77–9.

[11] For example of the writ, see Fitzherbert, *N.B.*, 66–8.

[12] For examples, see ibid. 249–51.

[13] For examples, see (1209) *Pleas Before the King of Justices*, vol. iv (Selden Soc., vol. 84), 212–13; *Fleta* (Selden Soc., vol. 72), 67.

[14] *De homine replegiando* was used as late as 1736; *Trebelock* 1 Atk. 633. In 1758, Wilmot J. suggested that it was still available as an alternative remedy in the case of a false return to habeas corpus: *Opinion* Wilm. 123. With infrequent exception, however, it was out of use after the medieval period: 9 Holdsworth, 106.

Hale said that mainprize 'hath still its use': II Hale *P.C.*, 142, but it too was essentially a medieval remedy. It was refused in *Jenke's Case* (1676) 6 St. Tr. 1190 on the grounds, *inter alia*, that it was not applicable in cases of committal by the Council.

Hale called *de odio et atia* 'a writ much out of use': II Hale *P.C.*, 147, although Coke had argued that it was still extant: 2 *Inst.*, 43, 55, 315.

to obtain release on bail or mainprize, the court did not call for an explanation of the cause of imprisonment so that its legality could be determined as in the case of habeas corpus. The prisoner was simply given a temporary release until the time came for trial. Later on, this could also happen on habeas corpus, where the prisoner was bailed, but the significant aspect of habeas corpus was to be that it brought the matter of the imprisonment fully before the court and provided the possibility for a fundamental and final determination. Most important of all, these medieval writs were not available where the imprisonment was by virtue of the Crown's order, and could not, therefore, be used by the lawyers of the seventeenth century in their contests with the Stuarts,[15] contests which were to establish habeas corpus firmly in the English constitution.

3. HABEAS CORPUS AND THE JURISDICTIONAL CONFLICTS

The cases which arose from the jurisdictional conflicts of the fifteenth and sixteenth centuries mark the transition of the writ of habeas corpus from a device to secure the physical presence of a party to undergo some other process, to an unequivocal demand for the reason for the applicant's detention so that the court could judge the sufficiency of that reason. The modern 'ad subjiciendum' form of the writ, 'to submit' the cause to scrutiny, was emerging.

(a) *Centralization and the Local Courts*

Habeas corpus proved to be a useful device in the struggle for control between the central courts of the crown and the local courts. There can be little doubt that its use in this contest fostered the concept of the writ requiring cause to be shown for the imprisonment. It was directed by the central courts against the local inferior jurisdictions and helped to channel the litigation, and the fees, towards a central administration. As it was important to be able to exert physical control over the parties in civil litigation, and as the ultimate sanction possessed by a court was attachment or committal, habeas corpus could be used to upset the course of litigation, and remove the sting from the efforts of the local courts to enforce their orders. At this

---

[15] See 3 St. Tr. 95.

level, habeas corpus was used by both the courts of common law[16] and by the Chancery[17] in their efforts to centralize the administration of justice.

Initially habeas corpus was used with either certiorari or privilege and sometimes with *audita querela*[18] to remove causes from inferior courts. By the middle of the fifteenth century, the issue of habeas corpus, together with privilege, was a well established way to remove a cause from an inferior court where the defendant could show some special connection with one of the central courts conferring a right to have the case tried there.[19] To protect its own jurisdiction and to rob the inferior court of litigation, the superior court had the defendant brought up and discharged. Perhaps somewhat closer to testing the legality of an imprisonment is the use of habeas corpus with certiorari, again a practice well established by the early 1400s.[20] Here, it was available as a means of discharge from inferior process where it could be shown that the cause was one over which the local court lacked competence. The procedure was a recognized method of chicanery,[21] and the habeas corpus was clearly subsidiary. It does, however, mark an important stage in the development of the idea that habeas corpus should be associated with the concept of testing the legality of cause: here, the idea of testing the capacity of the tribunal which had ordered the detention of the defendant.

There can be little doubt, however, that habeas corpus in its cum causa form was being used for this purpose independently of privilege or certiorari by the mid-fifteenth century, and in 1433 there is a statute[22] referring to the use.[23] Emerging in these cases was the

---

[16] Fitzherbert, *Abridg.* (1577), sub tit. 'Corpus Cum Causa'; *Spencer's Case* (1615) 1 Role 316; *Webb* (1616) 3 Bulst. 214.

[17] *Select Cases in Chancery* (Selden Soc., vol. 10), 8–9, 104–5, 121, all fourteenth-century examples. See also Spence, *Equitable Jurisdiction of the Court of Chancery* (1846), vol. i, 331, 687.

[18] *Quartermaynes* (1456) *Select Cases in the Exchequer Chamber* (Selden Soc., vol. 51), 162.

[19] See, e.g., *De Vine* (1456) O. Bridg. 288; Fitzherbert, *Abridg.* (1577), sub tit. 'Corpus Cum Causa'.

[20] An act in 1414 (2 Hen. V, St. 1, c.2) mentioned habeas corpus and certiorari in this context: cited by Cohen, 18 Can. Bar Rev., 14.

[21] Jenks, 538–9; Cohen, 18 Can. Bar Rev., 15–16 gives references to legislation from 1554 to 1614 to curb the practice.

[22] Hen. VI, c.10; cited by Cohen, 18 Can. Bar Rev., 15.

[23] For examples, see Fitzherbert, *Abridg.* (1577), sub tit. 'Corpus Cum Causa'; *Select Cases in the Exchequer Chamber*, vol. 2 (Selden Soc., vol. 64), 75, 76, 82. Habeas corpus continued to be used for this purpose well into the nineteenth century: *infra*, p. 161.

concept that habeas corpus required a cause to be shown for the imprisonment, and that the legality of the cause could be tested. The motives were practical: the central courts sought a method to spread their control. At the same time, however, habeas corpus was becoming less and less an ancillary procedure to obtain someone's physical presence, and more and more a remedy to secure release from imprisonment.

(b) *The Struggle Between Common Law and Equity*

Habeas corpus became one of the principal weapons in the struggle between common law and equity. At this level, the fact that the Court of Chancery also had the power to issue the writ meant that the same weapon was available to both sides. While the common law courts did make more use of habeas corpus, there is at least one case in the reports to show that the Court of Chancery also used the writ to interrupt the process of the King's Bench.[24]

Chancery's chief device to control common law litigation was, however, the injunction, and very early on, in 1482, the King's Bench made it clear that if the Chancellor used the power to grant injunctions to prevent litigants from suing at common law, habeas corpus would be available to release a suitor committed for breach of such an injunction.[25] As well as trying to enjoin suits altogether, Chancery often granted injunctions to restrain the enforcement of a common law judgment which violated the principles of equity, and the common law courts fought back by releasing on habeas corpus anyone committed for breach of an injunction.[26]

There are also examples of habeas corpus being used to protect the proceedings at law against interference from the Court of Requests,[27]

---

[24] *Carie and Denis* (1589) 1 Leon. 145.

[25] *Russell's Case* Y.B. 22 Edw. IV, 37, cited in Pound and Plucknett, *Readings on the History and System of the Common Law* (3rd ed. 1927), 197.

[26] A good example is *Glanvile's Case* (1614) Moore K.B. 838, where the Chancellor attempted to relieve against the common law judgment by issuing an injunction to restrain execution except upon equitable terms. The plaintiff was committed and then released on habeas corpus, Lord Coke holding that it was improper to go to Chancery after judgment at law. The power of the Chancellor to grant such injunctions was upheld in the end: 1 Holdsworth, 461–5. For other examples of this use of habeas corpus, see *R. v. Dr. Gouge* (1615) 3 Bulst. 115; *Apsley* (1615) 1 Rolle 192; *Anon* (1619) 1 Cro. Car. 580. An unusual case is *Blackwell* (1626) Benloe 301, 307 where habeas corpus *de bene esse* was given to a litigant who feared that he was going to be imprisoned by Chancery for contempt.

[27] *Humfrey* (1571) Dal. 82.

and of its use by the King's Bench and Common Pleas against the Admiralty.[28]

(c) *High Commission Cases*

The cases of the early years of the seventeenth century generally indicate a growing acceptance of habeas corpus as a device to test the legality of commitments, and in particular, there are numerous cases of prisoners being discharged or bailed having been committed by the High Commission.[29] Relief was awarded if the return failed to show a good cause for the imprisonment, and the courts were plainly not willing to accept the returns which did not make manifest that all had been within the powers conferred by law.

The High Commission cases particularly demonstrate the effectiveness of the writ where an attack was mounted against the jurisdiction of the tribunal ordering the committal.

In one case, Lord Coke C.J. demonstrated the fervour of the common lawyers' desire to control this extraordinary tribunal by saying: 'By the law of God, none ought to be imprisoned but with the cause expressed in the return of his imprisonment, as appeareth in the Acts of the Apostles.'[30]

4. HABEAS CORPUS AND EXECUTIVE COMMITTALS

(a) *Sixteenth Century and the Resolution of 1592*

Perhaps the most significant development in the law of habeas corpus came with its use to test the validity of executive committals. By the time of Elizabeth, it was becoming clear that the claim to a power to commit for reasons of state could be tested on habeas corpus. There are cases as early as 1567 in which habeas corpus was used by persons detained by order of the Privy Council to obtain their release on bail.[31] Before that, in 1560, habeas corpus had figured in a dispute over the prerogative to appoint a court officer,[32] and by 1587, in *Searche's*

---

[28] *Thomlinson* (1604) 12 Co. Rep. 104; *Scadding* (1608) Yelv. 134; *Hawkeridge* (1616) 12 Co. Rep. 129.
[29] See esp. *Hinde* (1576) 4 Leon. 21; *Roper* (1607) 12 Co. Rep. 45; *Throgmorton* (1610) 12 Co. Rep. 69; *Chancey* (1611) 12 Co. Rep. 82; *Bradstone* v. *High Commission* (1613) 2 Bulst. 300; *Hodd* v. *High Commission Court* (1615) 3 Bulst. 146; *Codd* v. *Turback* (1615) 3 Bulst. 109.
[30] *Codd* v. *Turback* (1615) 3 Bulst. 109.
[31] Cases collected at Moore K.B. 838.
[32] *Skrogges* v. *Coleshil* (1560) 2 Dyer 175a.

Case[33] and *Howel's Case*,[34] it was shown to be a remedy fit to challenge the authority of the crown. In the latter case, it was held that a commitment by the hand of one Privy Councillor was insufficient where no cause was shown, although the court added, by way of dictum, that such a committal by the whole Council would be upheld.

There are numerous other instances of prisoners of state being discharged or bailed on habeas corpus,[35] and by 1592, the practice was sufficiently troublesome to the Council to warrant a request that the judges state the principles upon which such prisoners were to be delivered. The judges resolved as follows:

> We think that if any person be committed by Her Majesty's commandment from her Person, or by order from the Councilboard, or if any one or two of her Council commit one for high treason such persons so in the case before committed may not be delivered by any of her Courts without due tryal by the law, and Judgment of acquittal, had.
>
> Nevertheless the Judges may award the Queen's Writs to bring the bodies of such persons before them, and if upon return thereof the causes of their commitment be certified to the Judges as it ought to be, then the Judges in the cases before ought not to deliver him, but to remand the prisoner to the place from whence he came, Which cannot conveniently be done unless notice of the cause in generality or else specially be given to the keeper or gaoler that shall have the custody of such prisoner.[36]

The statement is ambiguous. It suggests, on the one hand, that the sovereign and Council do have the power to commit pending trial without specifying the cause in the first instance, but on the other hand, it allows for the inference that if the cause be not specified, the judges do have the power to bail or discharge on habeas corpus.

The assumption underlying the *Resolution* was that legal charges would be brought against the prisoners and it was, perhaps, for this reason that the judges said that there should not be release on habeas corpus without trial. While this does indicate a certain tolerance for uncertain causes of committal, the *Resolution* did make it clear that habeas corpus was not to be precluded simply because an executive committal was involved, and there is, nascent, the idea of the writ requiring substantive legal justification for the imprisonment in all cases.

[33] 1 Leon. 70.   [34] Ibid.

[35] *Peter* (1586) 3 Leon. 194; *Hellyard* (1586) 2 Leon. 175; and see cases collected at Moore K.B. 838.

[36] And. 297. It seems generally accepted that Anderson's version of the *Resolution* is the accurate one, although there are others: 5 Holdsworth, App. 1. 495.

(b) *Early Stuart Period*

While the cases of the first part of the seventeenth century for the most part indicated a general acceptance that habeas corpus would always be available to test the legality of imprisonment, in their treatment of challenges to the executive or prerogative power, the courts began to show a certain lack of confidence. In one case,[37] a prisoner committed by the Council for contempt was bailed where the court was not satisfied that the behaviour had been contemptuous, but this was an exception. In 1610[38] the court had to take time to consider the case of *Addis* who had been detained by order of the Chancellor 'for certain matters concerning the King', as it was said to be the first time that exception had been taken to the generality of such a return. Unfortunately, there does not appear to have been a decision, but the case is indicative of judicial reluctance to become involved in matters of state. Indeed, even Lord Coke, one of the draftsmen of the Petition of Right, was hesitant. In 1614[39] he held that a prisoner was not bailable if committed by the Council, and again in 1615, in two separate cases[40] Coke refused to bail prisoners committed by the Council. It gradually became clear that the power to commit prisoners of state was being abused. The issue came to a head on an application for habeas corpus.[41]

(c) *Darnel's Case and the Petition of Right*

Darnel's Case, 1627,[42] was a case of major constitutional importance, and one which illustrates the extent of the development of habeas corpus by the early seventeenth century. It involved the clash between the Stuart claims of prerogative and the common law, and was, in the words of one of the judges, 'the greatest cause that I ever knew in this

[37] *Chambers' Case* (1628) Cro. Car. 133. Cf. *Chambers* (1628) Cro. Car. 168, where a similar committal by the Star Chamber, held to be 'one of the Courts of Justice', was upheld.

[38] Cro. Jac. 219.

[39] *Les Bruers' Case* 1 Rolle 134.

[40] *Ruswell* 1 Rolle 193; *Salkingstowe* 1 Rolle 219. *Ruswell* would seem to be the case which was cited in Parliament, much to Coke's embarrassment, fifteen years later, during the debate on the Petition of Right: 3 St. Tr. 81–2. Coke then repudiated the decision, saying that he had since looked further into the matter, and, invoking a novel qualification on stare decisis, that the decision need not be followed as it was not yet twenty-one years old.

[41] Walker, 44, 65 refers to unsuccessful Parliamentary bills to tackle the problem in 1593 and in 1621.

[42] 3 St. Tr. 1 (often referred to as *The Five Knights' Case*).

court'.[43] The fact that such a dispute could be raised on habeas corpus demonstrates that it had truly become, as Selden said, 'the highest remedy in law for any man that is imprisoned'.[44]

The facts of the case are, perhaps, well known and may be stated briefly. Charles I had resorted to a forced loan in an effort to raise revenue without Parliamentary sanction, and his agents had detained a number of subjects who refused to contribute. Of those detained,[45] five sought their freedom by way of habeas corpus. It is very likely that they intended to test the legality of the whole scheme of the forced loan, but the returns to the writs of habeas corpus simply stated that they were detained *'per speciale mandatum domini regis'*.[46] The case turned quite simply on whether that statement, or lack of statement, of the cause for committal entitled the court to bail the prisoners. The arguments were fully put in the King's Bench, and again, in even greater detail, in the Parliamentary proceedings which led to the Petition of Right. The central issue which reappeared at each stage of the argument was whether the court had to take it on good faith that there was substantive legal justification for the imprisonment, or whether the failure to disclose the grounds for the detention itself entitled the prisoners to be bailed until they were brought to trial. In other words, did the King possess a power which superseded the common law adjudicatory process, or was he always subject to a supervisory judicial power to inquire whether his actions complied with the law?

(i) *The Arguments.* Counsel for the prisoners placed great reliance on Magna Carta, and on statutes from the time of Edward III[47] which were said to confirm it and to define the concept of due process of law. How, it was asked, could the imprisonment be justified in the face of chapter 29 of the Great Charter: *'nullus liber homo capiatur vel imprisonatur ... nisi ... per legem terrae.'*[48] The Attorney-General's

---

[43] Ibid., at 31 per Doderidge J.

[44] 3 St. Tr. at 95.

[45] There were many more than five detained: Gardiner, *History of England, 1603–42*, vol. 6, 225, says that when the King ordered the release of these prisoners in January, 1628, seventy-six were freed or returned from banishment.

[46] There is some speculation that the judges may have been called in to advise how to frame the return so as to evade the question of the legality of the forced loan: Relf, 2–3.

[47] 25 Edw. III, c.4; c.9; 28 Edw. III, c.3; 36 Edw. III, Rot. Parl. no. 9 & 20; 42 Edw. III, c.3.

[48] The translation of the whole article given in 6 *Halsbury's Statutes* (3rd ed.), 404: 'No freeman shall be taken or imprisoned, or be disseised of his freehold, or liberties, or

answer was simple. Magna Carta did not define '*legem terrae*', and to rely on that phrase was mere question-begging. He insisted that the Charter had not impinged upon the prerogative of the King, a part of the law of the land, and that chapter 29 did not limit detentions to cases following conviction according to the course of law.[49]

There can be little doubt that the sovereign had long exercised a power of arbitrary committal where there was thought to be a threat to the safety of the realm.[50]

However, the cases[51] which were cited did not reveal an entirely clear picture. Some of the early cases tended to support the prisoners' case,[52] but the later ones probably favoured the Crown.[53] It seems to have been accepted that the cases could be divided into two categories. There were those where the return showed a committal by the King or Council, but specified the matter of the committal, and there were others where the return was general as in the case at bar. In the former, there was no doubt that the courts had bailed prisoners if the offence disclosed was either bailable or stated with insufficient particularity. In the second category of case, there was doubt about what the court had actually done. Where it appeared from the record that the court had bailed the prisoner, it was contended by the Attorney-General that this had been done after consultation with the Council as to the nature of the charges;[54] where the record showed that the prisoner had been remanded, counsel for the prisoners alleged that this simply meant that the court wished to consider the matter further, or even that the prisoner was remanded while sureties were arranged.[55]

free customs, or be outlawed, or exiled, or any other wise destroyed; nor will we not pass upon him, nor condemn him but by lawful judgment of his peers, or by the law of the land. We will sell to no man, we will not deny or defer to any man either justice or right.'

[49] 3 St. Tr. at 38–41. There was some authority to support the Attorney-General's argument that the power to bail in the case of a committal by King and Council had been taken away by the Statute of Westminster I: *Ruswell* (1606) 1 Rolle 193; Staunford, *Les Plees del Coron*, fol. 72. It was argued, on the other hand, that the statute only curtailed the powers of sheriffs to admit to bail, and left the powers of the judges untouched: 3 St. Tr. at 90–2. The court does not appear to have given effect to the Attorney General's argument, but cf. Jenks, 545, who was of the view that the statute played an important part in the Court's decision.

[50] Gardiner, op. cit. vol. 6, 214; 4 Holdsworth, 87.

[51] All the records cited are set out verbatim, 3 St. Tr. at 109–26.

[52] Esp. *Bildeston* (1344) cited at 3 St. Tr. 109.

[53] See 3 St. Tr. at 57–8, the cases being mostly from the time of Henry VII.

[54] 3 St. Tr. at 46–9.

[55] 3 St. Tr. at 97–109.

At the very least, the precedents showed that the courts were not precluded from bailing simply because the committal was by King or Council. At the very most, they showed that where the court could see for itself the basis for the committal it could bail if bail were seen to be appropriate. That left open an area in between which encompassed the narrow issue of the case, namely, whether a prisoner was bailable simply because the specific cause for committal had not been expressed.

The court placed special reliance on the Resolution of 1592, and Hyde C.J. confidently expressed the view that it laid down, 'that if a man be committed by the commandment of the king, he is not to be delivered by a habeas corpus in this court, for we know not the cause of the commitment'.[56] It was, perhaps, not so clear. The question presented in *Darnel* was whether the prisoners should be bailed, not delivered. Probably the judges in 1592 had not really considered the express point raised in *Darnel*: their *Resolution* certainly did not answer it. They said that a prisoner could not be delivered on habeas corpus without having been tried, and that he could only be tried if the cause were expressed. Beyond that, they did not express their views.

(ii) The Decision of the Court.   It is well known that the court refused to bail the prisoners, but it should be remembered that the judges apparently did not intend their determination to be a final one. They later said that a further application from the same prisoners would have been entertained the next day.[57] In the proceedings in Parliament which led to the Petition of Right, the issue was presented not so much in the form whether the court's decision should be overruled, but whether Parliament should answer the questions raised by the case which the judges had failed to answer.[58] On the other hand, as a practical matter, it would have been inconceivable for the court to have bailed the prisoners unless it had been made clear on the subsequent return that they were held on a bailable offence. Technically the court had not made a final determination, but it had clearly given in completely to the Attorney-General's argument and had decided that the prisoners should not be released on the grounds that the return was insufficient.

[56] 3 St. Tr. at 58–9.
[57] 3 St. Tr. at 160–3.
[58] The immediate cause for concern was the draft judgment which the Attorney-General proposed to have entered in the court rolls which was framed as a final judgment: 3 St. Tr. at 75; at 82, per Lord Coke: 'This draught of the Judgment, should it be entered, will sting us to death.'

There is no unanimity on whether the court came to the correct conclusion on the basis of the authorities.[59] It is, perhaps, fair to say that on the strictly legal arguments, the court could have easily come down on either side, and that the political pressures and, perhaps, the political convictions of the judges, tipped the scale in the King's favour.

(iii) The Petition of Right. The Petition of Right dealt with the main grievances of the day against Charles I—arbitrary taxation, billeting of soldiers and mariners, abuses through martial law proceedings, and perhaps most important, arbitrary imprisonment. Clause five set out the grievance that:

divers of your subjects have of late been imprisoned without any cause shewed; and when for their deliverance they were brought before your justices, by your majesty's Writs of Habeas Corpus, there to undergo and receive as the court should order, and their keepers commanded to certify the causes of their detainer; no cause was certified, but that they were detained by your majesty's special command, signified by the lords of your privy-council, and yet were returned back to several prisons, without being charged with any thing to which they might make answer according to the law.

Clause eight, the operative part, simply provides 'that no freeman in any such manner as is before mentioned be imprisoned or detained.'

There is some doubt about the formal legal nature of the Petition of Right.[60] It does not take the form of an ordinary statute, nor is it strictly an ordinary petition of right.[61] It seems to have been the product of compromise, and was probably considered at the time to be a declaration of the law given by the two Houses of Parliament in their judicial capacity and endorsed by the King.[62] Indeed, all during the debates, the proponents of the Petition insisted that they were merely

---

[59] Maitland, *Lectures on the Constitutional History of England*, 313, said that in refusing the prisoners bail the judges 'had, I think, the weight of precedents, even of modern precedents, against them; but practice had hardly been uniform, and we are not, I think, entitled to say that the judgment was plainly iniquitous'. Blackstone thought the judges had 'perhaps misunderstood the "arbitrary precedents"': 3 Bl. *Comm.*, 134. Hallam, *Constitutional History of England* (2nd ed.), vol. 1, 528–9, found the decision unsupportable. However, others have maintained that the decision was right in law, if wrong in principle: Adams, *Constitutional History of England*, 291; Jenks, 545; 6 Holdsworth, 37: 'We cannot say that their opinion was contrary to the later precedents.'

[60] Relf, 44–54. Hallam, op. cit. 531, called it a 'declaratory statute'.

[61] Relf, 47–9.

[62] Ibid. 54.

seeking to have the ancient laws of England observed. While Lord Coke had to admit at one point that the rights claimed were only implicitly conferred by the ancient laws,[63] there probably was a genuine feeling that the Petition did not enact new laws so much as re-assert old ones.

In the next section, it is shown how Charles I was able to evade the effect of the Petition, partly because of its uncertain legal form. However, by the second half of the seventeenth century, after the civil war and the restoration of the monarchy, these doubts about the force of the Petition of Right seem to have been forgotten. Since that time it has been accepted that it does deprive the executive of the power to detain solely for reasons of state in the absence of emergency legislation conferring such power.

(d) *Abuses Following the Petition of Right*

As early as 1629, events proved that Charles I was not going to let his power be limited by the Petition. Following an incident in the Commons, when the Speaker, on the instructions of the King, refused to put a question on tonnage and poundage, Selden and several other members of parliament were committed on the King's warrant.[64] They brought habeas corpus, and it was returned that they were detained 'for notable contempts ... committed against ourself and our government, and for stirring up sedition against us'.[65] This was hardly more satisfactory than the warrant in *Darnel's Case*, and certainly did not express a charge upon which the prisoners could be tried. The Attorney-General's argument in support of its sufficiency revealed the narrow view that the King and his advisers were taking of the Petition of Right. He first quoted the King's explanation of his assent to the Petition: 'It must be conceived that I have granted no new, but only confirmed the ancient liberties of my subjects.'[66]

The Attorney-General went on to explain:

A petition in parliament is not law, yet it is for the honour and dignity of the King, to observe and keep it faithfully; but it is the duty of the people not to stretch it beyond the words and intentions of the King. And no other

---

[63] Relf, 33.   [64] (1629) 3 St. Tr. 235.   [65] Ibid. at 240.
    [66] Ibid. at 281, quoting the King's statement of 26 June 1628. Before consenting to the Petition, Charles had called the judges in, and tried to get their assurance that it would not be interpreted so as to curtail his powers. The judges refused to give a clear answer: 1 Hallam, op. cit. 533–5.

construction can be made of the Petition, than to take it as a confirmation of the ancient liberties and rights of the subjects. So that now the case remains the same quality and degree, as it was before the Petition.[67]

The judges were, perhaps, a bit sceptical about this argument, but the King was able to prevent anything from being done, first by ordering the gaoler to refuse to bring the prisoners before the courts, and then by insisting that the opinion of all the judges be sought.[68] After the prisoners had spent the long vacation in gaol, Hyde C.J. and Whitelocke J. were summoned by the King, and they seem to have convinced him that the prisoners should be bailed.[69] They did, however, accept his proposal that the prisoners should also be required to put up sureties for good behaviour. This was seen as a request for an admission of guilt, and the offer was refused. Several of the members stubbornly stayed in prison until 1640 when Parliament again met after the ten year break.

The Petition of Right was again flouted in the *Shipmoney Case*, 1637,[70] when the judges acquiesced in the King's imposition of a tax without Parliament's sanction. At the same time, however, the reports from this period do yield cases of habeas corpus being used with effect, even in the case of committal by the King or Council. *Lawson's Case*[71] and *Barkham's Case*,[72] both in 1638, are clear instances of prisoners being bailed because the return revealed only a committal by the council without cause being specified. In other cases[73] the court insisted on granting the prisoner bail where time was sought to maintain a committal of Council, or, at least, forced the executive to proceed on indictment so that the prisoner would have his trial.[74]

(c) *Habeas Corpus Act 1640*

When Parliament finally met again in 1640, it set out to curtail the prerogative claim for the power of detention. The Habeas Corpus Act 1640 abolished all the conciliar courts, including the Star Chamber, and specifically provided that anyone imprisoned by order of the King

---

[67] 3 St. Tr. at 281–2.
[68] The text of the King's letters to the judges is given ibid., at 287–8.
[69] Ibid. at 288, quoting Whitelocke, *Memorials of English Affairs*, 14.
[70] 3 St. Tr. 825 at 1237: 'There was no new thing granted, but only the ancient liberties confirmed', per Finch C.J., referring to the Petition of Right.
[71] Cro. Car. 507.
[72] Cro. Car. 507. See also *Seeles* (1639) Cro. Car. 558.
[73] *Wolnough* (1639) Cro. Car. 552.
[74] *Freeman's Case* (1640) Cro. Car. 579.

or Council should have habeas corpus and be brought before the court without delay with the cause of imprisonment shown. The judges were required to pronounce upon the legality of the detention within three days time and bail, discharge or remand the prisoner accordingly.[75] A judge or other officer who failed to act in compliance with the statute was made subject to heavy fines and liable in damages to the party aggrieved.[76]

Yet a few months after this Act, which appeared to remove the means for evasion, the Grand Remonstrance was registered by the Commons, and it contained clauses complaining about the abuse of executive committals.[77] The Habeas Corpus Act 1640 had not been completely effective, and indeed, it was becoming increasingly clear that the crisis of State was not to be resolved by law alone.

(f) *The Protectorate*

From the period of the Protectorate, there are reports of cases which clearly show that the practice of executive committal without criminal allegation had by no means ended. An example is *Lilburne's Case*, 1653[78] where, by order of the Council of State, no return was made to the writ as the prisoner had been committed 'for the peace of the nation'. The judges meekly accepted: 'The Council of State have reason for what they do in this business.'[79] In another case,[80] the judges seemed to be ready to bail the prisoners, but changed their minds when directly threatened with loss of office by Cromwell.[81]

5. PROCEDURAL DEFECTS AND THE HABEAS CORPUS ACT 1679

(a) *Problems Associated with the Writ*

While playing a significant role in the constitutional struggles of the day, habeas corpus had been gradually becoming an accepted remedy

---

[75] s.6.   [76] ss.4,5.
[77] Arts. 11–15: Gardiner, *Constitutional Documents of the Puritan Revolution*, 209.
[78] 5 St. Tr. 371.
[79] Ibid.
[80] *Cony* (1655) 5 St. Tr. 935.
[81] Ibid. at 938. He is said to have told the judges that 'their Magna F***** should not control his actions which he knew were for the safety of the Commonwealth.' Cf. Ashley, *Magna Carta and the Seventeenth Century* (1965) 46, doubting the correctness of the account.

in the more ordinary cases. It continued to be used in civil suits but there are also instances in the seventeenth century of its use in used custody cases,[82] and to test the validity of ordinary criminal committals.[83] In *Dr. Alphonso's Case*,[84] the court ordered the release of a prisoner committed for unlawful medical practice by the College of Physicians, and in another case,[85] the court released an irate citizen who had been committed by his mayor for contempt.

By the time of the Restoration, it had become an accepted remedy, more or less in the form we now know. The deliberate efforts of the Stuarts, and then Cromwell, to flout the force of the writ had merely fixed in the popular conception the principle that the writ should be freely and quickly available to challenge any commitment. The writ had, however, evolved in an uncertain, sometimes precipitate, fashion from humble origins, and there were consequent procedural defects which could impair its operation despite the acceptance it had gained.

Perhaps the most important of these was the question whether or not the writ could be issued in vacation. The source of this difficulty may well have been in the original use of habeas corpus to remove civil cases from inferior courts. This could only be done in term, when the cause could be heard at Westminster. Practice may have been slow to catch up with the changing function of the writ.[86]

Coke[87] and Hale[88] both said that Chancery could issue writs in vacation; Hale added that the other courts could not. Wilmot, writing over 100 years later, claimed that before the 1679 Act, there had been an 'unsettled practice' for the judges of the King's Bench to grant the writ in vacation.[89] Subsequent to the 1679 Act, it was held that both Chancery[90] and the other courts[91] did have the power at common law to issue the writ in vacation, but the matter was of sufficient contemporary doubt to lead to the great abuse in *Jenke's Case* in 1676.[92] Both the Chief Justice of the King's Bench and the Lord Chancellor refused to grant the writ in the long vacation to a prisoner committed by the Council for advocating that Parliament be recalled. He was

---

[82] *Viner* (1675) 1 Freem. K.B. 522; *Leigh* (1674) 3 Keb. 433.
[83] *Lee* (1640) Cro. Car. 593; *R.* v. *Mayo* (1663) 1 Sid. 144; *Brice* (1640) Cro. Car. 593; *Bronker* (1647) Style 16.
[84] (1614) 2 Bulst. 259.   [85] *Hodges* v. *Humkin* (1613) 2 Bulst. 139.
[86] Jenks, 548.   [87] 2 *Inst.*, 53; 4 *Inst.*, 81.
[88] 2 *P.C.*, 147.   [89] Wilm. 81, at 94.
[90] *Crowley's Case* (1818) 2 Swanst. 1.
[91] Wilm. 94–100.
[92] 6 St. Tr. 1190 and see *Crowley's Case* (1818) 2 Swanst. 1, where further details are given.

unquestionably entitled to be bailed, but because of the uncertainty in the law, he was denied a remedy.

A similar question arose concerning the power of the Common Pleas to grant the writ in ordinary criminal cases. For a long time, the court had granted the writ where the applicant had the privilege of the court,[93] but there was some authority to the effect that since only the King's Bench could proceed upon the cause in a criminal case if the return were good, the Common Pleas should not act in such cases.[94] The Act of 1640 gave the Common Pleas jurisdiction over cases within its scope[95] on a par with the King's Bench and by 1670, in *Bushell's Case*,[96] the Common Pleas awarded habeas corpus in an ordinary criminal case, after which it came to be more or less accepted that the court had jurisdiction at common law to grant the writ.[97]

There were other abuses which were cause for concern.[98] Prisoners were moved from gaol to gaol so that it was impossible to serve the proper gaoler with the writ, and worse still, some prisoners were taken to Scotland or other places beyond the writ's reach.[99] There had also grown up the practice of simply ignoring or 'standing out' the original writ so that applicants had to sue out an 'alias' and even 'plures' writ before the gaoler could be forced to make a return.[100] Even prisoners who were successful and bailed or discharged could find themselves immediately rearrested and back in prison, left to start proceedings all over again.[101] Prisoners who were not entitled to immediate discharge were none the less thought to be entitled to a speedy trial and determination of their rights, but this did not always happen.[102]

(b) *Habeas Corpus Act 1679*

Efforts were made in Parliament to remedy these defects by

---

[93] *Wynne* v. *Boughey* (1666) O. Bridg. 570.

[94] *Rudyard* (1670) 2 Vent. 23; *Anon.* (1671) Carter 221; *Jones* (1677) 1 Mod. 235, 2 Mod. 198.

[95] s.6.   [96] Vaughan 135.

[97] *Wood* (1770) 2 Wm. Bl. 745.

[98] Many of these had been current for some time and were discussed in the debate on the Petition of Right: 3 St. Tr. at 182–5.

[99] In *Clarendon* (1668) 6 St. Tr. 291 at 330, 396, one of the charges was that he 'hath advised and procured divers of his majesty's subjects to be imprisoned against law, in remote islands, garrisons, and other places thereby to prevent them from the benefit of the law'.

[100] See the preamble to s.1 of the 1679 Act.

[101] Ibid. s.5.

[102] Discussed in detail *infra*, pp. 136–45.

legislation, and after several abortive bills,[103] the Habeas Corpus Act 1679 was finally passed.

Maitland said of the Act: 'I know no subject on which it is more difficult to lecture briefly, because it is altogether made up of details.'[104] The act is largely a piecemeal repairing of the common law. It by no means solved all the difficulties which were known to exist, and it can hardly be said that it was elegantly, or even clearly, drafted. Perhaps the most important thing the Act did was to find itself a place in the constitution and in the popular conception as a fundamental guarantee of liberty, and to demonstrate that abuses with respect to habeas corpus would not be tolerated. It accomplished reforms in two broad areas. First, it went some way to ensure that prisoners entitled to relief would not be thwarted by procedural inadequacy. The Act tried to ensure the availability of the writ at any time of the year[105] from any of the courts or judges at Westminster,[106] that the gaoler would obey the writ immediately,[107] that the judges would come to a speedy determination,[108] and that, if released, the prisoner would not be thrown back into prison.[109] There were also provisions to ensure that the prisoner would not be moved from prison to prison without proper authority[110] and that prisoners would not be taken to places beyond the reach of the writ,[111] and another section required the gaoler to provide the prisoner with a copy of the warrant so that the grounds for the detention would be known to permit an assessment of whether the writ should be applied for in the first place.[112]

Second, it contained provisions which were designed to ensure that even prisoners not entitled to immediate release would be brought to trial with as little delay as possible.[113]

Parliament took the extraordinary step of making the judges personally liable for punitive damages in the event of their unduly denying the writ in vacation.[114] This indicates not only that the measure was seen to be very important at the time, but that the legislators had

---

[103] 9 Holdsworth, 117. There were bills in 1668, 1669–70, 1673–4, 1675, 1676–7.
[104] *Lectures on the Constitutional History of England*, 314–15.
[105] s.9. S.3 provides that a prisoner who had been in custody for two terms without applying for the writ is not entitled to ask for the writ in vacation.
[106] s.2.   [107] s.1.   [108] s.2.
[109] s.5. Discussed in detail, *infra*, pp. 213–17.
[110] s.8, discussed in *Day* v. *The Queen* (1983) 153 C.L.R. 475.
[111] s.11.   [112] s.4.
[113] ss.6, 17, 18. Discussed in detail *infra*, pp. 136–45.
[114] s.9.

learned that the judges could not always be trusted to act according to the law.

The Act applied only to criminal cases, and even at that, it left many problems unsolved. The Act did not meet the problem of excessive bail, and the problem of controverting the truth of the return, solved in civil cases by the Act of 1816, is sometimes thought to remain to this day in criminal cases.[115] Moreover, in civil cases, the judges themselves solved many of the procedural problems without the help of legislation.[116] This merely demonstrates that the importance of the Act is perhaps explained not so much by what it actually did, but by the fact that it established the principle that the efficacy of habeas corpus is not to be thwarted.

The Act of 1679 marks the point at which the writ took its modern form. The practice on habeas corpus has changed through the years,[117] but the substance of its guarantee remains the same. The effect of the Habeas Corpus Acts of 1816 and 1862, and that of the Administration of Justice Act, 1960, together with the historical background to those acts is discussed in detail in subsequent chapters.[118]

[115] Discussed in detail *infra*, pp. 60–71.
[116] See Wilmot's *Opinion*, Wilm. 81.
[117] See Chapter X for a detailed discussion.
[118] See Chapters III, VIII and IX respectively.

2

Scope of Review

1. INTRODUCTION

The purpose of this chapter, together with the two chapters which follow, is to provide a comprehensive view of the scope of review which is available on habeas corpus.[1] This chapter deals broadly with questions of law; the next discusses the special problems which are encountered with questions of fact; and the third deals with the control of executive discretionary power on habeas corpus.

The definition of the scope of review on habeas corpus largely depends upon the general concepts of judicial review. One of the problems which must be faced in analysing any aspect of judicial review is that, to a certain extent, the cases defy being cast in conceptual moulds. The traditional guiding principle of review in English law, the concept of *ultra vires* or excess of jurisdiction,[2] has never been given a definition of predictive value. The jurisdictional principle supposes, in theory, that there is an area within which the inferior body is free to act, and even to err, without interference from the superior court. The definition of that area is, however, often narrowed to the point where administrative agencies are left virtually no margin of error. While deference to the expertise of specialized boards and tribunals may call for a more cautious judicial approach in certain contexts,[3] rarely if ever in a habeas corpus case where the liberty of the subject is at stake will the courts be prepared to decline to review a legal error on the ground that it does not go to jurisdiction.

In addition to giving jurisdictional error an almost limitless definition, the courts have adopted another technique to achieve review which is also to be found in the habeas corpus cases. This method is to

---

[1] *Pace*, Professor de Smith, *Judicial Review of Administrative Action* (4th ed. 1980), 600: 'Insuperable difficulties would frustrate any attempt to present a coherent and concise account of the scope of judicial review in habeas corpus proceedings, for the case-law is riddled with contradictions.'

[2] Cf. Oliver, 'Is the Ultra Vires Rule the Basis of Judicial Review?' [1987] P.L. 543.

[3] See e.g. *Canadian Union of Public Employees, Local 963* v. *New Brunswick Liquor Commission* [1979] 2 S.C.R. 227.

abandon the idea that review can only be based on jurisdictional error and to claim that in certain situations, any apparent error will allow for interference. The modern revival of error of law on the face of the record as grounds for review in certiorari,[4] together with the statutory duty imposed on certain tribunals to give adequate reasons for their decision[5] has proved to be an important source for review. In habeas corpus cases, it will be seen, there is a long tradition of review of this nature, and the decision of the House of Lords in the *Armah* case in 1968, discussed in detail later on has given[6] fresh impetus in this area.

The unmistakable trend is to broaden the grounds for judicial review to include virtually all errors of law.[7] If the court chooses not to classify the error as going to jurisdiction, it may well be possible to review it as an error on the face of the material before the court.

The scope of review on habeas corpus, it will be argued, demonstrates these characteristics. Because personal liberty is at stake, there has always been the possibility of a broad scope of review. The courts have shown themselves ready to mould concepts and definitions so as to achieve the power to give a remedy where a remedy seems to be needed.

The analysis of the scope of review on habeas corpus which follows leads to the conclusion that where the writ is seen to be an appropriate remedy against the sort of decision which is impugned, it is almost always safe to assume that a remedy will lie for any error of law. In other words, the determining factor is the type of decision under review, rather than the type of error alleged. This, however, only describes what the courts do, not what they say. The language of jurisdictional review is still used and it cannot be ignored. For this reason, the analysis proceeds along the lines dictated by the traditional language. This is the way the courts treat the matter, and the problems which may be encountered in the jurisdictional analysis must be understood. There can be little doubt but that jurisdictional review has always sounded more restrictive than it actually is. This chapter

---

[4] *R.* v. *Northumberland Compensation Appeal Tribunal, ex p. Shaw* [1952] 1 K.B. 338.
[5] Tribunals and Inquiries Act 1971, s.12. See *R.* v. *Immigration Appeal Tribunal, ex p. Khan (Mahmud)* [1983] Q.B. 790; *R.* v. *Knightsbridge Crown Court, ex p. International Sporting Club (London) Ltd.* [1982] Q.B. 304.
[6] [1968] A.C. 192, see *infra*, pp. 43–5.
[7] For discussion, see Emery and Smythe, 'Error of Law in Administrative Law' (1984) 100 L.Q.R. 612. Cf. Beatson, 'The Scope of Judicial Review For Error of Law' (1984) 4 O.J.L.S. 22, suggesting that error of law cannot serve as the definitional concept for judicial review.

suggests that at least in the law of habeas corpus, jurisdictional review, together with review for patent error, makes any significant or relevant error of law a ground for relief.

2. THE FORM OF REVIEW ON HABEAS CORPUS

The form of review available on habeas corpus may be described as follows. The writ is directed to the gaoler or person having custody or control of the applicant. It requires that person to return to the court, on the day specified, the body of the applicant and the cause of his detention. The process focuses upon the cause returned. If the return discloses a lawful cause, the prisoner is remanded; if the cause returned is insufficient or unlawful, the prisoner is released. The matter directly at issue is simply the excuse or reason given by the party who is exercising restraint over the applicant.

The problem of defining the scope of review on habeas corpus occurs where the propriety of the return depends on a prior decision, order, or determination. By what method and on what grounds can the court 'go behind' the warrant and review that determination?

Under modern practice, habeas corpus cases are not usually determined on a formal return, but on the affidavits of the applicant and respondent.[8] The idea of trying the case on the return is, therefore, somewhat misleading. It will be seen later on that the material before the court is not always as limited as it might have been under the old practice.[9] The technical considerations of the return have, however, largely shaped the scope of review on habeas corpus, and it is essential to keep those considerations in mind if the cases are to be properly understood.

When the writ actually issued, the only material which was brought before the court for consideration was the return of the gaoler. Holt C.J. pointed this out when he compared habeas corpus and certiorari: 'An habeas corpus does not remove the record though it does the cause, but a certiorari removes the record and cause too ... besides a certiorari goes to the judge but a habeas corpus to the officer...'[10]

When, for example, there has been a conviction or other judicial

---

[8] *Infra*, pp. 219–20.   [9] *Infra*, pp. 45–6.
[10] *Heatherington* v. *Reynolds* (1705) Fort. 269. See also *Fazakerly* v. *Baldoe* (1704) 7 Mod. 177, per Holt C.J.: '... for there is a difference in this respect between a habeas corpus and a certiorari: upon an habeas corpus we have not the record itself as we have upon a certiorari.'

order, the gaoler will usually have a written warrant by which justification for the detention is claimed, and the return must either annex or contain a copy of the warrant.[11]

From this formal point of view, habeas corpus may be described as a collateral method of attack.[12] The writ is directed to the gaoler rather than the person or tribunal ordering the detention. The issue for determination is in this sense one between the prisoner and the detainer,[13] and the prior determination is only incidentally or collaterally impugned. When a situation of collateral attack arises,[14] the court cannot review the correctness of the prior decision, but it may examine the question of jurisdiction.[15]

It is argued in this chapter, however, that in reviewing on the grounds of patent error,[16] the courts have gone beyond the bounds of collateral attack, and that such a concept is inadequate to describe the powers of review. Whatever the form, there can be little doubt that habeas corpus is seen by the judges as a remedy for review. In other words, it is not a form of proceeding which, from time to time incidentally brings into question the validity of a judicial or quasi-judicial act: it is one of the accepted remedies regularly used to test the validity of official action in constitutional law. The formally collateral nature of the attack has never properly defined the scope of review on habeas corpus.

At the same time, it should not be supposed that habeas corpus constitutes a form of appeal with the power to reconsider on the merits.[17] There is still a theoretical area within which the inferior court is free to err, and a decision within that area, although incorrect, may be immune from review. In practical terms, however, the margin for error has virtually vanished in those cases where habeas corpus is deemed to be the appropriate method of challenge. The purpose of

---

[11] See now Ord. 54, r.7, which requires the production of all documents upon which the imprisonment depends.

[12] For two of the rare instances where the courts have used the term 'collateral attack' to describe the powers of review on habeas corpus, see *R.* v. *Pantelidis* (1942) 79 C.C.C. 46 at 49 (B.C.C.A.); *Re Khattar* (1927) 47 C.C.C. 184 (N.S.S.C.).

[13] That this is somewhat artificial is demonstrated by the cases where the gaoler takes a position in argument in support of the prisoner, a third party (usually a foreign government seeking extradition) taking the other side: see, e.g. *Armah* v. *Government of Ghana* [1968] A.C. 192 at 217; *R.* v. *Governor of Brixton Prison, ex p. Gardner* [1968] 1 All E.R. 636 at 640.

[14] Rubinstein, *Jurisdiction and Illegality* (1965), 39–46 gives several examples of situations of collateral attack.

[15] *Ibid.* 36.

[16] *Infra*, pp. 34 *et seq.*

[17] See e.g. *Ex p. Corke* [1954] 2 All E.R. 440; *Ex p. Hinds* [1961] 1 All E.R. 707.

this chapter is really to describe the techniques which the courts have used to evolve this broad scope of review.

3. JURISDICTIONAL REVIEW

There are many instances of the effective use of habeas corpus where the basis of review is that the impugned proceedings were taken without jurisdiction. The concept of jurisdictional review seems to have emerged early in the history of the struggle between the common law courts and the other jurisdictions for control, and it has been seen how habeas corpus was used in the seventeenth century to challenge the wrongful exercise of jurisdiction by the High Commission and other prerogative courts.[18] The concept of review based on want of jurisdiction emerged with special strength in the magisterial law of the nineteenth century. The use of habeas corpus to review proceedings before magistrates demonstrates the use of the habeas corpus to achieve a broad form of jurisdictional review, and as many of the principles which evolved retain significance today, the cases warrant close scrutiny.

(a) *Magisterial Law—Review Based on Jurisdiction*

In the eighteenth and nineteenth centuries, the power of justices in summary matters was considerable, and the common law courts were eager to assert control over its exercise. The reason for the extensive use of certiorari and habeas corpus to question these proceedings was simply that no other method of challenge was available.[19]

(i) Basis for Review. To achieve control, the superior courts often placed great importance upon formal or technical matters in order to justify review. The rationale was explained by Holt C.J. as follows:

... the defendant is put to a summary trial different from magna charta; for it is a fundamental privilege of an Englishman to be tried by a jury ... Then, where a

---

[18] *Supra*, pp. 6–7.
[19] A writ of error did not lie to challenge a summary conviction: *R.* v. *Leighton* (1708) Fort. 173; *R.* v. *Lomas* (1694) Comb. 297. Before the Summary Jurisdiction Act 1879, the right of appeal by trial de novo to quarter sessions was granted only in some cases and before the introduction of appeal by stated case to the High Court by the Summary Jurisdiction Act 1857, there was no method, aside from the prerogative writs, to bring a conviction or warrant before a court of superior jurisdiction for review: see Paley, *Summary Convictions* (9th ed. 1926), 670 *et seq.*

penalty is inflicted, and a different manner of trial from magna charta instituted; and the party offending, instead of being openly tried by his neighbours in a court of justice, shall be convicted by a single justice of peace in a private chamber, upon the testimony of one witness; I fain would know, if on the consideration of such a law, we ought to adhere to the letter of the law, without carrying the words farther than the natural sense of them.[20]

The leading principle of magisterial law was that it had to appear from the face of the record that the court had acted within the statutory limits. By insisting that nothing could be presumed in favour of the validity of instruments issued by the magistrates and that jurisdiction had to appear on the face, the superior courts were able to control the magistrates closely even though the inquiry was confined to the record or warrant. In these early cases, jurisdictional review meant 'has the inferior court made jurisdiction manifest' rather than 'has the inferior court in fact acted within jurisdiction'.[21] By forcing the inferior courts to describe with great particularity their proceedings to avoid sins of omission, many sins of commission were revealed. It was upon this basis that the writs of certiorari and, to a large extent, habeas corpus, depended for their effectiveness.

(ii) Review of Warrants of Commitment. Habeas corpus was primarily used in magisterial law to review warrants of commitment. The rule that instruments issued by the inferior jurisdictions had to make jurisdiction manifest applied no less to warrants of commitment and it enabled the courts to exercise broad powers of review on habeas corpus. In a habeas corpus case, Coleridge J. explained the basis for review:

The question is whether the warrant, which the gaoler has returned, be a legal one. Of the conviction we know nothing, except through the warrant. By a legal warrant I mean a warrant which upon the face of it shews a right to detain: and that cannot exist unless there be jurisdiction in the magistrate. To deny that this must appear on the face of the proceedings, is to call into question one of the most important rules of the criminal law.[22]

This meant that even though the court only had the warrant before it,

---

[20] *R.* v. *Whistler* (1702) Holt K.B. 215.
[21] See e.g. *Re Douglas* (1842) 12 L.J.Q.B. 49, where the court (incorrectly) refused to look at affidavits to prove want of jurisdiction, but discharged the prisoner because the warrant did not recite the same matter and thereby make jurisdiction patent.
[22] *Re Peerless* (1841) 1 Q.B. 143 at 154.

pervasive jurisdictional review could still be exercised. For example, if a warrant of commitment upon a conviction for smuggling failed to show compliance with the special provisions of the statute which gave the justices jurisdiction over the accused taken at sea, the prisoner would be discharged.[23] Similarly, where the statute creating the offence stipulated that a complaint in writing[24] or on oath[25] had to be received, and the warrant failed to state that this had been done, the prisoner would be discharged, as would a prisoner committed upon conviction for desertion where the warrant failed to specify that he was a soldier who ought to have been with his corps.[26] In certain cases, magistrates were empowered to order imprisonment without register-ing a formal conviction.[27] When reviewing such orders, the superior courts seemed to require that the warrant bear the marks of both conviction and commitment,[28] and the prisoner would be discharged if the offence was inadequately stated in the information[29] or if the warrant failed to state the evidence[30] or to show that it was given to the prisoner's presence.[31]

It will be seen that statutory changes in the mid-nineteenth century took away the basis for this sort of review,[32] but modern examples are sometimes encountered. In one such Canadian case,[33] the court felt that it should only look at the warrant, but was prepared to discharge the prisoner because the warrant did not show jurisdiction on its face. The result may be proper, but it is submitted that this sort of reasoning is tortured. It will be seen that extrinsic material which shows want of jurisdiction may be brought before the court.[34] There can be little

[23] Ibid., *Kite & Lane's Case* (1822) 1 B. & C. 101.
[24] *R.* v. *Fuller* (1844) 2 Dow. & L. 98.
[25] *R.* v. *Lewis* (1844) 13 L.J.M.C. 46.
[26] *Re Douglas* (1842) 12 L.J.Q.B. 49.
[27] Most of these cases arose under the act of 1823 (4 Geo. IV, c.34) dealing with the relationship between master and servant and empowered magistrates to commit apprentices and workmen in certain situations.
[28] *Re Baker* (1857) 2 H. & N. 219. Cf. *Re Bailey, Re Collier* (1854) 3 E. & B. 607, a case of this type holding that if a conviction had been drawn up, the warrant need not be so particular.
[29] *Re Seth Turner* (1846) 9 Q.B. 80.
[30] *Re Hammond* (1846) 9 Q.B. 92; *Nash's Case* (1821) 4 B. & Ald. 295; cf. *Re Geswood* (1853) 23 L.J.M.C. 35, where the effect of the Summary Jurisdiction Act 1848 was held to overcome the same difficulty.
[31] *R.* v. *Tordoft* (1844) 5 Q.B. 933;
[32] *Re Gray* (1844) 2 Dow. & L. 539. *Infra*, pp. 30–1.
[33] *Re Munavish* (1958) 121 C.C.C. 299 (B.C.S.C.). See also Cartwright C.J. (dissenting) in *Sanders* v. *R.* [1970] 2 C.C.C. 57 (S.C.C.).
[34] *Infra*, pp. 75–6.

doubt that the basis for the decision in the Canadian case was that there really had been a jurisdictional defect, and basing the decision on the failure of the warrant to recite jurisdiction seems entirely artificial.

In any case, this reasoning was acceptable in the nineteenth century and it can be seen that the broad definition of jurisdiction together with the rule that nothing could be presumed in favour of the validity of summary proceedings made those proceedings especially vulnerable.

(*iii*) *Review of Convictions.* There are also cases where habeas corpus has been used to review an ordinary summary conviction.[35] There is no power to quash on habeas corpus[36] but the court could give relief if the conviction was shown to have been made without jurisdiction. The reason that there are relatively few reported habeas corpus cases in which a conviction is reviewed is undoubtedly that certiorari to quash, and later, appeal by case stated, are more convenient. Review on habeas corpus depends upon the idea of 'going behind' the conviction to find an error of jurisdiction. Theoretically this may always be done if there is jurisdictional error, but where the defect does not appear on the commitment, the more usual course has been to take direct proceedings to have the conviction quashed.

There are also instances of habeas corpus being used in conjunction with certiorari to review a conviction.[37] In these cases, both the commitment and the conviction are brought before the court, but the power to review the conviction is usually attributed to the certiorari rather than the habeas corpus.

It has been more recently held that habeas corpus is not to be used as a method of appealing summary convictions and this is discussed in more detail below.[38] Clearly, direct proceedings are more convenient but it is submitted that if the prisoner can show that the conviction is vitiated by jurisdictional error, the authorities permit the use of habeas

---

[35] *Re Authers* (1889) 22 Q.B.D. 345; *Re Clew* (1881) 8 Q.B.D. 511 (where, however, the order that the conviction be quashed indicates that there may have been certiorari as well); *Re Baker* (1883) 47 J.P. 666; *Re Thompson* (1860) 6 H. & N. 193 (application refused on the merits). See also the cases discussed *infra*, p. 41 where review was granted because of a mistatement of the offence in the warrant of commitment.

[36] *Bushell's Case* (1670) Vaughan 135 at 157: 'In all the precedents shew'd in the Common Pleas, or in any that can be shew'd in the King's Bench, upon discharging the prisoner by habeas corpus, nothing can be shew'd of quashing the orders or decrees of that Court that made the wrong commitment.'

[37] See e.g. *Ex p. Hopkins* (1891) 17 Cox C.C. 444, *infra*, pp. 51–2.

[38] *Ex p. Corke* [1954] 2 All E.R. 440, *infra*, pp. 31; 145–6.

corpus alone to review the conviction. In such a case, the error of jurisdiction could be brought before the court by affidavit.[39]

(*iv*) *Attempts to Curtail Review at Common Law.* While useful in cases of substantive error, the review of summary convictions which could be exercised on habeas corpus often depended upon insubstantial, technical errors, and attempts were made to curtail review in these unmeritorious situations. It was held in several cases[40] that the court would not consider an objection to the commitment which related to the validity of the conviction without first having the conviction itself brought up on certiorari.[41] In two other cases,[42] it was pointed out that the commitment need not contain everything the conviction contained, and that where the warrant recited that a good conviction had been made, the court would presume that it contained the requisites of validity. The theory was that the warrant was an instrument secondary to the conviction, and that so long as there was a good conviction, the prisoner should not benefit from a clerical or formal defect.

These attempts to limit review on habeas corpus were, however, not always followed. In some cases there were special reasons. For certain offences, no formal conviction was drawn up and only review of the warrant was possible.[43] In other cases, the right to certiorari was taken away by statute[44] and habeas corpus was the only means of redress. In most cases, though, the courts were simply unwilling to give up a potent measure of control over the inferior jurisdictions. If the warrant were defective for some technical reason unrelated to the conviction, it was said that a perfect conviction could not cure the defect.[45] In cases where the validity of the conviction as recited was impugned, the courts simply took the line that they could only assume that it was defective and that it was incumbent upon anyone who asserted it to be good to have it brought before the court.[46]

[39] *Infra*, pp. 75–6.
[40] *R.* v. *Hawkins* (1715) Fort. 272; *R.* v. *Elwell* (1727) 2 Str. 794; *R.* v. *Taylor* (1826) 7 D. & R. 622.
[41] The use of certiorari-in-aid of habeas corpus is discussed *infra*, pp. 51–3.
[42] *R.* v. *Helps* (1814) 3 M. & S. 331; *R.* v. *Rogers* (1822) 1 D. & R. 156.
[43] *Supra*, p. 27.
[44] *R.* v. *Chaney* (1838) 7 L.J.M.C. 65, which pointed out, however, that the crown could still ask for certiorari.
[45] *R.* v. *Fletcher* (1844) 8 J.P. 168; *R.* v. *Chandler* (1704) 1 Ld. Raym. 545; *R.* v. *James* (1822) 5 B. & Ald. 894.
[46] *Re Reynolds* (1844) 1 Dowl. & L. 846 (where the conviction had even been previously affirmed); *R.* v. *Chaney* (1838) 7 L.J.M.C. 65; *R.* v. *Timson* (1870) L.R. 5 Exch. 257; *Re Allen* (1860) 30 L.J.Q.B. 38; *Re Hammond* (1846) 9 Q.B. 92; *R.* v. *Tordoft* (1844) 5 Q.B. 933.

In one case, certiorari had issued to bring a good conviction before the court, but the court rejected the argument that the prisoner should be remanded since there was shown to be a valid conviction notwithstanding the defective commitment. Denman C.J. explained: 'As this is a proceeding which restrains the liberty of the subject, it ought to appear that the thing done was in perfect conformity to the statute.'[47]

(v) *Summary Jurisdiction Acts.* In the mid-nineteenth century, both the basis and the reason for this broad form of review were taken away by statute. The Summary Jurisdiction Act 1848 provided for simplified and abbreviated standard forms of conviction and commitment which had to be deemed legally sufficient.[48] The jurisdiction of the magistrate no longer had to appear on the face of the instrument,[49] and other mistakes were less likely to appear.[50] At the same time, Parliament took away the reason for the broad powers of review by providing adequate means of appeal.[51] The introduction of appeals to quarter sessions and of appeal by case stated to the High Court in all cases rendered the law of summary convictions less riddled with technicality, and at the same time, made redress more easily available if there was substantive error.

It was still possible to base a habeas corpus application on the misstatement of the offence in the warrant of commitment[52] until the Summary Jurisdiction Act 1879. This act abolished all review of warrants of commitment so long as there was a valid conviction or order to support the imprisonment. The provision has been brought forward to the present, and still represents the law:

... a warrant of commitment issued in pursuance of a valid conviction, or of a valid order requiring the person committed to do or abstain from doing

---

[47] *Re Elmy* (1834) 1 A. & E. 843.

[48] ss.17, 32 [repealed by Magistrates' Courts Act 1952, s.132, Sched. 6; see now Magistrates' Courts Rules 1981, r.16, 97].

[49] *Re Allison* (1854) 10 Ex. 561 at 568 per Platt B.: 'The learning of the cases prior to [the 1848 Act] has been swept away...'

[50] As Lord Sumner explained in his well-known dictum in *R. v. Nat Bell Liquors Ltd.* [1922] 2 A.C. 128 at 159: 'The Summary Jurisdiction Act ... did not stint the jurisdiction of the Queen's Bench, or alter the actual law of certiorari. What it did was to disarm its exercise. The effect was not to make that which had been error, error no longer, but to remove nearly all opportunity for its detection. The face of the record "spoke" no longer: it was the inscrutable face of a sphinx.'

[51] See *supra*, n. 19, p. 25. It is suggested that a habeas corpus case, *Re Baker* (1857) 2 H. & N. 219, allowing for a pervasive review on affidavits (see, *infra*, pp. 75–6) was the immediate cause of this provision: 26 L.J.M.C. 155 at 168.

[52] *R. v. Timson* (1870) L.R. 5 Exch. 247.

anything, shall not, if it alleges that the person committed has been convicted, or ordered to do or abstain from doing that thing, be held void by reason of any defect in the warrant.[53]

Even where the warrant of commitment is not covered by this provision, it seems that the court will be unlikely to order discharge on habeas corpus without looking at the conviction itself to see whether there is more than a technical defect in the commitment.[54]

The provision does not, however, rule out the review of summary proceedings on habeas corpus entirely. It still leaves the question of whether the conviction itself is a valid one. The English courts seem to dislike reviewing convictions on habeas corpus, but in an appropriate case, it is submitted that review of a summary conviction is still possible.

Lord Goddard C.J.'s admonition in 1954 is often taken to preclude any review of summary convictions on habeas corpus:

It is well that persons serving sentence passed on them by a competent court of summary jurisdiction should understand that habeas corpus is not a means of appeal. If they complain that they are wrongly convicted, they should appeal to quarter sessions. A person convicted by a competent court of summary jurisdiction cannot apply for a writ of habeas corpus.[55]

This does not necessarily preclude the use of habeas corpus to show want of jurisdiction, or in other words, to show that the conviction is not that of a 'competent court'. This does not depend upon habeas corpus being used as an appeal, and the existence of an alternate remedy here—appeal or certiorari to quash—should not exclude the use of habeas corpus.[56] It must be noted, however, that there does not seem to have been a case in nearly one hundred years where habeas corpus has been used in England for this purpose.[57] It would seem to be one situation where, whatever the theoretical possibilities, habeas corpus is no longer seen as an appropriate remedy.

The special considerations which virtually rule out any challenge to convictions on indictment are discussed in a separate section.[58]

[53] Magistrates' Courts Rules 1981, r.97(3).
[54] *R.* v. *Governor of Lewes Prison, ex p. Doyle* [1917] 2 K.B. 254 at 269; *Ex p. Leclerc* (1973) 21 C.C.C. (2d) 16 (Que. C.A.). Cf. *R.* v. *Allen* (1860) 30 L.J.Q.B. 38.
[55] *Ex p. Corke* [1954] 2 All E.R. 440.
[56] *Infra*, pp. 59–60.
[57] Cf. *R.* v. *Governor of Wormwood Scrubbs Prison, ex p. Boydell* [1948] 2 K.B. 193 reviewing the conviction of a court-martial on jurisdictional grounds. There are also many modern Canadian examples: see e.g. *Re Eustace* (1956) 116 C.C.C. 196 (B.C.S.C.); *Ex p. Hipke* [1968] 1 C.C.C. 66 (Sask. Q.B.).
[58] *Infra*, pp. 46–51; 145–6.

(*vi*) *Conclusion*. The scope of review on habeas corpus which evolved in magisterial law was really as broad as that available on certiorari. Habeas corpus was used where the defect appeared on the warrant of commitment, certiorari where it appeared on the conviction. A later section examines in detail the review of patent error,[59] a matter closely linked with jurisdictional review in magisterial law. Here, it has been seen how the rule requiring instruments to show jurisdiction on their face allowed the courts to exercise jurisdictional review, perhaps based on formalism, but probably allowing for review of most errors of law. As well as reviewing errors which appeared on the face of the warrant, in a few cases, habeas corpus was used as a remedy against an improper conviction where jurisdictional error could be shown by extrinsic evidence. This technique is closer to the modern practice, and modern examples are given later on.[60] While the Summary Jurisdiction Acts removed the basis for much of the review which had been exercised on habeas corpus, the principles which were developed in the cases are still valid.

(b) *Modern Examples of Jurisdictional Review*

There are many modern cases which illustrate the operation of jurisdictional review on habeas corpus. The courts are quite willing to grant relief where an inferior tribunal has stepped outside the limits of its authority by misconstruing a statute or by failing to base its decision upon the proper considerations. The law of extradition provides many examples where relief has been awarded on this basis, as in the cases where the offence alleged is not extraditable or 'political' within the meaning of the statute,[61] or where the committing magistrate has failed to follow the statutory procedures. Similarly, in the law of immigration, it is open to the applicant on habeas corpus to show that he or she is not a person subject to the statute or that the authorities failed to follow the requisite procedure.[62]

The modern practice is to permit the applicant to demonstrate jurisdictional error by affidavit, and this is examined more closely in the following chapter.

(c) *Ex p. Rutty*

While cases illustrating the application of jurisdictional review are to be found throughout this chapter and the next two, it may be useful to

---

[59] *Infra*, p. 34 *et seq.*   [60] *Infra*, pp. 75–6.
[61] *Infra*, p. 76.   [62] *Infra*, p. 119.

examine in detail the *Rutty* case[63] as it indicates the broad ambit of jurisdictional error in the modern cases. The case deals with a commitment under the Mental Deficiency Act 1913.[64] The Act allowed a magistrate to make an order of commitment to an appropriate institution where the individual was shown to be defective and where the individual had been 'found neglected'. The Divisional Court admitted affidavit evidence to show the facts which were before the magistrate, and then entered upon the question whether the applicant could be said in law to have been 'found neglected'. Hilbery J. explained the court's power on habeas corpus as follows:

> On an application for a writ of habeas corpus this court does not sit as a court of appeal. It will not re-hear the matters which were to be decided by the judicial authority. The court will, however, admit affidavit evidence to decide whether there was any evidence before the judicial authority such as would justify his finding that he had jurisdiction to deal with the patient and to make an order.[65]

In other words, it is open to the superior court on habeas corpus to examine the legal basis of the inferior tribunal's decision and to see for itself whether the correct legal test has been applied. If the court finds that the statutory provision has been applied to a person or situation which it considers in law to lie outside the ambit of the statute, the court will interfere on habeas corpus. There are some passages in the judgment[66] which suggest that the court may have entertained the 'heresy' found with some frequency in habeas corpus cases, that making a finding without evidence constitutes jurisdictional error.[67] The references to 'no evidence' in the decision probably arise from the wariness courts sometimes express against reviewing a question of fact on which conflicting evidence has been received by the inferior court, even where that question relates to jurisdiction.[68] It is submitted that the case may be interpreted as saying 'on the facts adduced, it cannot be said that this person falls within the definition of "found neglected"'. In that sense, there was no evidence before the court that she was such a person within the meaning of the statute.

By imposing its own interpretation of 'found neglected' and holding

---

[63] *R.* v. *Board of Control, Ex p. Rutty* [1956] 2 Q.B. 109.
[64] Committals under mental health legislation are discussed at length in Chapter VI.
[65] [1956] 2 Q.B. 109 at 119.
[66] Esp. ibid. at 124 per Lord Goddard C.J.
[67] Discussed in detail, *infra*, pp. 79–85.
[68] *Infra*, pp. 80–1.

that the magistrate had exceeded jurisdiction on the facts, the court adopted a very wide definition of jurisdictional error. The *Rutty* case is a good modern example of habeas corpus being used to review a decision on the grounds of jurisdictional error. It demonstrates the broad, perhaps all-encompassing definition of jurisdictional error, and shows that jurisdictional error can be brought before the court on habeas corpus by affidavit.[69]

(d) *Other Aspects of Jurisdictional Review*

Two other aspects of jurisdictional review are discussed in the next chapter which deals with the consideration of questions of fact on habeas corpus. The first is the doctrine of jurisdictional fact, a concept which allows the court to consider many questions of fact and law on habeas corpus, and which provides further evidence of the broad definition given to jurisdictional review.

The second is the review of the sufficiency of evidence. The readiness of the courts to review the sufficiency of evidence on habeas corpus contrasts with the traditional reluctance in the law of judicial review to enter the question. It indicates the broad scope of review which is available on habeas corpus and may have presaged developments in the general law of judicial review.

4. REVIEW OF PATENT ERROR

The second branch of review which is available on habeas corpus is to give relief on the grounds of patent error. This aspect of review, long neglected but now revived in the law of certiorari,[70] is that the superior court may examine the record or documents brought before it relating to the inferior court's proceedings and give a remedy where there is a patent error or 'error on the face of the record'. This may occur even where the error is not one which goes to jurisdiction. The principle marks a significant departure from the jurisdictional basis for review, although as the definition of jurisdiction broadens to include most errors of law, it may merely provide alternate grounds for giving relief.

It is sometimes supposed that habeas corpus is merely a form of collateral attack, but equally, it is often recognized that collateral attack does not adequately describe the powers of review which the court

---

[69] See further, *infra*, pp. 75–6.   [70] *Supra*, p. 22.

has.[71] While the attack is collateral in form, there are quite clearly reviewing powers akin to those available on direct review, and the basis for the exercise of these powers is not excess of jurisdiction but is closer to 'error on the face of the record'.

Quite plainly, relief may be granted in cases where the return to the writ is bad, yet free from jurisdictional error. The whole purpose of habeas corpus is to determine whether or not the gaoler can produce legal authority for the detention. If the reason or document returned is erroneous in law or, in certain cases, in fact, the detention is not justified. The nature of the review differs from that had on certiorari in that the whole record of proceedings is not necessarily brought before the court and there is no power to quash. But the return, as in the case of the record on certiorari, is subjected to a search for error on the face.

The powers of review available on habeas corpus resemble very closely those available on certiorari, and so far as review for patent error is concerned, were described by Lord Pearce as follows:

The High Court has always had the power by writs of habeas corpus and certiorari to correct any error of law provided that it is able to see that the error has occurred ... in certiorari difficult questions may arise as to whether an error appears on the face of the record ... In habeas corpus the question was whether an error appeared on the return of the writ.[72]

The significance of allowing for review based on patent error is that it allows for a remedy without requiring the classification of the error as going to jurisdiction. While it now seems that most errors of law may be said to go to jurisdiction, review for patent error provides an 'escape' where the error is one which is usually seen as being intra-jurisdictional. In the modern cases, the most important use of this technique has been to justify the review of the sufficiency of evidence in extradition committals and this is to be discussed in detail.[73]

The power of the court to act on a patent error depends upon the technical question of what 'it is able to see'. Under the old practice, this was controlled by the contents of the return to the writ. If the return was detailed and disclosed a good deal about what had happened, then the possibilities for review were that much greater. Habeas corpus cases have not been tried on formal returns for some

---

[71] Rubinstein, op. cit. 105–16; de Smith, *Judicial Review*, 600–3.
[72] *Armah* v. *Government of Ghana* [1968] A.C. 192 at 253–4.
[73] *Infra*, pp. 79–85.

time, and it will be seen that the material before the court for scrutiny cannot be determined by imagining what the return would have contained.[74] However, the concept of review for patent error depends on the notion of the return to the writ, and it will be useful to look at the older cases which developed the idea of reviewing errors actually disclosed on the return.

(a) *Bankruptcy Committal Cases*

It is perhaps best to start with the clearest examples of review of patent error. This is offered by the cases dealing with the review of committals by commissioners of bankruptcy in the nineteenth century. Until 1869[75] commissioners of bankruptcy had extensive powers to commit for contempt. The statute which empowered commissioners to commit where the answer of the person being examined was unsatisfactory also provided that the warrant of commitment had to contain a verbatim account of the material parts of the examination.[76] This meant that on habeas corpus the court had brought before it a record of what had gone on below, and could, therefore, exercise direct review over the commissioners.

Even in the early cases, before this statutory change, the courts had exercised wide powers of review on habeas corpus, and had strictly interpreted the powers of the commissioners.[77] The common law had laid the ground for wide review over the commissioners, and with the aid of the statute, habeas corpus became virtually a form of appeal, simply because the material was there for the court to see. Lord Eldon described the test for deciding whether or not the party examined should be committed as being:

... satisfaction to a reasonable mind: in the first instance, to the mind of the Commissioners, in the next, to the mind of the Judge, as it were, appealed to, upon a habeas corpus. Thus appealed to, the Court has to exercise its own opinion upon the reasonableness of the examination.[78]

It is clear that review went beyond the question of the jurisdiction of the commissioners, and went to the very merits of their decision. Abbot C.J. described what happened:

---

[74] *Infra*, pp. 45–6.
[75] Bankruptcy Act 1869, s.3.
[76] Bankruptcy Act 1732, s.17.
[77] *Bracy's Case* (1701) 1 Salk. 348; *Hollingshead's Case* (1702) 1 Salk. 351; *R. v. Nathan* (1730) 2 Str. 880.
[78] *Coombe's Case* (1816) 2 Rose 396 at 398.

... as far as concerns the liberty of the person, their [the commissioners'] decision is to be subject to review, upon the general question, whether the answers be or be not satisfactory; that for the purpose of such review, the whole examination be set forth in the warrant; and if upon review by the superior tribunals, the answers be thought satisfactory the party is liberated from his imprisonment.[79]

The statutory obligation to include the particular question or questions and the unsatisfactory answer was extended by the cases to require the inclusion of the whole examination.[80] In several cases the prisoner was discharged where part of the examination was omitted,[81] as the courts insisted upon being able to review all that had passed before the commissioners.

The bankruptcy cases illustrate how very flexible the scope of review on habeas corpus can be. Even though the court considered itself to be confined to the return,[82] a power of review akin to appeal was evolved. Habeas corpus was said to be the only way to question these committals,[83] and it was accordingly important that there be a sufficiently wide scope of review. These cases show that while the nature of review depends upon the rules relating to warrants and the return, these rules can be readily adapted, where considerations of policy so require.

(b) *Defining the Contents of the Return. The Seventeenth-Century Cases*

In the bankruptcy cases, the requirement for a full return was based on statute. Some of the earlier cases, which have been discussed in Chapter 1, are significant in that they established the common law requirement that the return show cause for the imprisonment. By holding insufficient those returns which failed to disclose sufficient details of the cause, the courts forced the inferior jurisdictions to make more of their proceedings openly appear. It has been seen how the early cases dealing with committals by the High Commission, Chancery, Admiralty and other bodies, together with the struggle over the prerogative and the Petition of Right, really established habeas corpus

---

[79] *Doswell* v. *Impey* (1832) 1 B. & C. 163 at 177. See also *Ex p. Oliver* (1813) 1 Rose 407.

[80] *Coombe's Case* (1816) 2 Rose 396; *Ex p. Oliver* (1813) 1 Rose 407; *Tomlin's Case* (1824) 1 Glyn. & Jam. 373.

[81] Ibid.

[82] *Crowley's Case* (1818) 2 Swanst. 1 at 75; *Coombe's Case* (1816) 2 Rose 396.

[83] *Crowley's Case* (1818) 2 Swanst. 1; *Ex p. Tomkinson* (1804) 10 Ves. Jun. 106; *Doswell* v. *Impey* (1823) 1 B. & C. 163.

as an effective remedy.[84] The rule requiring the process or warrants to show clearly the cause for the imprisonment was needed to ensure that the arbitrary or unlawful nature of the imprisonment could not be hidden from judicial scrutiny.

In many cases, the court went further than requiring cause to be shown in the sense of a valid order made within jurisdiction. The cases dealing with contempt committals are especially good examples of the broad controlling power the court could exercise on habeas corpus. It was held that sufficient details of the words alleged to be contemptuous had to be given so that the court could judge for itself whether the finding could be upheld.[85]

These cases are, of course, incidents in the struggle between the common law courts and the other jurisdictions. The common law courts were unwilling to countenance the claims of their rivals to a general power to imprison, especially for a cause so vague as contempt. The battle would have been lost had the King's Bench or Common Pleas been precluded from further investigation by a simple sentence or judgment. By requiring the process under which the prisoner was held to show cause for the imprisonment, the courts were able to achieve a broad and flexible power of review on habeas corpus.

However, perhaps the best example of the claim to a broad power of direct review depends not at all upon the struggle between the courts for control. In *Bushell's Case* in 1670,[86] Vaughan C.J. ordered the discharge of a juryman who had been committed for contempt by the London Court of Sessions. The contempt alleged was that he and the other jury members had refused to convict the accused on charges of unlawful and tumultuous assembly, and that the refusal to convict had been against the weight of the evidence.[87] Vaughan C.J.'s view that the return was insufficient and that he had the power to go behind the order of contempt suggests an extremely broad scope of review:

The Court hath no knowledge by this return, whether the evidence given were full and manifest, or doubtful, lame, and dark, or indeed evidence at all material to the issue, because it is not returned what evidence in particular, and as it was delivered, was given. For it is not possible to judge of that rightly,

---

[84] *Supra*, Chapter 1.
[85] See esp. *Chamber's Case* (1628) Cro. Car. 133; *Hodd* v. *High Commission Court* (1615) 3 Bulst. 146; *Codd* v. *Turback* (1615) 3 Bulst. 109.
[86] Vaughan 135.
[87] The trial is *Penn & Mead's Case* (1670) 6 St. Tr. 951.

which is not exposed to a man's judgment. But here the evidence given to the jury is not exposed at all to this Court, but the judgment of the Court of Sessions upon that evidence is only exposed to us; who tell us it was full and manifest. But our judgment ought to be grounded upon our own inferences and understandings, and not upon theirs.[88]

He did go further and express his view that, in any case, the jurors could not, in law, be held in contempt for finding against the evidence, but the decision itself did rest upon the insufficiency of the return. The case describes a pervasive power of review, based upon the rationale of the sufficiency of the return.[89] The court did not need to go outside the return: it simply required the return to contain such a complete account of the proceedings that a power of review in the nature of direct attack was achieved.[90]

The seventeenth-century cases do provide examples of effective review of patent error on habeas corpus. By requiring that the documents relied on to justify the detention should contain a complete legal cause, the courts provided themselves with a method whereby they could ask to see whatever they liked, or whatever was necessary, of the impugned proceedings.[91] What would suffice as a sufficient return was not defined with precision. Enough had to appear to satisfy the court that the imprisonment was a legal one, and the court did not have to be stymied by technical rules. In cases where the court felt that review was appropriate, requiring cause to be shown enabled the

[88] Vaughan 135 at 137.

[89] In a subsequent action for false imprisonment against the sessions judges *Hamond* v. *Howell* (1670) 2 Mod. 218) it was held that while the judges had acted incorrectly, they had acted judicially, and that therefore no action would lie. See comment on the case in IV Bacon Abridg. 120–1: '... [it was held that] though the imprisonment was illegal, yet that no action lay against the commissioners, because they acted as judges; and commissioners of oyer and terminer can no more be punished for an erroneous commitment than they can for an erroneous judgment; and the highest remedy the party in this case can have is a writ of habeas corpus.' See also *Bushell's Case* (1674) 1 Mod. 119.

[90] It is clear from *Bushell's Case* itself that the broad power of review would not always have been exercised. Vaughan C.J. acknowledged that a return showing a committal for treason or felony need not set out the facts upon which the charge was based: Vaughan at 142; and it is doubtful that he would have been willing to review a conviction of the Court of Sessions. See Oaks, 'Legal History in the High Court—Habeas Corpus' (1966) 64 Mich. L.R. 451, discussing the use of *Bushell's Case* as an authority by the United States Supreme Court in *Fay* v. *Noia* 372 U.S. 391 (1963).

[91] See e.g. *Hawkeridge's Case* (1616) 12 Co. Rep. 129, where the court asked the Marshal of the Admiralty to amend the return and bailed the prisoner when he refused to do so: 'for the insufficiency of the return which the court could not obtain to be amended, the said Hawkeridge was bailed ... upon an insufficient return the party ought to be bailed or discharged, as all our books and infinite precedents are'.

court to 'see' what it wished and grant review if it found error, without necessarily worrying about the jurisdictional classification.[92]

These cases do provide the basis, if one is needed, for the court to investigate certain errors without having to bring those errors within the rubric of 'jurisdictional error'. In the *Armah* case in 1968[93] the House of Lords seems to have revived this principle in practice. Should development of the principle require further authority, it should be remembered that when the closely analogous review for error on the face of the record in the law of certiorari was revived, the Court accepted the authority of the seventeenth-century cases.[94]

The High Court of Australia has held that a warrant of committal for contempt issued by a royal commission must set out on its face the cause for the committal and the nature of the contempt, for '[i]f that is not done, when a warrant is produced in answer to an application for habeas corpus, it is not possible to see whether a prisoner is held arbitrarily, or has been committed for lawful reasons.'[95] A similar principle has been acted on in Canada.[96]

(c) *Magisterial Law—Patent Error*

Patent error was also a basis for review in magisterial law. The principle here was that expressed in *Dr. Groenvelt's Case*: '... the cause

---

[92] See e.g. 1 Hale *P.C.*, 584: '[A warrant of commitment must] express the cause for which he is committed, namely felony, and what kind of felony ... it is necessary upon return of the habeas corpus out of the King's Bench, because it is in the nature of a writ of right or a writ of error to determine whether the imprisonment be good or erroneous.' For a later expression of the same idea, see *R.* v. *Bowen* (1793) 5 T.R. 156 at 158 per Kenyon C.J., '... no certiorari ought to have been granted to remove the order of sessions hither, because I think that the proper mode of obtaining relief in this case, if the defendant were entitled to it, is by habeas corpus, on a return to which the causes of commitment would be specified, and upon those the court would be enabled to form an opinion whether or not those causes were sufficient to justify his detention.'

[93] [1968] A.C. 192, *infra*, pp. 43–5.

[94] *R.* v. *Northumberland Compensation Appeal Tribunal, ex p. Shaw* [1952] 1 K.B. 338; see also *Ex p. Pickett* (1976) 28 C.C.C. (2d) 417 (Ont. H.C., aff'd C.A. at 422) at 421–2, referring to *Bushell's Case* '... as an authority for the proposition that habeas corpus was available at common law to attack imprisonment on grounds other than want of jurisdiction.... That case stands for a great principle.' See further, *infra*, n. 102, p. 41.

[95] *Ferraro* v. *Woodward* (1978) 143 C.L.R. 102 at 106, ordering release on habeas corpus where the warrant was defective.

[96] In *Braaten* v. *Sargent and A.G. for B.C.* (1967) 61 D.L.R. (2d) 678 (B.C.S.C.) it was argued on the basis of some old authorities that a committal for contempt by a Royal Commissioner was bad for not setting out the offence and the jurisdiction on its face: per Seaton J. at 689–90: 'It may be said that some of the authorities cited are very old and that the rights and remedies dealt with on these applications are of ancient origin. It would seem to me that the rights are still at least of equal importance today and that the remedies are still valid.'

of commitment ought to be certain, to the end that the party may know for what he suffers, and how he may regain his liberty.'[97]

The first branch of the rule, the idea that the process under which the prisoner was held had to 'show cause' for his imprisonment, often meant that the court could exercise a pervasive power of review. The importance of the rule that jurisdiction has to appear on the face of inferior proceedings has already been noted in the discussion of jurisdictional review. There can be little doubt, however, that the review of patent error often went beyond what would normally be regarded as jurisdictional review. For example in a smuggling case in 1821,[98] the return simply stated that the prisoner had been committed upon due proof as required by the statute[99] but the court held this to be insufficient:

... in as much as this Act trenches very strongly on the liberty of the subject, we must take care that its provisions are strictly pursued. This averment is one of a conclusion of law; it states that upon due proof the party was committed. Now whether that was so this return does not enable us to judge; for unless we know what the proof was which was given, it is impossible for us to tell whether it was the proof required by the Act of Parliament.[100]

This is reminiscent of the view expounded in *Bushell's Case*[101] on the use of the concept of 'cause shown' to provide a broad power of review.[102]

The cases where the prisoner has been discharged because the warrant fails to describe an offence fully or accurately can also be put under this head of proper cause shown.[103] In 1870 a court ordered the discharge of a prisoner convicted of vagrancy where the warrant of commitment failed to state that the highway frequented was a place of public resort.[104] There are many other cases where failure to state a

[97] (1702) 1 Ld. Raym. 213.   [98] *Nash's Case* (1821) 4 B. & Ald. 295.

[99] 57 Geo. III, c.87.

[100] 4 B. & Ald. at 297, per Abbot C.J.

[101] *Supra*, pp. 38–40.

[102] See also *Re Munavish* (1958) 121 C.C.C. 299 (B.C.S.C.); *Ex p. Lewis* (1975) 25 C.C.C. (2d) 124 (B.C.S.C.); *Ex p. Andrews* (1973) 15 C.C.C. (2d) 43 (B.C.S.C.) at 44 per Meredith J.: 'I am unable to determine from an examination of this warrant whether or not there was jurisdiction in the Court to issue the same.'

[103] It is arguable that these cases should be excluded from consideration as examples of patent error, and be properly seen as implementing the requirement that inferior process show jurisdiction on its face. It is submitted, however, that they are properly classified in the text because there was no pretence that the errors went to jurisdiction, nor would they ordinarily be so regarded.

[104] *Re Timson* (1870) L.R. 5 Exch. 257; following *Ex p. Jones* (1852) 21 L.J.M.C. 116; cf. *Ex p. Brown* (1852) 21 L.J.M.C. 113, *contra* on the substantive point.

constituent element of an offence[105] or a simple misstatement[106] of the offence in the commitment led to the discharge of the prisoner on habeas corpus.

As well as these substantive errors, there were other more technical forms of error which could vitiate a warrant of commitment. This is the second branch of the rule quoted above from *Dr. Groenvelt's Case* regarding the sufficiency of warrants, namely, that the prisoner should be able to see 'how he may regain his liberty'. The warrant had to be directed to someone in particular rather than ordering imprisonment in general terms.[107] It had to spell out the period of the imprisonment,[108] clearly state the amount of fine to be paid or sureties to be found before the prisoner could be discharged,[109] and a commitment which could be construed as allowing for a longer period of time than that authorized by statute was bad. The commitment had to be in writing, under the hand and seal of the justice,[110] and express the office and authority of the justice.[111] Where a commitment followed an unsuccessful distraint for the penalty, it had to appear that an adjudication of insufficiency had been made.[112] The courts granted relief in all these cases, and again, they are examples of review on the grounds of patent defect.

(i) Summary Jurisdiction Acts. It has been seen[113] that the effect of the Summary Jurisdiction Act 1848 was to remove the basis for full review by providing for brief, even bald convictions and warrants which disclosed little of the proceedings. The formal conviction and warrant of commitment became much less significant and direct appellate proceedings took the place of review on the prerogative writs.

While this has had the effect of lessening the importance of habeas corpus in the review of summary convictions almost to the vanishing point,[114] the principle of these earlier cases need not be rejected. They

---

[105] *R. v. Chaney* (1838) 7 L.J.M.C. 65; *R. v. King* (1843) 13 L.J.M.C. 43; *R. v. Brown* (1798) 8 T.R. 26; *Cavanagh* (1842) 6 Jur. 220.

[106] *R. v. Evered* (1777) Cald. 26; *R. v. Harpur* (1822) 1 D. & R. 222; *Ex p. Hill* (1827) 3 C. & P. 225; *Re Fischer* (1874) 8 S.A.L.R. 57.

[107] *R. v. Smith* (1731) 2 Str. 934.

[108] *R. v. James* (1822) 5 B. & Ald. 894; *Mash's Case* (1772) 2 W. Bl. 805; *Re Williams* (1874) 5 A.J.R. 160.

[109] *R. v. Catterall* (1730) Fitz-G. 266; *Rudyard's Case* (1670) 2 Vent 23.

[110] 2 Hawkins *P.C.*, c.16 s.13.

[111] Ibid.; *R. v. York* (1770) 5 Burr. 2684.

[112] *R. v. Chandler* (1704) 1 Ld. Raym. 545.

[113] *Supra*, pp. 30–1.

[114] *Supra*, pp. 30–2. Cases of patent error may still arise, however: see e.g. *R. v.*

demonstrate that if the court can 'see' the defect on habeas corpus, it can grant relief, and that the defect does not always have to be related to jurisdiction.

(d) *Armah* v. *Government of Ghana*

Perhaps the best modern example of review of patent error is *Armah* v. *Government of Ghana*.[115] There, the House of Lords was faced with the question of review of the sufficiency of evidence for a committal under the Fugitive Offenders Act. The problem of review on the grounds of no evidence is discussed in detail in another part.[116] For present purposes, it suffices to note that while review of this question has been allowed on habeas corpus in extradition cases on the grounds that such an error goes to jurisdiction, the accepted rule in the law of judicial review has been that making a finding with no evidence does not constitute a jurisdictional error.[117] In *Armah*, when faced with the contrast between previous practice on habeas corpus and the accepted rule that the question was not reviewable, at least two of the Law Lords put review for no evidence on the footing of review for apparent error, and a third seemed to acknowledge this as a possible view.

The opinion of Lord Reid, especially, demonstrates that even where a judge refuses to classify an error of law as going to jurisdiction, review may still be justified. His decision provides an excellent example of how review on habeas corpus tends to encompass all errors of law where the decision is of a type which the courts consider appropriate for review on habeas corpus.

Lord Reid clearly indicated that the superior court could review certain intra-jurisdictional errors, and that the sufficiency of evidence was such an error.[118] Lord Upjohn said that the power to review the evidence could be supported either as jurisdictional review or as being one of the questions of law, not going to jurisdiction, which could be examined.[119] Lord Pearce pointed out that the court could grant relief

Governor of Bedford Prison, ex p. Ames [1953] 1 All E.R. 1002, where it was held on habeas corpus that a warrant issued under the Money Payments (Justices Procedure) Act 1935 was bad since it specified an incorrect amount, and the applicant was accordingly released.

[115] [1968] A.C. 192.   [116] *Infra*, pp. 79–85.
[117] But cf. the cases which suggest that this is becoming an accepted ground of review, discussed *infra*, pp. 80, 84.
[118] [1968] A.C. 192 at 230, 235–5.
[119] Ibid. at 257.

on the basis of errors of law which it could see,[120] and he added that in the present case, the magistrate had fallen into jurisdictional error by asking the wrong question.[121] Lord Morris of Borth-y-Gest and Lord Pearson, dissenting, described the court's powers of review purely in terms of jurisdictional error, although Lord Morris admitted that the concept of jurisdiction was being stretched.[122] They both would have found sufficient evidence in the case before them to give the magistrate jurisdiction to commit.

The result is that one of their Lordships based his opinion solely on the grounds that the court could review certain questions of non-jurisdictional law, another held that non-jurisdictional questions of law could be entertained and that 'no evidence' could be considered as either an error of jurisdiction or simply as an error of law. A third held that apparent errors of law were reviewable, and added to this finding a jurisdictional analysis. There is, then, a majority view that the court can review certain errors of law without characterizing them as going to jurisdiction.

Both Lord Reid and Lord Pearce concerned themselves with the somewhat suspect proposition that the sufficiency of evidence could be reviewed. They both characterized the problem as being a technical one, namely, how do the depositions get before the court in the first place. Under the old practice, the court had to consider the case on the return of the gaoler, and since the depositions were not in his possession, they would not have been included in the return. Lord Reid and Lord Pearce both suggested that the practice of examining the deposition may have resulted from the procedure adopted in two of the earliest extradition cases, where, by agreement of counsel, the depositions were brought before the court as if on certiorari.[123] In fact,

---

[120] Ibid. at 253 (passage quoted *supra*, p. 35).

[121] Ibid. at 255: 'In addition to the point whether there was evidence which the magistrate could properly hold sufficient to raise a strong or probable presumption, the court can also consider the point whether the magistrate asked himself the right question, the answer to which was essential to his jurisdiction. If he did not do so, he did not properly assume his jurisdiction, and the superior court can interfere ... In my view, therefore, the learned magistrate was misled by the case of *Bidwell* [1937] 1 K.B. 305 [which dealt with the standard of proof required under the Fugitive Offenders Act 1881] into applying the wrong test. And had he applied the right test as laid down in plain words by the Act he could not properly have found that the evidence raised a strong or probable presumption.' This analysis, it is submitted, is further indication of the all-encompassing nature of jurisdictional error.

[122] Ibid. at 237–8.

[123] Ibid. at 234–5, 254. The two cases are *Re Tivnan* (1864) 5 B. & S. 645; and *Re Windsor* (1865) 6 B. & S. 522.

it would seem that in these early cases, the courts treated the matter just as they treated the review of domestic committals, and the practice of reviewing the depositions for the purpose of granting bail was adapted to meet the need of the extradition cases.[124] It is important to note that there does not appear to be a single case where the courts have felt that certiorari was actually needed,[125] and until *Armah*, it was never even mentioned. Moreover, the depositions are not usually regarded as part of the record to be returned on certiorari.[126] It would be a mistake, then, to treat *Armah* as just another certiorari case dealing with error on the face of the record. It should be recognized as confirming what had been accepted in so many of the earlier cases, namely, that patent error constitutes a ground for review on habeas corpus.[127]

(e) *When is a Defect Patent?*

In the old cases, the question of what defects were patent or apparent, and therefore subject to review, was defined by the return. In modern practice, the issue is usually tried on motion where the material is before the court on affidavit. The writ rarely issued and it is unusual to have a case tried upon a formal return.[128] Moreover, the *Armah* case suggests that the question of what errors of law are reviewable is not answered by imagining what might have been

---

[124] See further, *infra*, pp. 81–3.

[125] Cf., however, the Canadian practice, discussed *infra*, pp. 51–2.

[126] *R. v. Nat Bell Liquors* [1922] 2 AC.C. 128 (P.C.). In *Armah*, the following passage from IV Bacon Abridg. 122 was said to show that under the old practice, certiorari was required to bring up the depositions: 'If a person be in custody, and also indicted for some offence in the inferior court, there must, beside the habeas corpus to remove the body, be a certiorari to remove the record; for as the certiorari alone removes not the body, so the habeas corpus alone removes not the record itself, but only the prisoner with the cause of his commitment; and therefore, although upon the habeas corpus, and the return thereof, the court can judge of the sufficiency or insufficiency of the return and commitment, and bail or discharge, or remand the prisoner, as the case appears upon the return; yet they cannot upon the bare return of the habeas corpus give any judgment, or proceed upon the record of the indictment order or judgment, without the record itself be removed by certiorari; . . .' It is submitted, however, that the passage refers to certiorari to bring up the record so the court could proceed to *try* the prisoner on indictment: with respect to pre-trial proceedings, it states that on habeas corpus alone 'the court can judge of the sufficiency of insufficiency of the return and commitment and bail or discharge or remand the prisoner, *as the case appears upon the return.*' See also *infra*, pp. 129–30.

[127] Cf., however, Aronson and Franklin, *Review of Administrative Action* (1987), 665–7, suggesting that authority for proposition that habeas corpus is available to review for patent error is problematic.

[128] The practice, present and past, is discussed in more detail, *infra*, 218–21.

returned to the writ. In that case, the review was exercised over materials which would not necessarily have been brought forth on the return but which had been brought before the court simply as a matter of practice.

In fact, the cases provide very little guidance here. It is possible that the problem will not arise simply because it will be possible to characterize most errors of law as errors of jurisdiction. If, however, the jurisdictional approach proves to be resilient, there is the possibility of review for patent error. It has been seen how the courts have at times asked for 'full cause' for the imprisonment to be shown in order that they could 'judge for themselves' the legality of the detention.[129] Especially in cases where there is no other remedy available, it is difficult to imagine that the courts would be satisfied with a bald warrant or order of committal, and it is more likely that more material would be required. In the law of certiorari, where there is a similar problem of defining the record,[130] the courts have not been constrained by overly technical consideration in this regard.[131] There is every reason to suspect that a similarly inventive approach could be taken in habeas corpus. If there is an error of law which for some reason is not to be considered jurisdictional, it is submitted that the court could give relief by treating it as a patent error.

5. SUPERIOR COURT ORDERS AND CONVICTIONS

The writ of habeas corpus has never been used with effect where convictions or orders of courts of general common law jurisdiction are concerned.[132] These were the courts of superior jurisdiction, courts of

---

[129] *Supra*, pp. 37–40.

[130] Discussed by Abel, 'Materials Proper for Consideration in Certiorari to Tribunals' (1964) 15 U. of T.L.J. 102; Fitzgerald and Elliot, 'Certiorari: Errors of Law on the Face of the Record' (1964) 4 Melb. U.L.R. 552.

[131] *R.* v. *Chertsey JJ., ex p. Franks* [1961] 2 Q.B. 152, holding that the oral reasons of the justices constituted part of the record. Cf. the case comment (1961) 77 L.Q.R. 157 which concludes at 161: 'Perhaps it is not too bold to prophesy that in the end the sphinx may indeed prove to be a phoenix.' See also *R.* v. *Medical Appeal Tribunal, ex p. Gilmore* [1957] 1 Q.B. 574 (C.A.), holding that the count has power to require a tribunal to complete its record.

[132] It has been held in Canada, however, that habeas corpus is available to review an extradition committal made by a superior court judge, and that a full scope of review is available: *Re Meier and The Queen* (1983) 6 C.C.C. (3d) 165 (B.C.S.C.) (aff'd 8 C.C.C. (3d) 210, leave to appeal to S.C.C. refused, ibid.). In such a case, in order to avoid delay, the original judge may hear and refuse a habeas corpus application immediately after

assize, and quarter sessions, when trying matters on indictment, and now are the courts which exercise jurisdiction in the name of the Supreme Court, including in certain of its functions, the Crown Court.[133]

The common law provided only the most awkward and inadequate forms of redress in respect of an error made by a court of general jurisdiction. The only form of direct review available[134] was the writ of error, the inadequacy of which was generally acknowledged.[135] It removed the record of proceedings to be reviewed, but the court was restricted to dealing only with those errors which appeared on the face of the record, a document which disclosed nothing of the evidence or jury direction.[136] There were few instances where exception could be taken to the record and the courts held that if error were available, no other direct method of attack, such as certiorari, could be used.[137]

The common law protection against wrongful conviction was trial by jury and, as for contempt committals, it was felt that the authority of the courts would have been undermined had they been freely reviewable. There were no post-conviction remedies which would be considered adequate nowadays and the judges did not see the need to supply any. The common law and the jury guaranteed a fair trial and after that it was thought that there should be finality.[138]

While other direct methods of attack were excluded, the writ of habeas corpus could always exert its demand on the gaoler, and it was not precluded as a remedy simply because the conviction or order of a superior court was involved. However, as a practical matter, the courts have never allowed habeas corpus to be used as a means of reviewing

---

issuing the warrant of committal, so that the matter may be brought immediately before the Court of Appeal: *Re Federal Republic of Germany and Rauca* (1983) 4 C.C.C. (3d) 385 (Ont. H.C.); *R.* v. *Borle* (1985) 20 C.C.C. (3d) 285 (Alta. C.A.).

[133] Supreme Court Act 1981, s.29(3).

[134] There was some possibility of a new trial if appropriate procedural steps had been taken before trial: see 1 Stepehen, op. cit. 310–11.

[135] 1 Stephen, op. cit. 308–10; 1 Holdsworth, 215.

[136] 1 Stephen, op. cit. 308–10.

[137] *Rice* v. *R.* (1616) Cro. Jac. 404; *R.* v. *Bethel* (1702) 6 Mod. 17; *R.* v. *J.J.W. Riding Yorkshire* (1798) 7 T.R. 467; *R.* v. *Pennegoes* (1822) 1 B. & C. 142. As Gordon, 'Challenging Conviction by Habeas Corpus and Certiorari' (1959) 2 Crim. L.Q. 296, points out the courts used confusing language, describing such decisions as being by a court 'having competence to try the offence, ... having general jurisdiction over the offence,' or 'court of record,' but the test always appeared to have been whether the matter was a final judgment on a trial according to common law.

[138] See *infra*, n. 108, p. 145 for the history of appeals.

the decisions of superior courts.[139] Typical is the statement made by Denman L.J. in 1845 with reference to a superior court order: '[There is an] exception that runs through the whole law of habeas corpus, whether under common law or statute, namely, that our form of writ does not apply where a party is in execution under the judgment of a competent court.'[140]

It has been seen how techniques were developed by the courts to achieve review of inferior court decisions on habeas corpus. By marked contrast, proceedings and decisions of the common law courts were treated with a respect which made for finality.

In the first place, the presumption *omnia praesumuntur rite esse acta* was applied to instruments issued by the superior courts.[141] Regularity was presumed and a conviction or warrant could never be questioned for not patently showing jurisdiction. Even where the formal warrant or commitment was found to be defective, the courts have always regarded the error as one of form only where regular proceedings had led to its issue, and the prisoner would be remanded.[142] The technical approach so rigorously followed in the case of summary proceedings was simply not thought to be proper in the case of common law courts.

Moreover, the records of the common law courts have a kind of sanctity which even prevents a reviewing court from acting where an actual absence of jurisdiction is alleged.[143] It is invariably presumed that the court has acted regularly and in no case has the record of the proceedings been impeached on habeas corpus.

---

[139] In *Re Sparrow* (1908) 28 N.Z.L.R. 143, Chapman J. refused relief on the merits, but suggested that habeas corpus could be used against a superior court in a case of exceeded jurisdiction. See also *R.* v. *Collyer & Capon* (1752) Sayer 44, where habeas corpus was awarded against an unlawful sentence at quarter sessions: noted *infra*, p. 150. Cf. the Canadian cases discussed *supra*, n.132, p. 46.

[140] *Carus Wilson's Case* (1845) 7 Q.B. 984 at 1008.

[141] *Re Sproule* (1886) 12 S.C.R. 140; *In the Application of Harrod* [1978] 1 N.S.W.L.R. 331; *Peacock* v. *Bell* (1667) 1 Saund. 73 at 74. 'The rule for jurisdiction is, that nothing shall be intended to be out of the jurisdiction of a superior court, but that which specially appears to be so; and on the contrary, nothing shall be intended to be within the jurisdiction of an inferior court but that which is so expressly alleged.'

[142] *R.* v. *Bethel* (1702) 5 Mod. 19.

[143] *Re Sproule* (1886) 12 S.C.R. 140. A good example of this principle in operation is *Re Newton* (1855) 16 C.B. 97. The place of the commission of the offence as stated in the record was not within the jurisdiction of the Central Criminal Court. On habeas corpus, the court held that affidavits showing where the stated place was could not be admitted as the issue of the *situs* of the offence must be taken to have been decided against the prisoner by the jury. See also: *R.* v. *Carlisle* (1831) 4 C. & P. 415; *Re Clarke* (1842) 2 Q.B. 619. Cf. Lanham, 'The Reviewability of Superior Court Orders' (1988) 16 Melb. U.L.R. 603.

It has been suggested that the basis for the inviolability of Supreme Court orders in collateral proceedings is the rule that superior court judges have the power to decide the limits of their own jurisdiction.[144] This means that even if a superior court judge exceeds his jurisdiction, that is an error which he has jurisdiction to make. This, however, begs the question why, as a matter of policy, superior court judges should be given more than tentative power to decide the limits of their own jurisdiction. It is not unusual in direct appellate proceedings to see a higher court say that a superior court judge exceeded his jurisdiction.[145] The refusal to allow this to happen on collateral proceedings or on habeas corpus may be explained by the desire for certainty and stability of the judicial process at this level, and this policy perhaps accounts for the decided reluctance to make even a wrong decision subject to indirect attack.

It has been seen how there is a possibility of achieving a kind of direct review by requiring the instrument under which the prisoner is held to state fully the cause for the imprisonment. However, this branch of review on habeas corpus has been hopelessly crippled in the case of the superior courts by the refusal of the courts to require any more than a bald statement that an order was made.

The neglect of the power in this area stems from cases dealing with committals by Parliament for contempt. The refusal to require a full statement of the nature of the alleged contempt in the early cases was based on the theory that Parliament was a body beyond the ordinary jurisdiction of the courts. In the *Earl of Shaftesbury's Case* in 1677,[146] it was recognized that if the return had related to the order of 'an ordinary court of justice, it would have been [adjudged] ill and uncertain', but it was held that proceedings in Parliament were simply not justiciable.[147] However, in the eighteenth and nineteenth centuries, the authority of the cases of Parliamentary contempt orders was applied to the superior courts,[148] and the generality allowed Parliamentary committals was also allowed to those of the courts.

[144] Salmond, *Torts* (16th ed. 1973), 417; Rubinstein, op. cit. 11–12.
[145] See e.g. *Sirros* v. *Moore* [1974] 3 W.L.R. 459 at 474, per Buckley L.J.
[146] 1 Mod. 144.
[147] See also *R.* v. *Paty* (1704) 2 Ld. Raym. 1105 at 1106, per Gould J.: 'If this had been a return of a commitment by an inferior court, it would have been nought because it did not set out a sufficient cause of commitment; but this return being of a commitment by the House of Commons, which is superior to this court, is not reversible for form.'
[148] *Alexander Murray's Case* (1751) 1 Wils. 299; *Brass Crosby's Case* (1771) 2 W.Bl. 754; *Middlesex Sheriff's Case* (1840) 11 A. & E. 273; cases cited *infra*, n. 150, p. 50. See

The idea that the warrant and return must show enough to enable the reviewing court to judge the legality of the committal for itself was specifically held in 1861 to be inapplicable to superior court committals.[149] It was said that a simple statement of the court and of the fact of its adjudication would suffice. This merely confirmed the result reached in many other cases dealing with superior court orders[150] and made superior courts virtually immune from review on habeas corpus.

It has been recognized, however, that if the return to the writ itself shows vitiating illegality, or that the court was 'incompetent', then the prisoner will be released even where an order or conviction of a superior court is involved.[151] If, for example, it were returned that the prisoner had been convicted at quarter sessions for murder, an offence triable only at assizes, the prisoner would be discharged on habeas corpus.[152] The possibility of review has, however, remained theoretical and the superior courts have virtual immunity.

There is nothing inherent in the writ of habeas corpus which makes

now *Linnet* v. *Coles* [1987] Q.B. 555 (C.A.), holding that except in exceptional cases, habeas corpus cannot be used to challenge a committal for contempt of court, but that such committals should be tested by way of appeal pursuant to the Administration of Justice Act 1960, s.13.

149 *Ex p. Fernandez* (1861) 10 C.B.N.S. 3. The court also rejected the authority of the old cases dealing with committals by Chancery as being merely referable to the 'sort of contest going on at that time between the two jurisdictions' (at 33–4).

150 *Re Andrews* (1847) 4 C.B. 226; *Ex p. Partington* (1844) 6 Q.B. 649; *Re Dunn* (1847) 5 C.B. 215; *Dodd's Case* (1858) 2 De G. & J. 510; *Re Crawford* (1849) 13 Q.B. 613; *Brenan & Galen's Case* (1847) 10 Q.B. 492; *Carus Wilson's Case* (1845) 7 Q.B. 984; *Ex p. Lees* (1860) E.B. & E. 828; *Re Sproule* (1886) 12 S.C.R. 140; *Williamson* v. *Inspector-General of Penal Establishments* [1958] V.R. 330.

151 In *Burdett* v. *Abbott* (1811) 14 East 1 at 150, Lord Ellenborough said: '... if a commitment appeared to be for a contempt of the House of Commons generally, I would neither in the case of that court, nor of any other of the superior courts, inquire further: but if it did not profess to commit for a contempt, but for some matter appearing on the return, which could by no reasonable intendment be considered as a contempt of the court committing, but a ground of commitment palpably and evidently arbitrary, unjust, and contrary to every principle of positive law, or national [natural?] justice; I say, that in the case of such a commitment ... we must look at it and act upon it as justice may require from whatever Court it may profess to have proceeded.' See also *R.* v. *Paty* (1704) 2 Ld. Raym. 1105, per Holt C.J. (dissenting); *Middlesex Sheriff's Case* (1840) 11 A. & E. 273; *Ex p. Fernandez* (1861) 10 C.B.N.S. 3 at 60; Rubinstein, op. cit. 110. Cf. *Ex p. Hallett* (1841) 1 Legge 163 (N.S.W.), refusing relief where the return showed such an error. See also Lord Parker C.J.'s confusing remark in *Re Hunt* [1959] 1 Q.B. 378 at 383, a habeas corpus case dealing with a high court contempt committal: 'It may be that the true view is, and I think the cases support it, that though this court always has the power to inquire into the legality of the committal, it will not inquire whether the power has been properly exercised.'

152 *Re Sproule* (1886) 12 S.C.R. 140 at 205; *Ex p. Williams* (1934) 51 C.L.R. 545.

the review of an order of a superior court improper; it is simply that the rules concerning the orders of superior courts make it extremely difficult to establish the grounds for review. Habeas corpus became linked in the minds of the judges with certiorari and the jurisdictional basis for review. To a certain extent, it was seen as simply one of the methods used by superior courts to keep inferior courts within their jurisdiction. It became tied to a theory which was never applied to the common law courts.

Quite apart from these limitations, the judges were simply unwilling to claim a reviewing power over the decision of their colleagues. Trial by common law was thought to provide the subject with adequate protection, and the possibility of allowing a convicted person some method of challenging the correctness of a conviction by habeas corpus was viewed with considerable misgiving.[153]

6. CERTIORARI-IN-AID OF HABEAS CORPUS

It is often possible to ask for certiorari in conjunction with habeas corpus in order to bring the complete record of inferior proceedings before the court.[154] This technique is used much more frequently in Canada,[155] but provided certiorari is itself available to question the

[153] See e.g. what was said by Denman C.J. in *Carus Wilson's Case* (1845) 7 Q.B. 984 at 1009; 'The security which the public has against the impunity of offenders is, that the court which tries must be considered competent to convict. We could not interfere in this way without incurring the danger of setting at large persons committed for the worst offences.'

[154] For example, see *Re H.K. (An Infant)* [1967] 2 Q.B. 617.

[155] The view has been expressed that on habeas corpus alone, the court is confined to the warrant of committal: see, e.g., *Re Schumiatcher* [1962] S.C.R. 38; *R. v. Wood* (1924) 43 C.C.C. 382 (Ont.); *Ex p. Patterson* (1971) 3 C.C.C. (2d) 181 (B.C.S.C.); *Zamai v. R.* (1981) 24 C.R. (3d) 33 (B.C.S.C.). This probably stems from dicta in decisions of the Supreme Court of Canada under its former original jurisdiction in habeas corpus cases. The court was especially reluctant to open a collateral channel to review convictions, and narrowly defined its powers of review: *Re Trepanier* (1885) 12 S.C.R. 111; *Re Sproule* (1886) 12 S.C.R. 140; *Ex p. Macdonald* (1896) 27 S.C.R. 683; *Goldhar v. R.* (1960) 126 C.C.C. 337. It is now clear that these cases do not preclude jurisdictional review on habeas corpus alone: *The Queen v. Miller* [1985] 2 S.C.R. 613.

In several provinces there are special statutory provisions with respect to certiorari-in-aid:

Ontario: Habeas Corpus Act R.S.O. 1980 c.193, ss.5, 6; An Act for More Effectually Securing the Liberty of the Subject 1866, s.5; Nova Scotia Liberty of the Subject Act R.S.N.S. 1967 c.164, ss.7, 8; Prince Edward Island: Habeas Corpus and Certiorari Act, R.S.P.E.I. 1974 c.H-1, s.15. These seem to do little more than codify the common law, but are sometimes given credit for doing more. In *Re Jollimore and The Queen* (1986) 27

decision,[156] there is no reason to suppose that it is not just as possible in England.

In a case where it was used in 1891,[157] Coleridge C.J. made it clear that the certiorari added something to the powers of review: '... it might be that we should think it right to issue the certiorari to quash the proceedings, and yet it might be that ... the authorities ... might have a perfectly good answer to make in the way of a return to the habeas corpus.'[158] For example, a good return to habeas corpus could be given in a case where certiorari would allow the court to quash for error on the face of some document not brought up for the habeas corpus. The certiorari makes it easily possible for the court to examine the whole record, and to quash it if grounds are shown.

In many cases, certiorari-in-aid may have the effect of making the court more willing to provide relief where relief could be granted on habeas corpus alone. By bringing the whole record up, the court may be satisfied that there is real substance to the grounds of complaint. It would seem, however, that the same result may be achieved by simply bringing the material before the court by affidavit.[159]

Certiorari was regularly used in magisterial law for this purpose.[160] If the prisoner brought habeas corpus on the grounds of a defective warrant, it was open to the court to require that the conviction itself be

---

C.C.C. (3d) 166 (N.S.S.C.), it was held that in light of the Charter, the scope of review is as broad in cases falling outside the Nova Scotia Act.

The Ontario Act of 1866 seems to have merely been intended to allay doubts about issuing certiorari in vacation: *Re Mosier* (1867) 4 P.R. 64. It is said that it is the statute which allows the court to consider the depositions when committals are questioned, but the same result is reached in other provinces without similar legislation; *infra*, pp. 131–2.

[156] The Canadian courts have uncharacteristically given effect to a non-certiorari clause in criminal matters, and held that the same clause also bars certiorari-in-aid of habeas corpus: *Sanders* v. *R.* [1970] 2 C.C.C. 57 (S.C.C.); *Re Perry & Steele* (1959) 129 C.C.C. 206 (P.E.I.S.C.); *R.* v. *Keenan* (1913) 21 C.C.C. 467 (Ont. H.C.); cf. *Ex p. Worlds* [1968] 2 C.C.C. 88 (Alta. S.C.). It has been held, however, that the Federal Court Act, R.S.C. 1985 c.F-7, s.18, conferring exclusive jurisdiction on the Federal Court in relation to certiorari to review decisions of a federal authority, does not deprive the provincial superior courts of the power to issue certiorari-in-aid of habeas corpus where the issue is the validity of a decision of a federal authority, such as the National Parole Board or the authorities in a federal penitentiary: *The Queen* v. *Miller, supra*, n. 155, p. 52; *Cardinal* v. *Director of Kent Institution* [1985] 2 S.C.R. 643. See also Macdonald, 'L'Habeas corpus avec certiorari auxiliaire' (1980) 29 U.N.B.L.J. 228.

[157] *Ex p. Hopkins* (1891) 17 Cox C.C. 444.

[158] Ibid. at 449.

[159] *R.* v. *Mellor* (1833) 2 Dowl. 173; *Re Allison* (1854) 10 Ex. 561; *The Queen* v. *Miller* [1985] 2 S.C.R. 613; *In re Weetra* (1978) 18 S.A.S.R. 321 at 326.

[160] *Supra*, pp. 28–9.

brought up.[161] This could show that notwithstanding the defective recital of the conviction in the warrant, the conviction itself was a good one. Certiorari-in-aid was used here not to benefit the prisoner, but to demonstrate that there were valid proceedings to sustain the detention. The cases still show that certiorari-in-aid can be used to broaden the inquiry.

It is, however, perhaps more accurate to say that certiorari-in-aid facilitates rather than broadens review. Indeed, one of the reasons that certiorari-in-aid has not been used more frequently is undoubtedly because in many cases, the courts have acted just as if it had been used. The best example is to be found in the extradition cases where the court freely ranges over the whole record of the proceedings before the magistrate, and in no way confines itself to the warrant of commitment.[162] In fact, in weighing the evidence, the courts perhaps go further than would be allowed on certiorari.[163]

In *Khawaja* v. *Secretary of State for the Home Department*,[164] where the application was treated as one for habeas corpus along with judicial review to challenge an immigration detention order, Lord Wilberforce indicated that while distinct historically, in practice the two remedies should be effectively assimilated, and that for the purposes of the scope of review, both could be dealt with under 'a common principle'.

7. PRIVATIVE CLAUSES

As a general rule, the courts are unwilling to interpret any statute in such a way as to curtail habeas corpus jurisdiction unless the statute speci-fically refers to the writ.[165] There are few cases which directly consider the effect of a privative clause on habeas corpus review, but it would seem that such a clause will not prevent the court from considering the issue of jurisdictional error. It has been held, for example, that where a statute stipulates that a person detained 'shall be deemed to be in legal custody', the court will not be precluded from deciding whether

---

[161] *Supra*, p. 29. But cf. the cases where this was refused, *supra*, pp. 29–30.

[162] See esp. the discussion of *Armah*, *infra*, pp. 43–5. *Re Meier and The Queen* (1983) 6 C.C.C. (3d) 165 (B.C.S.C.) (aff'd 8 C.C.C. (3d) 210, leave to appeal to S.C.C. refused, ibid.).

[163] See e.g. *R.* v. *Botting* [1966] 2 O.R. 121 (C.A.).

[164] [1984] A.C. 74 at 99.

[165] See esp. *Cox* v. *Hakes* (1890) 15 App. Cas. 506.

or not powers under the statute have been properly pursued.[166]
In several Canadian cases, it has been held that a privative clause
will not prevent the court from deciding on habeas corpus whether
there was jurisdiction to make the order.[167] This is the familiar
reasoning used by the courts to avoid such clauses.[168]

The Supreme Court of Canada has held that '... because of its
importance as a safeguard of the liberty of the subject habeas corpus
jurisdiction can only be affected by express words.'[169]

The Canadian *Charter of Rights and Freedoms* explicitly accords
constitutional protection to the right of everyone on arrest or detention
'to have the validity of the detention determined by way of habeas
corpus and to be released if the detention is not lawful'.[170] In the light
of this constitutional guarantee, a provision on the Criminal Code
precluding review of a detention order pending trial will not stand in
the way of the remedy of habeas corpus.[171] Similarly, a privative
clause precluding review of the revocation of parole cannot deprive a
prisoner of resort to habeas corpus,[172] nor will the availability of a
statutory remedy, otherwise exclusive, preclude habeas corpus to
review a committal under provincial mental health legislation.[173]

---

[166] *R.* v. *Governor of Brixton Prison, ex p. Sarno* [1916] 2 K.B. 742; *Ex p. Sacksteder*
[1918] 1 K.B. 578 at 586; *Greene* v. *Secretary of State for Home Affairs* [1942] 1 K.B. 87 at
117 (C.A.).

[167] *Samejina* v. *R.* [1932] S.C.R. 640; *Masella* v. *Langlais* [1955] S.C.R. 263; *Maragos*
v. *Deguise* (1941) 77 C.C.C. 227 (Que. S.C.); *Re McCaud* (1964) 43 C.R. 252 (S.C.C.);
Pearce and Warden of Manitoba Penetentiary (1966) 55 D.L.R. (2d) 619 (Man. C.A.); cf.,
however, the cases under the War Measures Act, *infra*, n. 27, p. 99.

[168] See esp. *Anisminic Ltd.* v. *Foreign Compensation Commission* [1969] 2 A.C. 147.

[169] *The Queen* v. *Miller* [1985] 2 S.C.R. 613 at 624–5 per LeDain J. See also *Puharka*
v. *Webb* [1983] 2 N.S.W.L.R. 31, holding that habeas corpus to review an extradition
committal was not barred by reason of the fact that a statutory time-limit had been
exceeded, at 34–5 per Rogers J.: 'The remedy of habeas corpus is one of the most
treasured and long-standing heritages that this country has taken from the United
Kingdom. To surrender it in any case would be to cast away a treasured possession. It
should not be done without the most clear cut and measured terms of legislation.'

[170] s.10(c).

[171] s.459.1 (since amended to remove privative clause), struck down in *Re Kot and The
Queen* (1983) 10 C.C.C. (3d) 297 (Ont. H.C.) (appeal quashed 11 C.C.C. (3d) 96); *Re Jack
and The Queen* (1982) 1 C.C.C. (3d) 193 (Nfld. S.C.); following a case decided under the
Canadian Bill of Rights, which contained a similar provision: *Exp. Mitchell* (1975) 23 C.C.C.
(2d) 473 (B.C.C.A.). See also *Ex p. Clarke, ex p. White* (1978) 41 C.C.C. (2d) 511 (Nfld.
S.C.); *Re Swan and The Queen* (1983) 7 C.C.C. (3d) 130 at 142 (B.C.S.C.). Cf.
Believeau, 'Le contrôle judiciaire en droit penal canadien' (1983) 61 Can. Bar Rev. 735
at 793–6. For further discussion of the Bill of Rights provision, see *infra*, n. 179, p. 56.

[172] *Re Cadeddu and The Queen* (1982) 4 C.C.C. (3d) 97 (Ont. H.C.).

[173] *Reference Re Procedures and the Mental Health Act* (1984) 5 D.L.R. (4th) 577
(P.E.I.S.C.).

8. TRIVIAL DEFECTS

Several techniques have been devised to deal with the problem posed when an applicant relies on a legal defect of a trivial nature. The defect may, on a purely conceptual basis, appear to raise a sound objection. From the standpoint of convenience and doing what seems 'just', however, there may be every reason to refuse a remedy. Occasionally, in such a case, the courts use language which is too sweeping, and it is proposed to examine how such cases are actually dealt with.

(*i*) *Does the Defects go to Jurisdiction?* Defects may be classified as 'technical' or 'mere informalities', and the courts will, on that account, refuse to discharge the applicant even though there is an error in the proceedings upon which the detention is based.[174] This classification usually occurs when the court is deciding whether or not the defect affects the jurisdiction of the tribunal ordering the detention. In deciding whether an error goes to jurisdiction, as well as considering the intrinsic nature of the error, the courts are undoubtedly swayed by its gravity. The labels and language used are imprecise, but they do provide the verbal justification for refusing relief where it is not thought to be due. The classification itself is very much a subjective one for the judge.

To be weighed against this tendency to refuse relief where the defect appears not to be a serious one is the canon of construction which holds that all matters affecting the liberty of the subject are to be strictly construed.[175] This, it has been seen, was especially important in magisterial law,[176] and while the courts are perhaps less likely to apply it so strictly now,[177] it still does provide a vehicle for relief in certain cases.

[174] See e.g. *R. v. Bethel* (1702) 6 Mod. 19; *R. v. Governor of Brixton Prison, ex p. Servini* [1914] 1 K.B. 77; *R. v. Governor of Brixton Prison, ex p. Thompson* [1911] 2 K.B. 82; *Athanassiadis* v. *Government of Greece* [1969] 3 All E.R. 293 (H.L.); *Ex p. Henderson* (1929) 52 C.C.C. 95 (S.C.C.).

[175] For habeas corpus cases applying the rule see e.g. *Bracy's Case* (1701) 1 Salk. 348; *Re Allen* (1860) 30 L.J.Q.B. 38; *R.* v. *Nelson* (1908) 15 C.C.C. 10 (Ont. H.C.); *Re Royston* (1909) 15 C.C.C. 96 (Man. K.B.)) *Re Munavish* (1958) 121 C.C.C. 299 (B.C.S.C.); *R. v. Metropolitan Police Commissioner, ex p. Hammond* [1965] A.C. 810 at 834; *R. v. Bilinsky* [1941] 2 W.W.R. 285 (Man. K.B.); *Ex p. Andrews* (1973) 15 C.C.C. (2d) 43 (B.C.S.C.).

[176] *Supra*, pp. 25–32.

[177] See e.g. *R. v. Board of Control, ex p. Winterflood* [1938] 1 K.B. 420 at 426 per Lord Hewart C.J.: 'No doubt ... nothing is more important, or few things are more important, than liberty of the subject, and where one is dealing with an Act of Parliament providing

(*ii*) *Patent Defects in the Warrant of Commitment Following Conviction.*
There are now very few situations where an applicant will be able to
succeed on the grounds of some patent defect in the warrant of
commitment, unless that defect relates to a real error in the proceedings, or might affect the length of time the applicant will be detained.
Where imprisonment follows a valid conviction, it will be virtually
impossible to make out a successful case based on a defect in the
committal documents.[178] Legislation in most jurisdictions[179] requires
the court to refuse the writ if there is a proper conviction which could
support the detention. The source of so many habeas corpus proceedings in the nineteenth century has been effectively plugged. Even
where no such statutory provision is applicable, it would seem that the
court may refuse to order the release of the applicant where there is a
valid conviction.[180] Warrants of commitment tend now to be regarded
as a piece of machinery to implement the court's order, and unless an
error which vitiates the conviction itself is revealed, relief will be
refused.[181]

for the detention of a human being, it is necessary to be strict. But it is not necessary to
be unreasonable, and one has to consider what is the reasonable interpretation of these
words'; *R.* v. *Secretary of State for the Home Department, ex p. Iqbal* [1979] 1 All E.R. 675 at
684 per Lord Widgery C.J.: 'Even where the liberty of the subject is involved, the court
should strive not to be hamstrung by pointless technicalities.'

[178] *Supra*, pp. 30–1; *Olson* v. *The Queen* [1980] 1 S.C.R. 808.

[179] For the English provision, see *supra*, pp. 30–1. The Canadian Criminal Code
goes further and provides for an order allowing the court to 'take any proceedings, hear
such evidence or do any other thing that, in the opinion of the judge or court, will best
further the ends of justice': s.775. The section has been applied, for example, following a
successful challenge to committal proceedings: *R.* v. *Mishko* (1945) 85 C.C.C. 410 (Ont.
H.C.); *R.* v. *Cowden* (1947) 90 C.C.C. 101 (Ont. H.C.); *R.* v. *Churchman and Durham*
(1954) 110 C.C.C. 382 (Ont. H.C.); *R.* v. *Plouffe and Warren* (1958) 122 C.C.C. 291
(Ont. H.C.); cf. however *Re Joly and The Queen* (1978) 41 C.C.C. (2d) 538 (Ont H.C.);
following a successful application for failure to hold a ninety-day review: *Re Ferreira and
The Queen* (1981) 58 C.C.C. (2d) 147 (B.C.C.A.); and following a finding that
proceedings to revoke parole had been defective and that the applicant was entitled to
another hearing: *Re Mason and The Queen* (1983) 7 C.C.C. (3d) 426. The section was
held not to be inconsistent with s.2(c)(iii) of the Canadian Bill of Rights guaranteeing the
right to habeas corpus in *Ex p. Gooden* (1975) 27 C.C.C. (2d) 161 (Ont. H.C.); *contra: Ex
p. Amos* (1975) 24 C.C.C. (2d) 552 (B.C.S.C.). See also *R.* v. *Frejd* (1910) 18 C.C.C. 110
at 120 (Ont.): 'It is, in no sense, the purpose of any writ of habeas corpus to thwart the
due administration of justice.' per Meredith J.A., and *Ex p. Henderson* (1929) 52 C.C.C.
95 at 105 (S.C.C.): 'Courts should not permit the use of this great writ to free criminals
on mere technicalities.' per Rinfret J.

[180] *R.* v. *Governor of Lewes Prison, ex p. Doyle* [1917] 2 K.B. 254.

[181] See also *R.* v. *Mount* (1875) L.R. 6 P.C. 283, discussed *infra*, p. 148; *Pearson* v. *R.*
(1978) 5 C.R. (3d) 264 (Que. S.C.). The Canadian Criminal Code specifically provides
that a defect in the form of a warrant of committal shall not render the warrant void on

A similar line of reasoning has been applied even where the case does not involve a conviction, and if material is filed which satisfies the court that the defect in the warrant is a mere oversight, habeas corpus will be refused.[182] In some cases, there is specific statutory authority to correct defects on appeal, and in such cases, habeas corpus cannot be used to circumvent the statutory power.[183]

Amendments are allowed, even at a late stage in the proceedings,[184] and this, as well, will permit the respondent to cure a patent defect of an inconsequential nature. Where the return and the order or warrant give an invalid reason for the detention but the court determines upon investigation of the facts that a valid reason exists, habeas corpus will be refused, even where the party supporting the detention has taken no step to have the warrant or order amended or replaced.[185]

(iii) Inherent Discretion. A few cases[186] which rest on the inherent powers of the judges of the King's Bench to act as conservators of the peace are sometimes taken to stand for the proposition that the courts may ignore a defect where it appears that the prisoner is a person who, on the merits, ought to be detained. Apart from domestic criminal cases, where it seems that the judges can, on their own motion, remand a person for trial, it is extremely doubtful that the courts have the power to ignore illegality simply because it seems that the applicant really ought to be detained.[187] Such a power would make habeas corpus a discretionary remedy, and that it plainly is not.[188] In fact, it is probably safe to say that the courts rarely act on this principle

habeas corpus if it is alleged that the applicant was convicted and if there is in fact a valid conviction. For an application of this provision, see *Ex p. Leclerc* (1973) 21 C.C.C. (2d) 16 (Que. C.A.). Cf. *Ex p. Andrews* (1973) 15 C.C.C. (2d) 43 (B.C.S.C.), refusing to apply the section where a warrant of committal in default of payment of a fine failed to state the reason for immediate committal as required by s.722(7) of the Code (since repealed).

[182] *R.* v. *Governor of Brixton Prison, ex p. Pitt-Rivers* [1942] 1 All E.R. 207; *Ex p. Williams, re Seery* (1931) 48 W.N. (N.S.W.) 221. *Re Jack and The Queen* (1982) 1 C.C.C. (3d) 193 (Nfld. S.C.).

[183] See *Linnet* v. *Coles* [1987] Q.B. 555 (C.A.), applying the Administration of Justice Act 1960, s.13, which provides for an appeal from a committal for contempt.

[184] See *infra*, p. 182, where this is fully discussed.

[185] *R.* v. *Secretary of State for the Home Department, ex p. Iqbal* [1979] 1 All E.R. 675.

[186] Esp. *R.* v. *Marks* (1802) 3 East 157; *Ex p. Krans* (1823) 1 B. & C. 258; *Parker* (1839) 5 M. & W. 32.

[187] *Ex p. Besset* (1844) 6 Q.B. 481; *R.* v. *Wishart* (1910) 18 C.C.C. 146 (Ont. C.A.) Cf. *Re Terraz* (1878) 39 L.T. 502 and see *R.* v. *Governor of Brixton Prison, ex p. Percival* [1907] 1 K.B. 696 and *R.* v. *Governor of Brixton Prison, ex p. Shuter* [1960] 2 Q.B. 89, holding that the court has the power to remit an extradition case for further hearing.

[188] *Infra*, pp. 58–9.

except in cases of trivial defect when the same thing could be otherwise justified.

An exception seems to have been made, however, in certain cases involving a person confined on account of mental disorder. There, the courts sometimes do refuse to order the release of the applicant even though a valid legal objection has been made, where it appears that the person is dangerous. The exercise of this power is discussed in greater detail in a subsequent chapter.[189] It seems to rest upon the *parens patriae* principle, and the notion that the best interest of the patient requires protective custody notwithstanding some legal defect. In the absence of such special considerations, the courts do not exercise this kind of broad discretionary power.

9. NON-DISCRETIONARY NATURE OF HABEAS CORPUS

In principle, habeas corpus is not a discretionary remedy: it issues *ex debito justitiae* on proper grounds being shown.[190] It is, however, a writ of right rather than a writ of course,[191] and there is a long-established practice of having a preliminary proceeding to determine whether there is sufficient merit in the application to warrant bringing in the other parties.[192]

This means, simply, that it is not a writ which can be had for the asking upon payment of a court fee, but one which will only be issued where it is made to appear that there are proper grounds. While the court has no discretion to refuse relief, it is still for the court to decide whether proper grounds have been made out to support the application. The rule that the writ issues *ex debito justitiae* means simply that the court may only properly refuse relief on the grounds that there is no legal basis for the application and that habeas corpus should never be refused on discretionary grounds such as inconvenience.[193] While it

---

[189] *Infra*, pp. 157–8.
[190] Wilmot, *Opinion, infra*, n. 193, p. 59. *Hobhouse* (1820) 3 B. & Ald. 420; *Re Edwards* (1873) 42 L.J.Q.B. 99; *Ex p. Nowlan* (1804) 11 Ves. Jun. 511; *Jenkes* (1676) 6. St. Tr. 1190 at 1207–8; *R.* v. *Governor of Pentonville Prison, ex p. Azam* [1973] 2 W.L.R. 949 at 960–1, 969, 970 (C.A.); de Smith, *Judicial Review*, 372. See also Habeas Corpus Act 1640, s.4; Habeas Corpus Act 1679, s.9, making judges liable in damages for unduly denying the writ in certain cases.
[191] See e.g. *Hobhouse* (1820) 3 B. & Ald. 420; *Ex p. Corke* [1954] 2 All E.R. 440; *Re Wood* (1927) 48 C.C.C. 146 (N.S.S.C.).   [192] *Infra*, pp. 218–20.
[193] The balance between requiring proper grounds to be shown and saying that the

may be necessary as a practical matter to have an initial screening of the application, it is an important safeguard of liberty that the writ not be refused on discretionary grounds. Plainly, the court is given considerable leeway in deciding whether the application has a sound legal basis, and it has been observed that an element of judicial discretion is necessarily involved at this stage.[194] However, if the prisoner does raise an arguable issue there is no room for discretion: the matter should proceed to hearing so that a full and proper determination can be made. The non-discretionary nature of habeas corpus is an important difference between it and the other prerogative writs.[195]

10. ALTERNATIVE REMEDIES

Since habeas corpus is not a discretionary remedy the existence of an alternate remedy does not afford grounds for refusing relief on habeas corpus.[196] Whether the other, perhaps more direct, remedy could still be used, or whether the applicant has forgone the right to use it, its existence should not preclude or affect the right to apply for habeas corpus.

This principle has not been universally followed, however, and there are cases where the writ has been refused because an appeal was thought to be more appropriate.[197] Where a statute confers specific jurisdiction on an appellate court to cure a defect which would result in

writ is one of right was explained by Wilmot J. in his *Opinion* Wilm. 81 at 83: '[The writ is] the birthright of the people, subject to such provisions as the law has established for granting [it]. These provisions are not a check upon justice, but a wise and provident direction of it.' Cf. *Re Keenan* [1972] 1 Q.B. 533 at 544; *Ex p. Tirey* (1971) 21 D.L.R. (3d) 475 at 480 (Alta. S.C.T.D.), suggesting that discretionary grounds might exist. See also the mental illness cases, *supra*, Chapter VI, where the courts have acted on an inherent *parens patriae* discretion to refuse to discharge certain patients.

[194] *Infra*, pp. 218–19.
[195] de Smith, *Judicial Review*, 372–6, 510.
[196] *Re B.* [1972] N.Z.L.R. 897; *R.* v. *Governor of Pentonville Prison, ex p. Azam* [1973] 2 W.L.R. 949 at 960–1, 969, 970 (C.A.); *R.* v. *Secretary of State for the Home Department, ex p. Mughal* [1973] 1 W.L.R. 1133 at 1136 per Lord Widgery C.J. (aff'd [1974] Q.B. 313).
[197] *R.* v. *Commanding Officer of Morn Hill Camp, ex p. Ferguson* [1917] 1 K.B. 176; *Re MacIntosh* [1942] O.W.N. 645 (H.C.); *Re Perry and Steele* (1959) 129 C.C.C. 206 (P.E.I.S.C.); *Re Hazlett* [1930] N.Z.L.R. 777; *Re Keogh* (1889) 15 V.L.R. 395; *Goldhar* v. *The Queen* [1960] S.C.R. 431; *Reference Re Procedures and the Mental Health Act* (1984) 5 D.L.R. (4th) 577 (P.E.I.S.C.) holds that habeas corpus is not available where there is a statutory remedy, but then goes on to say that s.10(c) of the Charter of Rights and Freedoms preserves the right of habeas corpus notwithstanding the statute.

the applicant being released, it has been held that habeas corpus is not
available.[198] Some of these cases may depend upon a finding that the
error alleged did not go to jurisdiction and there can be little doubt
that a right of appeal may influence the court to characterize an error
as being non-jurisdictional.[199] This is especially true in cases where it
is sought to challenge a criminal conviction on habeas corpus. The
courts have shown a certain determination to restrict the growth of
collateral methods of attacking convictions.[200] They seem to prefer to
have the matter raised by appeal, although it must be said that this is a
tendency rather than a rule of universal application.[201]

Conversely, in a situation in which the prisoner has no other
recourse, if it can be shown that there is an error in the proceedings,
the judges will rarely refuse a remedy on the grounds that the error is
not properly reviewable on habeas corpus. In this sense, the absence of
an alternative remedy may seem to have the effect of broadening the
scope of review.[202]

(a) *Remedies Which May Take the Place of Habeas Corpus*

While habeas corpus may be 'the most usual remedy by which a man
is restored again to his liberty if he have been against law deprived of
it',[203] there are several other remedies which may serve the same
function. Certiorari, prohibition, mandamus, or declaration may be
used in many situations to have the effect of securing the release of a
prisoner on the grounds that the detention is not authorized by law.

(*i*) *Declaration.* Perhaps the most interesting of these is the

---

[198] *Linnet* v. *Coles* [1987] Q.B. 555 (C.A.).

[199] See e.g. Rubinstein, op. cit., 49–50; *R.* v. *Commanding Officer of Morn Hill Camp,
ex p. Ferguson* [1917] 1 K.B. 176 at 180 per Darling J.: 'He desired a more expeditious
remedy, but that is no reason why this court should be permitted to enlarge its
jurisdiction. The court is not to be called upon to entertain appeals from all magistrates
who decide wrongly as soon as the decision is given.' Cf. 11 Hals. (3d) 26, citing the case
for the wide proposition that an appeal precludes habeas corpus. Cf. also the cases
refusing an appeal and holding certiorari to be more appropriate where jurisdictional
error is alleged: noted and criticized by Wade, (1969) 85 L.Q.R. 18, 20.

[200] *Infra*, pp. 145–6.

[201] Certiorari is frequently used to quash magistrates' decisions: see e.g. *R.* v.
Wakefield J.J., ex p. Butterworth [1970] 1 All E.R. 1181; and see *R.* v. *Brighton JJ., ex p.
Robinson* [1973] 1 W.L.R. 69 at 71, allowing certiorari where the appropriate remedy was
to file a statutory declaration because 'perhaps on balance an injustice might be done if
the order were refused', per Widgery C.J.

[202] The best examples are perhaps the extradition cases, *infra*, pp. 81–4.

[203] *Bushell's Case* (1670) Vaughan 135 at 136, per Vaughan C. J.

declaration.[204] This remedy is granted in an ordinary civil action, and it therefore has the advantage of allowing for discovery and full hearing on the facts, procedures which have not been developed on habeas corpus. Also, it is seen in several places in this book that the action for declaration has been used in place of habeas corpus where the writ is inappropriate for various technical reasons.[205]

Declaration does have the disadvantage of taking longer to come to trial than habeas corpus, although this may be mitigated by bringing it on proceedings for summary judgment.[206] The courts are perhaps unlikely now to hold that a declaration should be refused because another remedy would be the usual one,[207] and in any case, it has not been suggested that it should be refused simply because habeas corpus is available. A declaration does not formally quash the impugned decision nor does it result in an order which may be directly enforced. While habeas corpus is also declaratory in that it does not quash the impugned decision (in fact, it may often be used to secure a declaration as to personal status),[208] it does result in an order of release which can be directly enforced.

(ii) Civil Action of False Imprisonment. False imprisonment is not a remedy which takes the place of habeas corpus as it will not ordinarily be used to obtain immediate release from a restraint, but it does afford one means of redress for anyone who has been unlawfully imprisoned. It will be seen later on that it may be used in situations for which habeas corpus is inappropriate, namely, where there is present justification for the detention, but where there has been some prior illegality.[209]

When an action of false imprisonment challenges the validity of a judicial or quasi-judicial decision, it would seem that the possible grounds for relief are narrower than they would be on habeas corpus. A civil action in damages will only succeed where there has been an

---

[204] Zamir, *The Declaratory Judgment* (1962), 100–1 maintains that the declaration may be used in place of habeas corpus just as it is often used in place of the other prerogative writs.

[205] *Infra*, n. 87, p. 184 (habeas corpus inappropriate because the sentence being contested had not yet started to run); *infra*, n. 24, p. 168 (applicant not in actual custody).

[206] As in *Hancock* v. *Prison Commissioners* [1960] 1 Q.B. 117 (declaration as to length of sentence).

[207] de Smith, *Judicial Review*, 534–5.

[208] Especially in the cases where habeas corpus is used in effect to secure a determination of status in the law of immigration: *infra*, pp. 119, 173.

[209] *Infra*, pp. 179–82.

absence or excess of jurisdiction.[210] Moreover, it by no means follows that success on habeas corpus, even on the grounds of jurisdictional error, will afford the basis for an action in false imprisonment.[211] The matter is not *res judicata*, and in any case, the parties are different.

11. CONCLUSION

It is submitted that this review of the cases reveals that the scope of review on habeas corpus is very flexible. When review is possible, the issue of jurisdiction is open, and the broad definition given to that term will usually make an error of law subject to review. Apart from jurisdictional review, there is the further possibility of review for patent error, the limits of which are only to be determined by what material the court will examine.

Perhaps the most important factor in any given case is to consider the nature of the decision or proceeding to be reviewed. With respect to certain proceedings, habeas corpus is thought by the courts to be an inappropriate remedy, and in those cases it will be virtually impossible to get relief even though relief may be theoretically possible. The best example is perhaps the refusal of the English courts to review convictions by common law courts, even where an error of jurisdiction is alleged. More recently, this reluctance seems to have spread to summary convictions as well, and it can probably be said that habeas corpus will simply not be used by the courts as a means to review convictions.

On the other hand, where the decision is one in respect of which there really is no other form of redress, or is one concerning which habeas corpus has become the accepted remedy, the courts will wield

---

[210] *Cave* v. *Mountain* (1840) 1 M. & G. 257; *Kemp* v. *Neville* (1861) 10 C.B.N.S. 523; Salmond, *Torts* (16th ed. 1973), 417–19. Cf. the cases before the Justices Protection Act 1848, collected and discussed by Rubinstein, op. cit. 172–6, 181–2, which seem to rest on patent defect in the warrant of commitment. Where the action is brought against a judicial officer, the defence of judicial immunity will be encountered but an action will lie if the defendant exceeded jurisdiction: *In re McC. (A Minor)*, [1985] A.C. 528. In *R.* v. *Manchester City Magistrates' Court, ex p. Davies* [1988] 1 W.L.R. 667, in proceedings for judicial review, justices were found to have exceeded their jurisdiction in committing the applicant to prison, and were held liable in damages. Cf. *Morier* v. *Rivard* [1985] 2 S.C.R. 716.

[211] There are several cases where habeas corpus has succeeded, but where false imprisonment failed: see e.g. *Hamond* v. *Howell* (1670) 2 Mod. 218; *Budd* v. *Anderson* [1943] K.B. 642; *Johnston* v. *Robertson* (1908) 13 C.C.C. 452 (N.S.S.C.).

whatever powers of review are necessary to give relief where it is thought that something has gone wrong. There are very few cases to be found in this category where relief has been refused because the court's powers of review were insufficient.

In other words, the significant matter for consideration is the nature of the decision to be reviewed rather than the nature of the error alleged. When a court is faced with the sort of decision for which habeas corpus is seen to be an appropriate remedy, it will rarely refuse a remedy because an error of law cannot be properly classified. The traditional language of jurisdictional review is often used, but it should not be supposed on that account that there is a significant range of legal error which lies beyond the reach of the powers of review on habeas corpus. It has been shown that even errors of law which are usually considered to be intra-jurisdictional, can be reviewed on habeas corpus by treating them as patent or apparent errors.

3

Consideration of Questions of Fact

1. INTRODUCTION—RULE AGAINST CONTROVERTING THE RETURN

The purpose of this chapter is to examine problems, both substantive and procedural, which relate to the determination of issues of fact on habeas corpus. It is sought to show when the court can enter a factual inquiry, and how it can proceed to determine the facts.

At the core of the supposed difficulty in dealing with questions of fact on habeas corpus is the common law rule against controverting the facts in the return. The discussion of how questions of fact are dealt with must, then, start with a detailed discussion of the content and scope of this rule.

The source of most of the early learning on the question of controverting the facts in the return is the *Opinion on the Writ of Habeas Corpus*, delivered by Mr. Justice Wilmot to the House of Lords in 1758.[1] The common law rule stated by Wilmot J. was that the judges were bound by the facts as set out in the return unless there was the verdict of a jury or a judgment on demurrer in an action for false return[2] which determined the facts to be otherwise:

The court says [to the gaoler] 'Tell the reason why you confine him.' The Court will determine whether it is a good or bad reason; but not whether it is a true or a false one. The Judges are not competent to this inquiry; it is not their province, but the province of a jury, to determine it: 'ad questionem juris, non facti, judices respondent.' The writ is not framed or adapted to litigating facts: it is a summary short way of taking the opinion of the Court upon a matter of law where the facts are disclosed and admitted ... [I]f the facts are controverted, they must go to a jury; and when the return to a habeas corpus is made and filed, there is an end to the whole proceeding, and the parties have

---

[1] Wilm. 81. The Bill before Parliament which was the occasion for the *Opinion* is discussed *infra*, p. 68. For other statements of the rule, see 11 Hals. (4th ed.), 794–5; 2 Hawkins *P.C.*, c.15 s.78; IV Bacon *Abridg.*, 135; *Greene* v. *Secretary of State for Home Affairs* [1942] A.C. 284 at 291–5 per Visc. Maugham.
[2] The action for false return is discussed, *infra*, pp. 65–6.

'no day' in Court; and therefore it is impossible that a proceeding, by way of trial, should be grafted upon it.[3]

Wilmot J. said: '[I have] looked through the books as carefully as I can' but failed to find any instance of the truth of the return being controverted by affidavit.[4]

Wilmot J. was undoubtedly correct in his assertion that there was a common law rule against controverting the return,[5] although it is doubtful that the real reason for refusing to decide matters of fact was the absence of the jury. The maxim *ad quaestionem facti non respondent judices* only applied to a limited class of factual questions, namely, questions of ultimate fact raised on pleadings.[6] Habeas corpus did not involve a *lis inter partes* and no issue was joined[7] so that, technically, such issues did not arise. It is because the writ did not raise such ultimate factual issues that there was no jury, but that did not necessarily mean that if factual issues did arise, they could not be decided.[8] In other words, the common law rule may be regarded as an assertion that habeas corpus was not to take the place of trial by jury for the ultimate determination of guilt or innocence. This, however, did not prevent the courts from determining certain factual issues which did arise.

It was suggested that the way the matter could be tried by a jury was by the action of false return. This, however, seems to have been a remedy which was much talked about but seldom used. There are many dicta to the effect that such an action is available,[9] and it was also

---

[3] Wilm. 107.

[4] Wilm. 110. Aside from the absence of positive precedent, Wilmot relied on *Bagg's Case* (1615) 11 Co. Rep. 93b: and dicta in *Hawkeridge's Case* (1616) 12 Co. Rep. 129; and *Smith* (1614) Godbolt 219. All of these refer back to a case in the Year Books, 1431 (9 H.6.44a) found in Fitzherbert, *Grand Abridg.* (1577), sub tit. 'Corpus Cum Causa'; also referred to by Wilmot at 112 and translated as follows: 'If the cause appear to us sufficient in itself, notwithstanding it be false, it is enough for us upon the return, which the whole court agreed. And if he had not returned that he was his villein, this shall not make an issue here, whether he be his villein or not: wherefore, if you cannot prove but that the cause is sufficient in itself, he shall be sent back again.'

[5] As shown by *Bagg's Case* (1615) 11 Co. Rep. 93b, there was a similar problem in mandamus. This was cured by statute: Acts of 1710 (9 Anne, c.25) and 1831 (1 Wm. IV, c.21).

[6] Thayer, *Treatise on Evidence at the Common Law* (1898), 185 *et seq.*

[7] See further, *infra*, pp. 201–2.

[8] For cases where facts were determined, see *infra*, pp. 66–8.

[9] *Smith's Case* (1614) Godbolt 219; *Braithwaite* (1669) 1 Vent 19; *R.* v. *Majorem Rippon* (1705) 1 Ld. Raym. 563; *R.* v. *Lyme Regis* (1779) 1 Doug. 149; *R.* v. *Rogers* (1823) 3 D. & R. 607.

said that anyone who returned falsely was liable to indictment.[10] While there are at least two reported cases of actions for false return[11] (the plaintiff failed in both to make out a case), it was a remedy of dubious value in a situation where the law should have provided more speedy and effectual relief.

Even by Wilmot's time, however, there were several situations in which the courts did consider questions of fact on habeas corpus. Affidavits were freely admitted in proceedings before trial in criminal matters.[12] Facts were also tried on habeas corpus with privilege,[13] and in a case decided by Lord Mansfield, where it was alleged that the applicant was improperly held in a mad-house: 'The court thought it fit to have a previous inspection of her, by proper persons, physicians and relations; and then to proceed, as the truth should come out upon such inspection.'[14] The courts were especially ready to consider the facts in cases of impressment[15] and there was nothing like unanimity in favour of Wilmot's formulation of the common law rule. In fact, there would seem to have been a preponderance of judicial opinion which favoured a more liberal construction.[16] Indeed, if Wilmot's *Opinion* itself is closely examined, it will be seen that he, along with

---

[10] *Viner's Case* (1675) 1 Freem. K.B. 522.

[11] *Elwell* v. *The Birmingham Canal Co.* (1846) 6 L.T.O.S. 431; *Cobbett* v. *Hudson* (1852) 19 L.T.O.S. 166.

[12] *R.* v. *Greenwood* (1739) 2 Str. 1138; *Farington's Case* (1682) T. Jones 222; *Captain Kirk's Case* (1704) 5 Mod. 454; *Barney* (1701) 5 Mod. 323. In *Jackson* (1717), ref. to in 2 Hawkins P.C., 169 and IV Bacon *Abridg.*, 136, the court went very far indeed in acting on such evidence: '... it appeared that the prosecutor himself, if anyone, was guilty, and carried on the present prosecution to screen himself: and thereupon the court, in consideration of the unreasonableness of the prosecution, and the uncertainty of the time when another sessions of Admiralty might be holden, admitted Jackson to bail, and committed the prosecutor till he should find bail to answer the facts contained in the affidavits.'

[13] *Hutchins* v. *Player* (1663) O. Bridg. 272; *De Vine's Case* (1456) cited in O. Bridg. 288 at 305.

[14] *R.* v. *Turlington* (1761) 2 Burr. 1115.

[15] See e.g. *Goldswain* (1778) 2 Wm. Bl. 1207 at 1211; 'And [the court] declared that they could not wilfully shut their eyes against such facts as appeared on the affidavits, but which were not noticed on the return.' There are many other cases of impressment where the facts were examined: *King* (1674) Comb. 245; *Good* (1760) 1 Wm. Bl. 251; *Drydon* (1793) 5 T.R. 417; *Young* (1808) 9 East 466; Gude, *Crown Practice*, 281–6.

[16] Of the nine other judges who delivered opinions to the House of Lords in 1758, five thought that the return could be controverted: 15 Parl. Hist. 898 *et seq.* A sixth judge, unable to actually deliver his opinion, also took this more liberal view: 20 St. Tr. 1374, quoting an exerpt from Dodson's *Life of Foster*. In addition, Lord Mansfield strenuously opposed the bill because he thought that the law already permitted what the Bill sought to achieve: (1758) 15 Parl. Hist. 900–1.

other judges, did admit that in practical terms, the scope of the rule was narrow, and that questions of fact could often be entertained.

(a) 'Confessing and Avoiding' the Return

The first escape from the stricture of the rule was to permit the introduction of matters of fact which could be said to be consistent with the return, but which did show circumstances which vitiated the justification offered for the imprisonment.

The cases of *Swallow* v. *London Corporation*[17] and *Gardener's Case*,[18] both treated by Wilmot, are examples of this. In both cases, the prisoner was allowed to rely on extrinsic matters of fact which vitiated the grounds for the imprisonment without actually contradicting any fact in the return. In *Gardener*, the court went so far as to command 'a plea to be drawn, comprising all this matter, which was done; and then it was confessed, and the party discharged.'[19]

Wilmot J. acknowledged that the return could be 'confessed and avoided', pointing out that the grafting of a plea on the proceedings still ensured that the matter would come before the jury.[20] These cases really are early examples of the principle of 'jurisdictional facts' at work, and as will be seen, this concept has since developed to enable the court to consider issues of fact in many of the situations where the rule against controverting the return might be thought to apply.[21]

(b) Proceeding by Rule and Motion Rather than on the Return

A way of proceeding which seems to evade, more directly, the rule against controverting the return was indicated by the case of *White*,[22] also discussed by Wilmot. There, the return to habeas corpus certified that the applicant had been properly impressed into naval service. The applicant sought to adduce facts which showed that he was exempt from impressment. This could, perhaps, now be classified as an instance of jurisdictional facts, and the court would have no difficulty in entering the factual inquiry. The judges, however, apparently

---

[17] (1666) 1 Sid. 287.
[18] (1600) Cro. Eliz. 821; *sub nom St. John's Case* 5 Co. Rep. 71.
[19] Cro. Eliz. 821. In *R.* v. *Burnaby* (1703) 2 Ld. Raym. 900, a certiorari case, Holt C.J. would have followed *Gardener* and permitted a plea showing facts which impugned the conviction, but the majority doubted the authority of *Gardener*, and held that a judgment could not be pleaded to, and that an action would have to be brought against the justices to question the facts upon which they had found their jurisdiction.
[20] Wilm. 111–12.
[21] *Infra*, pp. 72–6.
[22] *R.* v. *White* (1746) 20 St. Tr. 1376.

thought that the statement in the return precluded any direct consideration of the facts, and they adopted the innovating procedure of making a rule after the return had been filed which required the impressment commissioners to show cause why the prisoner should not be released. Wilmot J. approved this manner of proceeding and maintained that it did not violate the rule against controverting the return since everything was done on the motion for the rule.[23]

The significant aspect of this reasoning is that it indicates that the prohibition against controverting the return was a purely technical matter, and could be avoided so long as an actual return was not involved. The modern practice is to try habeas corpus matters on motion, and the writ rarely actually issues.[24] Even where it does issue, it is usually only after the substantive rights have been determined. There is also no difficulty in bringing all interested parties into the proceedings.[25] On the basis of Wilmot's acceptance of the result in *White*, this, if nothing else, suggests that the rule against controverting the return need no longer trouble us.

(c) *Habeas Corpus Act 1816 and the Present Scope of the Common Law Rule*

The occasion in 1758 for Wilmot's *Opinion* was a proposal before the House of Lords which would have, inter alia, expressly made possible inquiry by the court into the truth of the return.[26] Pressure for the reform resulted from doubts about the capacity of the courts to deal properly with issues of fact in cases where the applicant sought to adduce evidence proving exemption from impressment.[27] The bill was rejected, perhaps because the methods already noted had been developed to deal with such cases, notwithstanding the rule.

In 1816 a similar measure was passed as the Habeas Corpus Act 1816,[28] and it abolished the rule against controverting the truth of the

---

[23] Wilm. 126–7.   [24] See *infra*, pp. 218–20.   [25] Ord. 54, r.2(2).

[26] The full text of the Bill is given in (1758) 15 *Parl. Hist.* 871–4.

[27] The debate in the Commons on the Bill (15 *Parl. Hist.* 874–97) seems to have been more a debate on the wisdom of impressment itself than on the wisdom of the particular reforms to the law of habeas corpus.

[28] The Act of 1816 is in substance the same as the bill of 1758, and it is said that its passage was due wholly to the efforts of one man, Mr. Serjeant Onslow, and the Act was apparently called 'Mr. Serjeant Onslow's Act' for a certain time: Fry, *Report of the Canadian Prisoner's Case* (1839), 26. Onslow's bill was rejected by the House of Lords when first introduced, having passed through the Commons with little difficulty. He brought the bill forward again on the strength of his select committee's report on the inadequacy of the law as it stood. The bill passed, apparently with no difficulty in either

return in all cases where the applicant is confined 'otherwise than for some criminal or supposed criminal matter and except persons imprisoned for debt or by process in any civil suit'.[29]

The relevant sections are:

s.3 In all cases provided for by this Act, although the return to any writ of habeas corpus shall be good and sufficient in law, it shall be lawful for the justice or baron, before whom such writ may be returnable, to proceed to examine into the truth of the facts set forth in such return by affidavit or by affirmation ... and to do therein as to justice shall appertain ... [and it is further provided that if doubtful as to whether or not the return is true, the justice or baron can bail the person restrained and bring the matter before the full court for determination].

s.4 The like proceeding may be had in the court for controverting the truth of the return to any such writ of habeas corpus awarded as aforesaid, although such writ shall be awarded by the said court itself, or be returnable therein.

The reason why these provisions of the Act were not extended to criminal cases was probably the fear that it would lead to trying people on affidavits.[30] It would seem that commitment for a 'criminal or supposed criminal matter' implies some previous judicial investigation, and that the Act will apply to cases where the applicant has been arrested and is held on suspicion of a criminal charge, but has not yet been brought before a court.[31]

The intended effect of the Act of 1816, then, was probably to encompass all situations in which the detention did not rest on a judicial determination or order. The Act also covers non-criminal committals on judicial authority, except where the party is committed

---

House: IV Bacon *Abridg.*, 147. The report of the special committee is found in 31 *Parl. Deb.* 891, and the debate on its report, in 32 *Parl. Deb.* 542. There does not appear to be a report of any debate on the bill itself.

[29] s.1
[30] *Ex p. Beeching* (1825) 6 D. & R. 209 at 211–12, per Abbot C.J.: 'The object of the [1816 Act] was to give the party a summary remedy by controverting the truth of the return, instead of putting him to an action for false return. There is very good reason for not permitting the truth of a return to be traversed where the party is charged with a crime, for that would be trying him upon affidavits; but here we are not called upon to try whether these persons have committed an offence, or that which may be called an offence.'
[31] *Ex p. Beeching* (1825) 6 D. & R. 209 at 211–12, where the Act was held to apply to the application of a prisoner charged under the smuggling Acts, who alleged he was taken to the wrong town and held for an unreasonable time without trial. See also *Carus Wilson's Case* (1845) 7 Q.B. 984 at 1010, per Patterson J.: '[It is meant], as I understand it, to except all cases of proceedings at law, and to include merely cases where parties are detained without any authority.'

in execution. The exception which is still of significance is criminal causes and in all criminal cases to which the Act does not apply, the respondent will rely on some judicial authority or warrant for the detention.

It is submitted, however, that in terms of actual result, there is no discernible difference between cases which fall within the Act and cases which fall without. Inquiry into the facts which lie behind an order always rests on the basis of jurisdictional review, and the doctrine of jurisdictional facts, discussed below.

Indeed, even in the law of certiorari, where there can now be no doubt about the admission of extrinsic evidence to 'traverse' the return and show want of jurisdiction, there once existed a similar problem.[32] The old rule in certiorari has long been forgotten, but that in the law of habeas corpus is still remembered. In practical terms, however, there has been little more difficulty about questioning facts which go to jurisdiction in habeas corpus than in certiorari.

While the Act is often relied on to justify a factual inquiry,[33] the same result can almost always be achieved through the jurisdictional facts doctrine. The courts have really never been prevented by the common law rule from reviewing facts essential to the jurisdiction or authority underlying the order for detention.

From time to time the courts do advert to the Act of 1816 as providing justification for looking at evidence which controverts the answer given by the respondent. In *Rutty*,[34] for example, Lord Goddard C.J. attributed to the 1816 Act the power to inquire into a fact which the other two judges treated as jurisdictional. At the same time, however, he stated that the court would not enter the inquiry if

---

[32] *R.* v. *Burnaby* (1703) 2 Ld. Raym. 900, Rubinstein, op. cit. 70–4; de Smith, *Judicial Review*, 110.

[33] For cases applying the Act (or its equivalent in Commonwealth jurisdictions) see: *Ex p. Beeching* (1825) 6 D. & R. 209; *Re Walmington* (1846) 6 L.T.O.S. 315; *Ex p. West* (1861) 2 Legge 1475 (N.S.W.); *Ex p. Fitzpatrick* (1893) 32 N.B.R. 182 (N.B.); *Re Davidson* (1915) 8 O.W.N. 481 (Ont. H.C.).

[34] *R.* v. *Board of Control, ex p. Rutty* [1956] 2 Q.B. 109. Lord Goddard's remarks were followed by Lord Parker C.J. in *R.* v. *Governor of Brixton Prison, ex p. Ahsan* [1969] 2 Q.B. 222 (discussed *infra*, pp. 86–91) where, again, the basis for review was plainly jurisdictional: see Parker C.J.'s own remarks quoted *infra*. See also *Greene* v. *Secretary of State for Home Affairs* [1942] 1 K.B. 87, where Lord Goddard said that the Privy Council decision in *Eshugbayi Eleko* v. *Officer Administering the Government of Nigeria* [1931] A.C. 662, rested on the 1816 Act. The Privy Council decision does not mention the Act. In *Ex p. Budd* [1942] 2 K.B. 14, 22–3 (C.A.), Lord Greene, M.R. delivering the opinion of the court, described the effect of the 1816 Act in terms of jurisdictional review: 'It is clear that there may be many matters into which the court can and will inquire under the

the magistrate had some evidence to support the finding. It is difficult to see how it could be said that the court is 'determining the truth of the return' if it will only interfere where there is no evidence. More recently, Lord Scarman described s.3 of the Act, which allows the court to examine the truth of the return, as 'the beginning of the modern jurisprudence the effect of which is to displace, unless Parliament by plain words otherwise provides, the *Wednesbury* principle in cases where liberty is infringed by an act of the executive'.[35]

It has repeatedly been held that nothing in the Act of 1816 requires the respondent to supply the facts by affidavit,[36] which would facilitate an inquiry into the facts. In short, the rule against controverting the return may safely be regarded as a harmless relic of the past. The remote possibilities of a mistake of identity[37] or a mistake about the existence of an order[38] on the part of the gaoler could perhaps raise the spectre of the rule. There are, however, many ways around the rule which have been used since Wilmot's time and before,[39] and it is inconceivable that a court would not give relief.

section if occasion arises, for example, the bona fides of the Secretary of State, the genuineness of the detention order itself, and the identity of the applicant with the person referred to in the order. Similarly, if, for example, a regulation empowered the Home Secretary to obtain any person who was in fact an alien, the court could inquire into the nationality of the applicant, since, if it transpired that he was not in fact an alien, his detention would be ultra vires. In all these instances the court would be inquiring into questions relevant to the matter in hand, namely, the legality of the detention.'

[35] *Khawaja* v. *Secretary of State for the Home Department* [1984] A.C. 74 at 110, referring to *Associated Provincial Picture Houses Ltd.* v. *Wednesbury Corporation* [1948] 1 K.V. 223 (C.A.).

[36] *Leonard Watson's Case* (1839) 9 A. & E. 731; *Greene* v. *Secretary of State for Home Affairs* [1942] A.C. 284; *Ex p. Budd* [1942] 2 K.B. 14 (C.A.).

[37] Mistaken identity was a factor in *Ex p. Docherty* [1960] Crim. L.R. 835 (where the authorities conceded an error had been made); *Re Thompson* (1888) 5 T.L.R. 540 (where the court acted). See the passage quoted from *Ex p. Budd* [1942] 2 K.B. 14 (C.A.) *supra*, n. 34, p. 70 suggesting that the court would review an error of identity. See also *R.* v. *Secretary of State for the Home Department, ex p. Iqbal* [1979] 1 All E.R. 675 (aff'd, C.A. at 685), where the factual inquiry under the 1816 Act disclosed that although the return failed to disclose a valid cause, there was in fact a lawful reason for the detention, and hence the writ was refused.

[38] In *Middlesex Sheriff's Case* (1840) 11 A. & E. 273 at 296–7, Coleridge J. suggested that the Act of 1816 only related to the existence of the order: 'It is contended that affidavits may be received to explain the facts returned. But the return states simply an adjudication of contempt. There is nothing in the affidavits referred to which controverts the fact of such an adjudication; and if the house had jurisdiction to make it, we can no more inquire by affidavit whether they came to a right conclusion in doing so than we could in the case of a like adjudication by the Court of Common Pleas.' See also *R.* v. *Dunn* (1840) 12 A. & E. 599.

[39] Including repudiation of the rule, or quashing a wilfully false return and

2. JURISDICTIONAL FACTS

Certain questions of fact are said to be 'jurisdictional' and therefore open to review by the superior courts.[40] Such questions are sometimes called 'preliminary' or 'collateral' or questions of 'precedent fact'. They are preliminary in the sense that they are logically prior to a determination of the main issue, and such issues are collateral to the issue that the tribunal is asked to decide ultimately. These terms describe the situation where the powers granted to an inferior jurisdiction can only be applied to a certain class of persons or things. While the inferior body may have to decide for itself initially whether or not the person or thing in question comes within the class upon which its powers may be exercised, the courts have said that its decision on this question is merely tentative[41] and is open to review as such a decision determines the jurisdictional bounds of the tribunal.

Professor Wade points out that very often, the label 'jurisdictional law' may be more appropriate than 'jurisdictional fact'.[42] In many of the cases which apply the jurisdictional fact principle, there is no real dispute as to the objective facts, and the real issue is to determine the correct legal principles which should be applied to those facts. It will be seen later on[43] that the courts have experienced difficulty in

committing the gaoler for contempt. In *Leonard Watson's Case* (1839) 9 A. & E. 731 at 805, Lord Denman expressed his doubts about the incontrovertibility of the return, and also said at 804: 'if there were anything like a wilful falsehood committed, it would be the subject of the severest punishment the Court can inflict.' Cf. this statement as reported by Fry, one of the junior counsel in the case in a pamphlet, 'Report of the Canadian Prisoner's Case' (1839) at 96: 'I believe that if there had been anything like wilful falsehood in this matter, and that this had been done for fraudulent purposes, *the return would have been quashed*, and the person who made it severely punished' (emphasis added).

[40] For general discussions, see Wade, *Administrative Law* (5th ed. 1982), 249–72 and 'Anglo-American Law: More Reflections' (1966), 82 L.Q.R. 226, 229–32; de Smith, *Judicial Review*, 114–19; Rubinstein, op cit. 214–18; Bentley, 'Jurisdictional or Collateral Issues' [1962] Public Law 7; Mullan, 'The Jurisdictional Fact Doctrine in the Supreme Court of Canada—A Mitigating Plea' (1972) 10 O.H.L.J. 440. For the argument against the doctrine, see Gordon, 'The Relation of Facts to Jurisdiction' (1929) 45 L.Q.R. 459 and 'Jurisdictional Fact: An Answer' (1966) 82 L.Q.R. 515.

[41] Cf. *R.* v. *Commissioners for Special Purposes of the Income Tax* (1888) 21 Q.B.D. 313 at 319, per Esher M.R., pointing out that in some cases, Parliament may give the tribunal power to make a binding decision on matters which determine the limits of jurisdiction. It would be exceptional, however, for a court to accept such a curtailment of its supervisory jurisdiction: 1 Hals. (4th), 63.

[42] 'Anglo-American Administrative Law—More Reflections' (1966) 82 L.Q.R. 226, 241.   [43] *Infra*, pp. 76–9.

deriving appropriate methods to determine the facts when there actually is a dispute. In any event, the concept of jurisdictional fact will often justify the admission of extrinsic evidence and the determination of factual issues on habeas corpus.

It has been argued that this concept of jurisdictional fact is logically insupportable[44] and admittedly, there can be little doubt that it is difficult to distinguish a jurisdictional fact from a non-jurisdictional one.[45]

The jurisdictional fact doctrine is a controversial one precisely because it permits courts to review decisions of boards and tribunals on virtually any ground. In some contexts, a higher degree of judicial deference to the expertise of administrative agencies and tribunals is called for, and the reach of the jurisdictional fact doctrine has been curtailed.[46]

On habeas corpus, however, the courts may be expected to continue to use the concept, together with the all-encompassing definition of jurisdiction discussed in Chapter 2, to ensure effective and thorough review. Without this means of review, state officials and inferior tribunals would be left free to decide the limits of their powers for themselves, and the courts have long considered that such unfettered powers would be intolerable with respect to the liberty of the subject.

Such issues of fact have frequently arisen and have been reviewed in habeas corpus cases. The principle was clearly enunciated by Wills J. in the case of *Re Guerin*.[47] There the learned judge had little difficulty in holding that as only non-British nationals were subject to extradition under the treaty, a finding of fact which led directly to the conclusion that the prisoner was not British, was open to review:

With respect to the power of this court to review the finding of the magistrate upon the question of nationality, which is a question for the magistrate in the first instance, it is a well established principle that where a matter of fact which is cardinal to the existence of a magistrate's jurisdiction is collateral to the

[44] See Gordon, op. cit.
[45] Compare, for example, the *Guerin* case, discussed *infra*, n. 47, and the *Ferguson* case, noted *infra*, n. 54, p. 75. In the former, it was held that the question of nationality was jurisdictional where no British person could be extradited; in the latter, the fact of ordinary residence was held not to be jurisdictional where persons 'ordinarily resident' could be detained.
[46] See, e.g., *Canadian Union of Public Employees, Local 963* v. *New Brunswick Liquor Corp.* [1979] 2 S.C.R. 227. For analysis of subsequent Canadian developments, see Mullan, 'The Supreme Court of Canada and Jurisdictional Error: Compromising New Brunswick Liquor?' (1987–8) 1 C.J.A.L.P. 71.
[47] (1888) 60 L.T. 538 further discussed *infra*, n. 115, p. 85.

subject of inquiry, the decision of the magistrate is not final, and the court has a right to inquire into the sufficiency of the evidence upon which the magistrate acted, as being a matter on which his jurisdiction to hear the case at all is based.[48]

The most recent example is the decision of the House of Lords in *Khawaja* v. *Secretary of State for the Home Department*,[49] dealing with the detention of an individual admitted to the United Kingdom, but subsequently detained as an illegal entrant on the ground that he had gained entry by fraud or deception. A line of earlier cases, including a previous decision of the House of Lords itself,[50] held that the court would not review such orders so long as the immigration officer had reasonable grounds for belief in facts that would sustain the detention order.[51] Those cases were overruled, and the House of Lords held that the power to detain could only be validly exercised if the prisoner was in fact an illegal entrant, and hence the court was called upon to review the facts to determine whether that 'precedent fact' had been established.[52]

There have been many other examples of such review of factual questions in habeas corpus cases.[53] While many of these depend upon

---

[48]   Ibid. at 541. See also, *infra*, n. 78, p. 78.

[49]   [1984] A.C. 74.

[50]   *Zamir* v. *Secretary of State for the Home Department* [1980] A.C. 930.

[51]   *R.* v. *Secretary of State for the Home Department, ex p. Hussain* [1978] 1 W.L.R. 700 (C.A.); *R.* v. *Secretary of State for the Home Department, ex p. Choudhary* [1978] 1 W.L.R. 1177 (C.A.); *R.* v. *Secretary of State for the Home Department, ex p. Akhtar* [1981] Q.B. 46 (C.A.); *R.* v. *Secretary of State for the Home Department, ex. p. Iqbal* [1979] 1 All E.R. 675 (aff'd C.A. at 685). Cf., however, *Azam* v. *Secretary of State for the Home Department* [1974] A.C. 18 at 34; *R.* v. *Secretary of State for the Home Department, ex p. Ram* [1979] 1 W.L.R. 148; *R.* v. *Secretary of State for the Home Department, ex p. Kahn* [1980] 1 W.L.R. 569 (C.A.). The restrictive view taken in these cases attracted sharp criticism: Jones, 'The Role of Habeas Corpus in Immigration Cases' (1979) 95 L.Q.R. 171; Newdick, 'Immigrants and the Decline of Habeas Corpus' [1982] P.L. 89; Blake, 'The Death of Habeas Corpus' (1980) 130 New L.J. 772; Macdonald, *Immigration Law and Practice* (1983), 416–21; British Institute of Human Rights, *The Habeas Corpus Act, Is it Becoming Less Effective* (1980); Newdick, 'Habeas Corpus: Zamir to Khawaja' [1983] P.L. 213.

[52]   Cf. the situation where an immigrant is detained at point of entry by an officer. Here, the House of Lords held, the statute contemplates a certain procedure which confers specific powers and the review on habeas corpus will accordingly be more limited: 'If leave to enter is refused, that decision can plainly only be challenged on the now familiar grounds on which the court has jurisdiction to review a public law decision committed by statute to an administrative authority.' ([1984] 1 A.C. at 122 per Lord Bridge of Harwich.)

[53]   See e.g. *Re Eggington* (1853) 2 E. & B. 717, allowing evidence that the prisoner was arrested on Sunday, a condition which vitiated further proceedings; *Swan* v. *Dakins* (1855) 16 C.B. 77, allowing evidence of circumstances making the prisoner privileged from arrest in a civil cause; *Re Bailey, Re Collier* (1854) 3 E. & B. 607, reviewing the

a broad definition of jurisdiction, a definition which has not been invariably applied,[54] there can be little doubt that this is a well-established basis for entertaining issues of fact on habeas corpus.

(a) *Admission of Extrinsic Evidence*

It is clear that fresh evidence cannot be received on a non-jurisdictional issue.[55] In other words, the court will not entertain the argument that the inferior body came to the wrong decision on the facts, so long as those facts do not go to jurisdiction, and it would now seem, so long as the inferior body had reasonable evidence to support its finding.[56] While the powers of review may be broad in some respects, the courts have made it clear that habeas corpus does not constitute a form of appeal. This rule applies even where the facts come to light after the time of the impugned proceedings,[57] unless, it would seem, such evidence tends to show fraud.[58]

It is equally clear, however, that where an inferior body's decision is questioned on jurisdictional grounds, evidence relevant to that issue can be admitted by the court on habeas corpus. Thus, in cases of 'jurisdictional fact', the court will receive affidavit evidence which is relevant to that issue.[59] Similarly, it may be necessary to bring other

existence of a master and servant relationship, a prerequisite for a conviction under the statute in question; *Re Authers* (1889) 22 Q.B.D. 345, allowing evidence to show that the magistrate erred having found a previous conviction which led him to award a harsher penalty; *Shin Shim* v. *R.* [1938] S.C.R. 378, reviewing the issue to citizenship to overcome a deportation order.

[54] See e.g. *R.* v. *Morn Hill Camp (Commanding Officer), ex p. Ferguson* [1917] 1 K.B. 176, a case under the Military Service Act 1916 which deemed all males 'for the time being ordinarily resident in Great Britain' to have been called up for service. The applicant sought to impugn the magistrate's finding that he was 'ordinarily resident', but the court, adopting the restrictive theory of jurisdiction expounded in *R.* v. *Bolton* (1841) 1 Q.B. 66, refused to entertain the issue.

[55] *Schtraks* v. *Government of Israel* [1964] A.C. 556. The suggestion was made in *Ex p. Castioni* [1891] 1 Q.B. 149 by Hawkins J. that the court could receive evidence on any point, but the suggestion has never been followed and was disapproved in the *Schtraks* case.

[56] Review of sufficiency of evidence is discussed *infra*, pp. 79–85.

[57] *Schtraks* v. *Government of Israel* [1964] A.C. 556 at 580 per Lord Reid: 'Owing to the restricted character of habeas corpus proceedings a court is not concerned with anything that comes to light after committal', pointing out that fresh evidence was for the Home Secretary in the exercise of his discretion. See also *Ex p. Schtraks* [1964] 1 Q.B. 191. For a case where this rule was applied to the benefit of the prisoner, see *R.* v. *Governor of Brixton Prison, ex p. Sadri* [1962] 3 All E.R. 747.

[58] *Ex p. Schtraks* [1964] 1 Q.B. 191 at 199 per Salmon J.; *Ex p. Enaharo* [1963] Crim. L.R. 568; cf. *Ex p. Corke* [1954] 2 All E.R. 440, refusing to review a conviction on the grounds that it had been obtained on perjured evidence.

[59] *Supra*, n. 53, p. 74; *Khawaja* v. *Secretary of State for the Home Department* [1984]

jurisdictional defects before the court by way of affidavit, and there is ample authority for this.[60] As Lord Hodson pointed out in the *Schtraks* case, the rule is the same as on certiorari.[61]

Good examples are the cases under the Extradition Act where the court admits evidence tending to show that the offence was of a political nature[62] or evidence that the offence was not extraditable in some other respect.[63] Evidence may also be admitted to show that the tribunal was improperly constituted,[64] or to prove what transpired at proceedings for which there is no transcript.[65] The prerequisite to the reception of extrinsic evidence is simply that it relates to the issue of jurisdiction.[66]

3. PROCEDURAL PROBLEMS AND ISSUES OF FACT

It has been noted that in many of the cases which apply the jurisdictional fact principle there is no real dispute as to the objective

A.C. 74 at 101 per Lord Wilberforce. For a review of the Canadian cases on this point, see Sharpe, 'Habeas Corpus in Canada' (1975–6) 2 Dal. L.R. 241 at 264–6.

[60] Cases cited *supra*, n. 53, p. 74 and *infra*, nn. 62–4. For further examples see: *Re Baker* (1857) 2 H. & N. 219; *Re Thompson* (1860) 6 H. & N. 193; *Re Lampon* (1834) 1 Mont. & Ayr. 245; *Re Cavenett* [1926] N.Z.L.R. 755; *Ah Sheung v Lindberg* (1906) V.L.R. 323; *The Queen* v. *Miller* [1985] 2 S.C.R. 613, repudiating the narrower view expressed in *Mitchell* v. *The Queen* [1976] 2 S.C.R. 570. cf. *Re Smith* (1858) 3 H.&N. 227, refusing to look at evidence relating the matter of territorial jurisdiction.

[61] [1964] A.C. 556 at 605–6.

[62] See e.g. *Re Kolczynki* [1955] 1 All E.R. 31; *Schtraks* v. *Government of Israel* [1964] A.C. 556 at 597, 605–6 (although Lord Reid at 580–1 thought that admission of such evidence was specifically contemplated by the statute); *R.* v. *Governor of Brixton Prison, ex p. Keane* [1970] 3 All E.R. 741 at 744 (aff'd [1972] A.C. 204), a case under the Backing of Warrants (Republic of Ireland) Act 1965. See also *R.* v. *Governor of Brixton Prison ex p. Perry* [1924] 1 K.B. 455; *R.* v. *Governor of Holloway Prison, ex p. Siletti* (1902) 87 L.T. 332. The Fugitive Offenders Act 1967, s.8(4) makes specific provision for the admission of such evidence. Cf., however, *Re Nobbs* [1978] 1 W.L.R. 1302, holding that the issue of whether an offence specified in a warrant pursuant to the Backing of Warrants (Republic of Ireland) Act 1965 was a political offence did not go to jurisdiction and that where no evidence on the issue had been adduced before the justices, affidavit evidence could not be received on habeas corpus.

[63] See e.g. *Kossekechatko* v. *A.G. Trinidad* [1932] A.C. 78 (P.C.).

[64] *Ex p. Johnson* (1915) 17 W.A.L.R. 149; *R.* v. *Boyle* (1868) 4 P.R. 256 (Ont.).

[65] *R.* v. *Board of Control, ex p. Rutty* [1956] 2 Q.B. 109.

[66] The Review of Justices' Decisions Act 1872, permits a justice to file an affidavit setting forth the grounds for his decision and any facts which he considers have a material bearing upon the question in issue, where his decision is questioned in a Superior Court by a rule to show cause or other process issued upon an *ex parte* application.

facts, and the real issue is to determine the correct legal principles which should be applied to those facts.[67] Indeed, from time to time, the courts have expressed an unwillingness to enter questions of fact on applications for prerogative writs where conflicting evidence has been presented, even though the matter at issue may be one which relates to jurisdiction.[68] The reason for this is the procedural difficulty, real or supposed, of entertaining complicated factual inquiries on applications for prerogative writs, rather than any doubt about the correctness of the theory of jurisdictional facts.[69] It is proposed here to discuss the problems which may be encountered in this respect on habeas corpus proceedings.

It has been shown that the common law rule against controverting the facts in the return did not always prevent the courts from entering questions of fact. The rule probably did, however, prevent the courts from developing adequate machinery to deal with the relatively limited range of factual questions which can arise on habeas corpus. This is a defect which habeas corpus shares with the other prerogative remedies, but it is submitted that the problem is more imagined than real.

(a) *Cross-Examination on Affidavits*

Under the present rules of court, the only potentially useful provision for dealing with factual inquiries which applies to habeas corpus and the other prerogative remedies is the rule which permits a deponent to be cross-examined on his affidavit.[70] This rule, frequently used in other proceedings,[71] is used only in exceptional cases in the context of judicial review.[72]

---

[67] *Supra*, p. 72–3.   [68] See *infra*, pp. 80–1.

[69] Professor Wade, 82 L.Q.R. 230, calls this 'one of the collection of defects from which the prerogative remedies suffer and which have long cried out for reform'. Cf. de Smith, *Judicial Review*, 140: 'The general principle is a sound one in so far as the Divisional Court is ill-equipped to evaluate conflicting evidence on the basis of affidavits.'

[70] Ord. 38, r.2(3).

[71] Supreme Court Practice (1985), 567–8. See *Comet Products U.K. Ltd.* v. *Hawkex Plastics Ltd.* [1971] 2 Q.B. 67 at 77, per Cross L.J.: 'It is, I think, only in a very exceptional case that judge ought to refuse an application to cross examine a deponent on his affidavit.' *O'Reilly* v. *Mackman* [1983] 2 A.C. 237 at 283 per Lord Diplock: '[cross-examination] should be allowed whenever the justice of the particular case so requires.' There is a flexibility in the mode of proceeding: the examination may be conducted before a judge, a master, or examiner: *Supreme Court Practice* (1985), 568.

[72] See e.g. *R.* v. *Stokesley, Yorkshire JJ., ex p. Bartram* [1956] 1 W.L.R. 254, a certiorari case where it appeared that a court order had been improperly altered. See

There is authority for cross-examination of deponents on habeas corpus. In *Barnardo* v. *Ford*,[73] the House of Lords held that the respondent could be cross-examined on the return and in the *Eshugbayi Eleko* case, it was made plain that even oral evidence could be taken and the deponents cross-examined.[74] In *Khawaja*, Lord Wilberforce stated that findings of fact could be made 'by the use of affidavit evidence or cross-examination upon them or oral evidence'.[75] Lord Bridge of Harwich suggested that in the past, perhaps the discretion to permit cross-examination had been 'too sparingly exercised',[76] although he warned that cross-examination should not be ordered where burdensome, as in the case of overseas witnesses. The modern practice is to try the matter on affidavits[77] and it is submitted that where there is conflicting evidence on a question of fact which is properly before the court on habeas corpus, relief should not be denied on account of unnecessary concern over the procedural difficulty. It is understandable that the courts should wish to keep habeas corpus as an uncomplicated summary remedy, but this should surely not be at the expense of denying relief in a proper case.

(b) *Trial of an Issue*

There are several nineteenth- and early twentieth-century cases where the courts simply directed the trial of an issue on a question of fact which arose on habeas corpus.[78] At the time this practice was

also *R.* v. *Kent JJ., ex p. Smith* [1928] W.N. 137 where leave to cross-examine on certiorari was refused. In Canada, cross-examination is routinely available in such cases.

[73] [1892] A.C. 326 at 340.

[74] *Eshugbayi Eleko* v. *Officer Administering the Government of Nigeria* [1931] A.C. 662 at 675 per Lord Atkin. Cf. *R.* v. *Secretary of State for Home Department, ex p. Mughal* [1973] 3 W.L.R. 647 at 652 per Denning M.R.: 'It was unheard of for a man applying to habeas corpus to be cross-examined.'

[75] [1984] A.C. 74 at 101.

[76] Ibid. at 124–5.

[77] *Infra*, p. 219.

[78] *Re Guerin* (1888) 60 L.T. 538 at 540, per Willis J.: 'As there are contradictory affidavits it will be necessary, if the point is to be considered, for the court to order an issue to be tried to determine whether the prisoner is entitled to the status of a native born subject or not. As to our jurisdiction to do this, I have no doubt that it is the only means at the disposal of this court by which it can inform itself upon such a matter of fact.' *Re Andrews* (1873) L.R. 8 Q.B. 153; *R.* v. *Douglas* (1888) as reported in Short & Mellor, *Crown Practice* (2nd ed. 1908), 323. See also *Ex p. Gregory* [1901] A.C. 128 at 129 (P.C.), where it was said that the court had such a power; see also the Canadian cases cited *infra*, n. 6, p. 157 and *Ex p. Vorhauer, Re Steep* (1967) 87 W.N. (Pt. 1) N.S.W. 36.

adopted, there was no express provision in the rules for it[79] and the example of these cases could, perhaps, be followed today. The most satisfactory solution might be to adopt a rule expressly providing for this in all proceedings for prerogative relief.[80] If the substantive law allows or requires the court to deal with a question of fact, it is inexcusable to pretend that procedural difficulties prevent a thorough investigation.[81] Allowing for the trial of an issue provides for a flexible way of dealing with questions of fact, and adds no complication to the ordinary case where the facts are not in dispute.

4. REVIEW OF SUFFICIENCY OF EVIDENCE

The orthodox rule in the law of judicial review has been that a determination cannot be said to have been made outside a tribunal's jurisdiction solely because it was made without evidence. The classic statement of the rule is that of Lord Sumner in the *Nat Bell Liquors* case in 1922:

A justice who convicts without evidence is doing something which he ought not to do, but he is doing it as a judge, and if his jurisdiction to entertain the charge is not open to impeachment, his subsequent error, however grave, is a wrong exercise of jurisdiction which he has, and not a usurpation of a jurisdiction which he has not ... To say that there is no jurisdiction to convict without evidence is the same thing as saying that there is jurisdiction if the decision is right, and none if it is wrong ...[82]

The rule stated by Lord Sumner has a compelling logic, but it does

[79] Short & Mellor, op. cit. 337, discussing Crown Office Rule 231 (1906) (which was dropped in the 1938 revision) which specifically provided for trial of an issue. 'This is a new rule, and provides authority for that which the court has on occasion done without authority.'

[80] Cf. the reforms suggested by the Law Commission, *Report on Remedies in Administrative Law* (No.73, 1976), recommending discovery, interrogatories, and attendance for cross-examination.

[81] For recent examples, see *Re Mitchell and The Queen* (1983) 42 O.R. (2d) 481 (H.C.), where the detention order of a habitual criminal was challenged and a trial of an issue was directed to determine whether the applicant was still a danger to society; *Re Reddekopp and The Queen* (1983) 6 C.C.C. (3d) 241 (Ont. H.C.), directing the trial of an issue to determine whether the applicant had in fact broken the terms of a conditional pardon.

[82] *R. v. Nat Bell Liquors* [1922] 2 A.C. 128 at 151–2 (P.C.). See also *Davies v. Price* [1958] 1 W.L.R. 434 (H.L.). The rule is not always followed in Canada: see Elliot, 'No Evidence: A Ground for Judicial Review in Canadian Administrative Law?' (1972–3) 37 Sask. L.R. 48.

rest upon the term 'jurisdiction' being given what Lord Reid has called its 'narrow and original sense of the tribunal being entitled to enter on the inquiry in question'.[83] This definition of jurisdiction has not been the one favoured by the courts,[84] and while the 'no evidence' rule has been retained, a broader definition of jurisdictional error has meant that the full effect of the rule can be avoided. A finding made without evidence constitutes an error of law.[85] It will often be wrong and lead to an unjust result. As might be expected, the courts have found ways to provide a remedy where a decision has been made without evidence.[86] In habeas corpus cases there has been astonishingly little difficulty in openly reviewing decisions on the grounds of no evidence, and until recently, the courts have based this review on the grounds of jurisdictional error. In 1968 in the *Armah* case,[87] it was suggested that the proper basis for review was that a finding made without evidence constituted an error of law, reviewable because it appeared on the documents before the court. The purpose of this section is to examine the unusual willingness of the courts to review for want of evidence on habeas corpus, and to discuss briefly the implications that this has in the law of judicial review.

(a) *'No Evidence' or Jurisdictional Fact?*

Before doing this, it may be useful to note one confusing aspect of reviewing questions of fact. Courts sometimes use the language of 'no evidence' in cases which deal with jurisdictional fact and vice versa. There is, it is submitted, a logical difference between reviewing a finding of a jurisdictional fact, that is, a preliminary or collateral question, and reviewing the sufficiency of evidence to support the principal finding, or a finding on the merits. The first situation involves a determination of whether the circumstances presented constitute a situation with which the tribunal has power to deal. The other involves the tribunal's factual decision on the ultimate question which it is empowered to decide.

However, the two categories are not always kept distinct, and it is often difficult to say which sort of case the court thinks it has before

---

[83] *Anisminic Ltd.* v. *Foreign Compensation Commission* [1969] 2 A.C. 147 at 171.

[84] *Supra*, p. 21.

[85] For the possibility of review for error on the face of the record, see *infra*, n. 108, p. 84.

[86] Wade, *Administrative Law* (5th ed. 1982), 287–95.

[87] *Armah* v. *Government of Ghana* [1968] A.C. 192, discussed in detail, *supra*, pp. 43–5 and *infra*, pp. 84–5.

it.[88] Even where there is a clear issue of jurisdictional fact which has been brought into question, the courts sometimes express reluctance to deal with the issue if the inferior court has already weighed conflicting evidence on that very question.[89] It is sometimes said that the issue will only be dealt with if there is 'no evidence' to support the finding.[90] Such reluctance would seem to violate the principle that no inferior body can make a conclusive determination on an issue which affects its own jurisdiction. If the question is one which the tribunal has no conclusive power to decide, it is difficult from a theoretical point of view to see why its decision should be more binding when there has been evidence than it is when there has not been evidence. The rationale is, perhaps, simply the unwillingness of the courts to decide disputed questions of fact on the prerogative writs.

On the other hand, on occasion, when faced with an issue of fact which is the very essence of that which the inferior tribunal does have the power to decide, the courts treat the matter as one of 'jurisdictional fact'. An extreme example of such reasoning is provided by some of the extradition cases which seem to rest on the notion that the extradition statute gives the magistrate the power or jurisdiction to commit only on condition that there be sufficient evidence,[91] whereas such a theory would make all questions of fact, questions of jurisdictional fact.

(b) *Review of the Sufficiency of Evidence in Extradition Committals*

In any case, review of 'no evidence' on habeas corpus has been especially important in the extradition cases. Where extradition is sought to a country other than the Republic of Ireland, the accused person is brought before a magistrate's court and evidence of the alleged offence is presented. If the magistrate's court finds that the evidence would be sufficient to warrant the accused's committal for trial if charged with an indictable offence committed within the jurisdiction of the court, a committal order is made pending delivery of the accused to the foreign authorities who sought his extradition.[92] In

---

[88] See e.g. *Re Bailey* (1854) 3 E. & B. 607; *Re Authers* (1889) 22 Q.B.D. 345; *R. v. Board of Control, ex p. Rutty* [1956] 2 Q.B. 109; *Re Sage* [1958] Crim. L.R. 258; all habeas corpus cases which use confusing language in this context.

[89] *R. v. Fulham, Hammersmith & Kensington Rent Tribunal, ex p. Zerek* [1951] 2 K.B. 1 at 11–14, per Delvin L.J.; *Segal v. City of Montreal* [1931] S.C.R. 460 at 473; de Smith, *Judicial Review*, 139–41.

[90] *Supra*, nn. 88 and 89.

[91] See e.g. *Re Arton* [1896] 1 Q.B. 108 at 113; *Re Galwey* [1896] 1 Q.B. 230 at 236; *R. v. Governor of Brixton Prison, ex p. Shure* [1926] 1 K.B. 127.

[92] The Extradition Act 1870, ss.9, 10, for extradition to specified foreign countries;

the case of an Irish fugitive, the magistrate's court acts upon a sufficient Irish warrant, and is not required to hear evidence which makes out a *prima facie* case against the accused.[93] In all cases, the prisoner must be told that there is the right to apply for a writ of habeas corpus.[94]

It has never really been doubted that the courts would review the sufficiency of the evidence for the committal. The question is the source of the power to do so. At least until 1968 and the *Armah* decision, this was said to be based on jurisdictional review.[95] Whatever justification the courts have given for reviewing the evidence, it would seem most likely that the practice began simply by following what used to be done in reviewing domestic committals. This is admittedly speculative, but it is seen in the discussion of the use of habeas corpus in criminal proceedings that until the end of the nineteenth century, it was the regular practice of the courts to review the sufficiency of evidence for committals for trial in domestic cases.[96] Extradition committals have always taken the same form as committal for trial, and initially, the habeas corpus cases dealing with extradition seem to have simply followed the same practice.[97] In domestic criminal cases, the basis for review was never regarded as jurisdictional. The court was not exercising a power of review so much as its inherent jurisdiction to grant bail. Before bailing the accused, the court wanted to be informed of the nature of the evidence against him, and the depositions were examined.[98] If the evidence was weak, the court would bail or even dis-

the Fugitive Offenders Act 1967, s.7, for extradition to designated Commonwealth countries. Under the Fugitive Offenders Act 1881, there had to be a 'strong or probable presumption that the fugitive committed the offence mentioned in the warrant'. This was held in *Armah* v. *Government of Ghana* [1968] A.C. 192, to require a higher standard of proof.

[93] Backing of Warrants (Republic of Ireland) Act 1965, s.2(2); *Re Arkins* [1966] 3 All E.R. 651; *R.* v. *Governor of Brixton Prison, ex p. Keane* [1970] 3 All E.R. 741.

[94] Extradition Act, s.11; Fugitive Offenders Act, s.8(1); Backing of Warrants Act, s.3(1). These provisions merely require that the prisoner be informed of his common law rights: they do not extend rights in themselves: *R.* v. *Governor of Holloway Prison, ex p. Siletti* (1902) 87 L.T. 332.

[95] *Infra*, p. 84.

[96] *Infra*, pp. 128–30.

[97] Cf. *Re Tivnan* (1864) 5 B. & S. 645; *Re Windsor* (1865) 6 B. & S. 522. These two cases were referred to in the *Armah* decision: [1968] A.C. 192 and 234–5, 254, where it was noted that the depositions were examined by the court, having been brought before the court by agreement. See further, *supra*, n. 126 p. 45. See also *R.* v. *Lavaudier* (1881) 15 Cox C.C. 329, where the depositions were examined 'with consent of counsel for the Crown.'

[98] *Infra*, p. 130.

charge the accused.[99] In this way, the habeas corpus application provided a general method of review over preliminary criminal proceedings.

The same approach would seem to have been adopted in the early extradition cases, and the power to review the evidence which originated with the use of habeas corpus to obtain bail was continued. However, towards the end of the nineteenth century, a summary application for bail replaced habeas corpus, and the writ was used less and less to review preliminary criminal proceedings.[100] The nature of review exercised on habeas corpus became more closely tied to the jurisdictional principle. The writ continued to be used in extradition matters in the way it had been used in domestic cases, but as the domestic practice faded away, the courts began to use the language of jurisdictional review to explain the basis for their action. Quite simply, the judges worried more about what they were doing than why they could do it. They did, however, foster the apparent heresy that 'no evidence' goes to jurisdiction, a heresy which somehow was confined to the extradition cases.

The courts acted ostensibly on the principle that 'no evidence, went to jurisdiction in many cases.[101] A good example is the case of *Re Galwey* in 1896, where Lord Russell C.J. said: '... we should, after the order of committal, be entitled to review the magistrate's decision, not in the sense of entertaining an appeal from it, but in the sense of determining whether there was evidence enough to give him jurisdiction to make the order of committal ...'[102] Strangely enough, the judges never seem to have concerned themselves with the accepted rule regarding 'no evidence'. At times the phrase 'no evidence' misled them into thinking that they could only interfere if there was absolutely no evidence.[103] In most cases, however, the phrase was interpreted to mean no evidence reasonably capable of supporting the finding.

[99] Ibid. [100] *Infra*, p. 134.
[101] *Ex p. Huguet* (1873) 12 Cox C.C. 551; *R. v. Maurer* (1883) 10 Q.B.D. 513; *Re Arton* [1896] 1 Q.B. 108; *Ex p. Siletti* (1902) 87 L.T. 332; *R. v. Vyner* (1903) 68 J.P. 142; *R. v. Governor of Brixton Prison, ex p. Shure* [1926] 1 K.B. 127; *R. v. Governor of Brixton Prison, ex p. Servini* [1914] 1 K.B. 77; *R. v. Governor of Brixton Prison, ex p. Mourat Mehmet* [1962] 2 Q.B. 1; *Schtraks v. Government of Israel* [1964] A.C. 556; *R. v. Delisle* (1896) 5 C.C.C. 210 (Que. Q.B.); *Ex p. Lillywhite* (1901) 19 N.Z.L.R. 502; *Collis v. Smith* (1909) 9 C.L.R. 490.
[102] [1896] 1 Q.B. 230 at 236.
[103] *Ex p. Siletti* (1902) 87 L.T. 332 at 334; *R. v. Governor of Brixton Prison, ex p. Servini* [1914] 1 K.B. 77. Elliot, (1972–3) 37 Sask. L.R. 48, suggests that according to the Canadian authorities, it may be that a finding made with absolutely no evidence does constitute a jurisdictional error.

In *Armah*,[104] apparently for the first time, the courts were called upon to reconcile the review of evidence in the extradition cases with the accepted rule that 'no evidence' does not go to jurisdiction. Of the five law lords who sat, Lord Pearson and Lord Morris of Borth-y-Gest (both dissenting on the merits) supported the review of sufficiency of evidence on the grounds of jurisdictional error, although they admitted that the meaning of jurisdiction was being stretched. In the majority, Lord Pearce accepted the possibility of review of sufficiency of evidence as an intra-jurisdictional error which the court is able 'to see' on the material before it, but added a jurisdictional analysis independent of the view that 'no evidence' goes to jurisdiction.[105] Lord Upjohn was satisfied that reviewing the evidence could be based either on the grounds of jurisdictional review, or of review of an error of law apparent on the material before the court.[106] Lord Reid based the review solely on the grounds that the superior courts could review certain intra-jurisdictional errors of law, and that in the extradition cases, the sufficiency of evidence was such an error.[107]

A finding made without evidence has always been regarded as an error of law, and where such an error of law was apparent on the face of the record, it could be reviewed on certiorari.[108] However, after the Summary Jurisdiction Act 1848, the conviction no longer had to recite the evidence,[109] and the depositions themselves were not normally regarded as part of the record.[110] This meant that while reviewing 'no evidence' as an error of law on the face of the record remains theoretically possible,[111] for practical reasons it is rarely, if ever, actually used.

The *Armah* case revives the concept of patent error of law as a grounds for review on habeas corpus.[112] But that apart, the courts do seem willing to assimilate such errors of law as making a finding

---

104   [1968] A.C. 192.

105   Ibid. at 255; *supra*, n. 121, p. 44.

106   Ibid. at 257.

107   Ibid. at 230, 234–5. *Armah* has been followed in Australia: *Bedgood* v. *Keeper of Her Majesty's Penitentiary at Malabar* [1975] 2 N.S.W.L.R. 144.

108   For the cases on certiorari, see Paley, op. cit. pp. 329–38. Habeas corpus cases which may be put in this category are *Nash's Case* (1821) 4 B. & Ald. 295 (discussed *supra*, p. 41: *Re Hammond* (1846) 9 Q.B. 92.

109   The effect of the Act is discussed in more detail *supra*, pp. 30–1. See also *Re Geswood* (1853) 23 L.J.M.C. 35, where its effect on reviewing want of evidence on habeas corpus is discussed.

110   *R.* v. *Nat Bell Liquors* [1922] 2 A.C. 128 (P.C.).

111   *R.* v. *Malony* [1910] 2 I.R. 695.

112   *Supra*, pp. 43–5.

without evidence to errors of jurisdiction.[113] Whether the technical justification for review is patent error of law or error of jurisdiction, it can be said that it now seems that review for want of evidence may well become an established ground for review not only in habeas corpus, but in administrative law generally.[114]

5. BURDEN OF PROOF

In any situation which requires a court to determine an issue of fact, properly placing the burden of proving that fact may be of decisive importance. There are two considerations here. First, there is the issue of the evidential burden: who is required, as a tactical matter, to come forth with evidence in order to put a point in issue? When a genuine issue of fact is raised, a second question arises—that of the legal burden. If the evidence on both sides is evenly balanced and the court is unable to decide the question either way, the issue of fact must be decided against the party who bears the legal burden.[115]

(a) *Evidential Burden and Legal Burden*

There are two types of burden to be distinguished on habeas corpus and the issue will be confused unless care is taken to analyse what

[113] See Lord Diplock's discussion of the *Armah* decision in *R.* v. *Governor of Pentonville Prison, ex p. Sotiriadis* [1974] 2 W.L.R. 253 at 275; *Government of the Federal Republic of Germany* v. *Sotiriadis* [1975] A.C. 1 at 30. See also Wade, *Administrative Law*, at 293.

[114] In Canada, statutory provisions specifically provide for the review of the sufficiency of evidence: see e.g. Judicial Review Procedure Act, R.S.O. 1980, c.224, s.2(3); Federal Court Act, R.S.C. 1985 c.F-7, s.28(1)(c).

[115] The entirely remarkable but apparently unnoticed circumstances of the *Guerin* case illustrate the uncertain approach taken by the courts. Having been committed for extradition, Guerin brought habeas corpus proceedings on the ground, inter alia, that he was a British subject and therefore not liable to be extradited under the governing treaty. There was conflicting evidence and the court directed the trial of an issue on the question: (1888) 60 L.T. 538. At the trial, the jury was instructed that the onus was on Guerin to prove his nationality: (1888) 5 T.L.R. 160. Its finding was that it was not satisfied that he was British, and it was consequently held that he should be extradited: (1888) 5 T.L.R. 188. Almost twenty years later, Guerin escaped from Devil's Island and returned to England, only to be again committed for extradition. Again habeas corpus proceedings were brought and again Guerin relied on the same claim to British nationality. This time the court held that Guerin should be discharged on the grounds that it had not been shown that he was non-British: (1907) 51 Sol. J. 571. The facts were the same but the court held that the burden was cast upon the authorities to prove that he was non-British, and that they had not satisfied that onus.

happens at the various stages of the proceedings. At the outset, the applicant has an evidential burden to meet. The writ does not issue of course, but only on proper grounds being shown.[116] The order or warrant which purports to justify the detention will benefit from the ordinary presumption of regularity. The applicant does not put it in question simply by bringing the application. As a tactical matter, a case must be made casting doubt on the validity of the detention. Where the case rests on matters of fact, enough evidence to raise the possibility of a favourable inference will have to be presented.

This tactical burden of adducing evidence is not to be minimized. In many cases, it may present an almost insurmountable hurdle in the way of the applicant. Especially where the case involves a challenge to an executive order under broadly construed discretionary powers, the burden of adducing evidence may be the most decisive factor.[117]

If the applicant does succeed in raising an issue as to the validity of the detention, the question becomes: does the legal burden rest with the prisoner to satisfy the court of what is alleged or does it rest with the authorities to substantiate what they have done? Who will lose if the court cannot decide one way or the other?

(b) *Legal Burden—Non-Judicial Orders*

The leading case on the burden of proof in habeas corpus is the 1969 decision of the Divisional Court in *Ahsan*.[118] In *Ahsan*, it was alleged by the applicant that the immigration officer who had ordered his detention under the Commonwealth Immigrants Act 1962, was without authority to make such an order. In view of the statute and the procedure adopted by the officer, the crucial issue before the court was whether the prisoner had been examined within twenty-four hours of his arrival in England. It was only in that circumstance that the statute authorized the detention order. It was held, with one dissent, that the legal burden was cast upon the party called upon to justify the imprisonment. While clearly suspicious of the truth of the applicant's

---

[116] *Supra*, pp. 58–9.

[117] Examples of this are provided by the *Greene* case, discussed *infra*, and *R.* v. *Secretary of State for Home Affairs, ex. p. Soblen* [1962] 3 All E.R. 373 (C.A.), discussed in detail, *infra*, pp. 122–3. Professor de Smith comments on this point as follows: 'Considerable difficulty is likely to be found in getting a case on to its feet by establishing a prima facie case of abuse of power.' *Judicial Review*, 333. Cf., however, *Re Lawlor* (1977) 66 Cr. App. R. 75, granting habeas corpus on the ground that a committal pursuant of the Backing of Warrants (Republic of Ireland) Act 1965 had been obtained in bad faith for an ulterior purpose.

[118] *R.* v. *Governor of Brixton Prison, ex p. Ahsan* [1969] 2 Q.B. 222.

story, the court held that since the burden rested with the authorities, and as it could not decide the question of fact one way or the other, the issue had to be decided in the prisoner's favour.

In coming to this conclusion the court distinguished the decision of the House of Lords in *Greene* v. *Secretary of State for Home Affairs*.[119] In *Greene*, where the prisoner sought to impugn a ministerial order of internment, it had been said that the burden was on the prisoner to bring forth facts which tended to vitiate the order. The court characterized the power to intern as being a subjective one, and this meant that the only relevant issue on habeas corpus was the good faith of the minister. Whether or not the minister actually did have reasonable cause did not matter: he or she only had to think that there were such grounds. The applicant had said that he did not know why he was detained and the Secretary had not given the facts upon which the order was based. The court was, therefore, dealing with an absence of facts rather than with disputed facts. The decision merely amounted to saying that there was an evidential burden or an initial onus of adducing evidence which rested with the applicant and that a state-ment of ignorance of the grounds for the order did not constitute such evidence. Admittedly, there is language in the decision which suggests that a broader proposition was being advanced,[120] but the issue of the legal burden of proof, where there are genuinely disputed facts, did not arise. The *Ahsan* case may be taken for the proposition that where an issue of fact is raised, the legal burden rests with the respondent. While the *Ahsan* rule was doubted for a period in a line of immigration cases,[121] it has been fully reinstated by the decision of the House of Lords in *Khawaja* v. *Secretary of State for the Home Department*.[122]

(c) *Judicial Orders*

In *Ahsan*, the court emphasized that it was dealing with an executive order, and not with the order of a judicial officer.[123] It may be asked whether this should make any difference to the question of placing the legal burden of proof. It is certainly not difficult to find dicta in habeas

---

[119] [1942] A.C. 284, discussed in detail, *infra*, pp. 101–8.

[120] 'I am of the opinion that where on the return an order or warrant which is valid on its face is produced it is for the prisoner to prove the facts necessary to controvert it ...' per Goddard L.J. in the Court of Appeal [1942] 1 K.B. 87 at 116 adopted by Visc. Maugham [1942] A.C. 284 at 295.

[121] See *supra*, nn. 50 and 51, p. 74.

[122] [1984] A.C. 74.

[123] [1969[2 Q.B. 222 at 231.

corpus cases, both before and after the *Ahsan* decision, which suggest that the onus is on applicant to satisfy the court of the facts which entitle him or her to release,[124] but most (if not all) of these statements may be explained as failing to distinguish between the two sorts of burden.[125]

It is submitted that the *Ahsan* rule should be taken as one of general application. Lord Parker's statement of the principle of the case is as follows: '. . . once the applicants allege that a state of affairs upon which the jurisdiction of the immigration officers depended did not exist, it was for the respondent to show that it did'.[126] It is upon this same principle of jurisdictional review that the courts act when a judicial order is involved and there is no reason why the burden of proof should be differently placed. The court will undoubtedly be more willing to go into the facts in a case like *Ahsan* where the order was made by an immigration officer, but if issues of fact which relate to the jurisdiction of a judicial body are raised, then, it is submitted, the legal burden should still rest with the respondent.

(d) *Standard of Proof*

Is the standard of proof that of proof beyond a reasonable doubt, derived from the criminal law, or the civil standard of the balance of probabilities? Both *Ahsan*[127] and *Eshugbayi Eleko*[128] indicated that as the

---

[124] *Ex p. Weber* [1916] 1 A.C. 421 at 424; *R. v. Brixton Prison (Governor) ex p. Soblen* [1962] 3 All E.R. 641 at 657; *R. v. Governor of Pentonville Prison, ex p. Fernandez* [1971] 2 All E.R. 24 (aff'd [1971] 2 All E.R. 691); *Pearce* v. *Warden of Manitoba Penitentiary* (1966) 55 D.L.R. (2d) 619 (Man C.A.), 631n (aff'd S.C.C.); *R* v. *Sanders* [1968] 4 C.C.C. 156 (B.C.C.A.), (aff'd S.C.C. [1970] 2 C.C.C. 57); *Ex p. Branco* [1971] 3 O.R. 575 (H.C.); *Re King* (1873) 1 N.Z. Jur. 83. Cf., however, statements the other way in: *King-Emperor* v. *Vimlabai Deshpande* (1946) 115 L.J.P.C. 71; *Ex p. Rowan* (1930) 54 C.C.C. 197 (B.C.S.C.); *R. v. Carter, ex p. Kisch* (1934) 52 C.L.R. 221 at 227. See also the cases which hold that the court should lean in favour of the prisoner in interpretation of statutory provisions: *R. v. Secretary of State for Home Affairs, ex. p. O'Brien* [1923] 2 K.B. 361 at 393; *Eshugbayi Eleko* v. *Governor Administering the Government of Nigeria* [1931] A.C. 662; *R. v. Boyle* (1868) 4 P.R. 256 (Ont.); *Re McCaud* [1970] 1 C.C.C. 293 (Ont. H.C.); *Re Ange* [1970] 5 C.C.C. 371 (Ont. C.A.).

[125] But see *Re Mitchell and The Queen* (1983) 42 O.R. (2d) 481 (H.C.), holding that where an inmate challenged an habitual criminal detention order as a violation of Charter rights, the onus was on the inmate to show that he or she no longer constituted a danger to society. Cf. *Re Reddekopp and The Queen* (1983) 6 C.C.C. (3d) 241 (Ont. H.C.), holding that the onus was on the crown to prove that the applicant's conditional pardon had been properly revoked for breach of the conditions.

[126] [1969] 2 Q.B. 222 at 233.

[127] *R. v. Governor of Brixton Prison, ex p. Ahsan* [1969] 2 Q.B. 222.

[128] *Eshugbayi Eleko* v. *Officer Administering the Government of Nigeria* [1931] A.C. 662 at 670 (J.C.P.C.)

liberty of the subject was at stake, proof had to be beyond a reasonable doubt. However, in *Khawaja*, Lord Scarman held the criminal law formulation to be inappropriate. At the same time, however, it was emphasized that the court should take into account that the liberty of the subject was at stake, and that 'The reviewing court will therefore require to be satisfied that the facts which are required for the justification of the restraint put upon liberty do exist.'[129] Lord Scarman stressed flexibility of the civil standard, a feature which permitted the court to insist upon a high standard of proof, while at the same time avoiding an unduly technical or rigid approach inappropriate for judicial review.

(e) *Effect of Rules Regarding Burden of Proof Peculiar to the Proceedings Being Questioned*

There may be a tendency to treat the issue of onus of proof as one which depends upon the rules governing the particular proceedings which are being questioned on habeas corpus. In those cases where the court reviews a decision on the merits, as in the extradition cases where the sufficiency of evidence is weighed,[130] it is clear that the burden of proof is not affected simply because the proceedings are questioned on habeas corpus. In such a case, the court is deciding whether the evidence before the lower court meets the requisite standard. However, where the issue is the power of the tribunal to order the detention of the applicant, the burden of proof should depend upon the law of habeas corpus. The issue of jurisdiction, or of some fact upon which jurisdiction depends, is not one which an inferior body can conclusively determine for itself, and the rules which concern the burden of proof for issues which are within the tribunal's competence are not applicable. Undoubtedly, it will take more in some cases than in others for the applicant to discharge the evidential burden, but once that is achieved, the legal burden should always be the same.

(f) *Burden of Proof Where Other Remedies are Used*

If the law is to be consistent, it should treat the issue of burden of proof in the same way whatever remedy is used to attack the validity of the order to detain. It is useful, then, to see what happens when an attack is mounted by other remedies.

The question of placing the burden of proof will arise when the

[129] [1984] A.C. 74 at 113.　　　　[130] *Supra*, pp. 81–5.

court characterizes an issue as one of 'jurisdictional fact'. Where the jurisdiction of a tribunal is directly attacked on certiorari or prohibition, the rule with respect to the burden of proof seems somewhat unsettled. The courts are, in fact, reluctant to decide issues of fact where there is conflicting evidence, but when they do, the tendency is to consider that the legal burden as well as the evidential burden rests with the applicant.[131]

However, when a decision is attacked in collateral proceedings, it is well established that it is up to the party who relies on the validity of the decision to show that the circumstances requisite for the tribunal's jurisdiction actually did exist.[132] If the case involves the decision of a superior court, the *omnia praesumuntur rite esse acte* principle will apply.[133] Inferior court orders, however, have never properly benefited from the protection of the rule, and the party who relies on an inferior decision must establish its validity.[134]

The House of Lords has held[135] that where proceedings are taken to challenge the legality of imprisonment, whether by way of habeas corpus or judicial review, the rules derived from habeas corpus are to be applied. Hence the scope of review of the factual inquiry and the burden of proof will be applied consistently according to a common principle. Whatever the formal nature of the proceedings, the burden will be on the party seeking to uphold the detention.

This approach is consistent with the well-established principle in the law of false imprisonment that once the plaintiff establishes the imprisonment, the burden of proving justification lies with the defendant.

Lord Atkin called it: '... one of the pillars of liberty is that in English law every imprisonment is prima facie unlawful and that it is for the person directing the imprisonment to justify his act.'[136] The rule applies with no less vigour where an action is brought against an inferior judicial officer on the grounds that he or she exceeded

---

[131] *R. v. Fulham, Hammersmith and Kensington Rent Tribunal, ex p. Zerek* [1951] 2 K.B. 1 at 10–11; *R. v. City of London etc. Rent Tribunal, ex p. Honig* [1951] 1 All E.R. 195 at 198; de Smith, *Judicial Review*, 120.

[132] *Briscoe* v. *Stephens* (1824) 2 Bing. 213; *Mayor of London* v. *Cox* (1867) L.R. 2 H.L. 239 at 263; de Smith, *Judicial Review*, 120; cases cited *infra*, n. 137, p. 91.

[133] See *Supra*, pp. 46–51.

[134] *Supra*, n. 132.

[135] *Khawaja* v. *Secretary of State for the Home Department* [1984] A.C. 74.

[136] *Liversidge* v. *Anderson* [1942] A.C. 206 at 245 (dissenting). See also *Holroyd* v. *Doncaster* (1826) 3 Bing. 492; *Hicks* v. *Faulkner* (1878) 8 Q.B.D. at 167 at 170 (aff'd (1882) 46 L.T. 127 (C.A)); 15 Hals. (3rd), 268.

jurisdiction in committing the plaintiff.[137] If, therefore, the rule were adopted that the prisoner on habeas corpus must bear the burden of proof, a prisoner could fail on habeas corpus to gain release and yet succeed in damages against the magistrate simply because of a difference in the rules about burden of proof. This would only happen in a close case, but such a result would be intolerable.

Moreover, the rule in the law of false imprisonment depends upon the policy of the law to protect personal freedom,[138] a policy which should be furthered with at least as much vigour in the law of habeas corpus.

(g) *Conclusion*

It is submitted that the *Ahsan* and *Khawaja* decisions correctly place the burden of proof of disputed facts on the respondent, and that the principle of the case should be taken as one of general application, whether an executive or judicial order is concerned. The burden of adducing evidence to impugn the order will rest with the prisoner, but the legal burden, or the ultimate burden of satisfying the judge, should rest with the respondent. The legal burden only comes into play in a case where the facts are evenly balanced. If the facts are so uncertain as to require the legal rule to tip the scales one way or the other, there can be little doubt but that the rule should favour the prisoner.

Once the applicant has adduced sufficient evidence to displace the presumption of regularity of official acts, it is submitted that the rule in false imprisonment, as well as the general rule in the criminal law which places the legal burden squarely with the prosecution, provide sound analogies. They demonstrate that where personal liberty is at stake, the prisoner is to be given the benefit of any doubt. Placing the burden on the respondent follows the fundamental assumption which underlies the law of habeas corpus, namely, that the restraint of freedom should only be permitted where the party restraining can clearly show justification.

---

[137] *Carrat* v. *Morley* (1841) 1 Q.B. 18; *Houlden* v. *Smith* (1850) 14 Q.B.D. 841; Rubinstein, op. cit. 127; *Re McC.* (*A Minor*) [1985] A.C. 528.

[138] Although it owes its origin to the fact that it is an action in trespass.

4

Habeas Corpus and the Executive

I. INTRODUCTION

The purpose of this chapter is to examine the use of habeas corpus where the liberty of the subject is restrained on account of an order made by the executive branch of government. This is but one aspect of the question of the review of executive action by the courts. The issue here is simply the extent to which the courts should control the exercise of discretionary powers. Broad discretionary powers may be conferred which affect even such basic rights as personal freedom, but the judges can control the exercise of executive discretion when they wish to do so by defining the lawful limits of the power granted, and by making certain that the official has acted within those limits. This chapter examines the extent to which the principle that government officials must always be able to justify their action when called upon to do so before a court of law has been implemented on habeas corpus.

The central theme of the chapter is the control of discretion. Discretion implies a certain choice between alternate courses of action, none of which can be said to be right or wrong. Conceptually, in controlling discretion, the courts do not involve themselves with this choice, often called the merits of the case, but rather define the limits of choice, or decide on the appropriate range of choice. In certain contexts, Parliament may intend to confer a broad range of choice, and it will be inappropriate for the courts to second-guess the decisions reached by specialized agencies or tribunals. On the other hand, where personal liberty is at stake, the courts might be expected to assume a more aggressive role.

The treatment of discretionary powers on habeas corpus is complicated by the fact that it is usually only in an emergency or in time of war that the executive assumes power to restrict judicial freedom. It has already been observed that the recent trend in habeas corpus is to narrow significantly discretionary powers and to broaden the scope of review. [1]

---

[1] See esp. *Khawaja* v. *Secretary of State for the Home Department* [1984] A.C. 74, discussed *supra*, p. 74.

There is, however, the opposite tendency in time of crisis to leave the executive power a full range of choice unfettered by judicial review. Although war-time cases are often said to be an unreliable guide to how the courts now act, it is in time of national peril and crisis that discretionary powers to detain are conferred. For this reason, the war-time cases are of continuing significance to the law of habeas corpus. If it is misleading to treat the war-time cases as being indicative of how the courts might now act,[2] it is perhaps every bit as dangerous to assume that the new-found interventionist approach would be vigorously pursued in time of national crisis. Both tendencies must be examined and the underlying policy considerations must be weighed.

2. EMERGENCY POWERS—TESTING THE LEGALITY OF THE POWER TO DETAIN

(a) *The Seventeenth Century: Darnel's Case and the Petition of Right*

One of the most important legal issues which arose during the great constitutional struggle of the seventeenth century was the question of the supposed prerogative power of the Crown to detain the subject without presenting a criminal charge. In *Darnel's Case*[3] in 1627, discussed fully in Chapter 1, the return to a writ of habeas corpus stated that the prisoners were detained *'per speciale mandatum regis'*. No justification other than the King's special command was given for their arrest and imprisonment. Despite strong arguments to the contrary, the court sided with the King and held this to be a proper return. Many of the Parliamentarians were strongly opposed to such an extraordinary prerogative power as the courts were willing to allow. This matter and others regarding the King's claims of prerogative power were debated in Parliament,[4] and the result was the Petition of Right. Among other things, the Petition of Right abolished the power of detention which had been confirmed in *Darnel's Case*. The King and Council were thereby deprived not only of the power to enforce the collection of money behind the back of Parliament, but also of the power to lock up, without laying a criminal charge, those who were considered to be dangerous to the security of the State.

For present purposes the most significant issue which arose was

---

[2] See e.g. de Smith, *Judicial Review*, 290: 'Wartime and immediate post-war decisions ought not to be treated with reverence'; Wade, *Administrative Law*, 406.
[3] 3 St. Tr. 1. [4] *Supra*, pp. 13–14.

whether, in order to protect the liberty of the subject adequately, it was necessary to deprive the executive of all discretion to order the arrest and detention of those subjects thought by the executive to be a menace to the safety of the realm. The answer was unequivocal. The common law, strengthened by the Petition of Right, allowed no such discretion, and from this time on, only the express will of Parliament has been capable in law of conferring emergency powers of arrest and detention. From this point, the review of emergency detention becomes an exercise in statutory interpretation. Claims for wide executive power to detain in the name of public safety continued to be made, but thereafter, always under the guise of Parliamentary sanction.

(b) *Habeas Corpus Suspension Acts*

The first method adopted to confer emergency powers was that of the popularly called 'Habeas Corpus Suspension Acts'. The effect of these acts was not so sweeping as their name would suggest. They followed, for the most part, the same form from the first such enactment in 1688.[5] As will be seen, Parliament ceased using this method of giving emergency powers in the nineteenth and twentieth centuries and adopted more extreme measures to meet the danger posed by the Irish troubles and the threat of total war.

The most important operative provision of a suspension act was that any person in prison on or after the date when the act took effect by reason of a warrant of the Privy Council, signed by six Privy Councillors, or by warrant of one of the Secretaries of State, for high treason, suspicion of high treason, or for treasonable practices, should be neither bailed nor tried unless by order of the Privy Council.

This gave no power to arrest or detain any person other than on a charge of treason. Its effect was to increase the period of time for which a person so charged could be held without trial.[6] There was not so much a suspension of habeas corpus itself as a suspension of one of the rights secured by the writ, namely the right to be either tried or released. Most subjects continued to enjoy the protection of the writ. Indeed, it appears that even a prisoner charged with treason could still apply for habeas corpus to determine the sufficiency of the warrant[7] or

---

[5] 1 Will. & Mary, c.7. For a list of the suspension acts, see Forsyth, *Cases and Opinions on Constitutional Law* (1869), 452. Cf. the suspension of habeas corpus by President Lincoln during the American Civil War: *Ex p. Merryman* 17 Fed. Cas. 144 (1861); *Ex p. Milligan* 71 U.S. (4 Wall.) 2 (1866).

[6] The life of a suspension act was always expressly limited, usually to one year.

[7] *R. v. Despard* (1798) 9 T.R. 736.

the legislative authority of the individuals authorizing the warrant.[8]

Extreme powers were given to the executive, but powers nonetheless distinctly limited by law. On its face, a suspension act gave no general power to arrest and detain people simply because they were thought to be dangerous, although the effect was to deprive a suspected traitor of the opportunity to have guilt or innocence determined. It is entirely likely that the powers given by the acts were abused on occasion, and to avoid any doubts about the personal liability of those who had purported to act pursuant to these powers, Parliament invariably passed an act of indemnity.[9] In the absence of such an act, an action, or even an indictment, would lie against anyone who had abused the powers conferred,[10] and it has been suggested that where the powers were maliciously abused, even an act of indemnity would not protect the defendant.[11] In any event, as Dicey pointed out,[12] the minister of state could only hope that indemnity would be given, and perhaps had to guard against arbitrariness lest the legislators be provoked to withhold their protection. It is quite a different matter to legitimate, *ex post facto*, acts which appear to have been necessary for reasons of state, than to give at the outset, unlimited powers in the fear that they may become necessary.

(c) *Modern Emergency Powers*

The significant aspect of twentieth-century experience with emergency powers has been the use of statutes conferring broad powers to enact subordinate legislation. In other words, Parliament has not itself conferred defined powers of discretionary arrest and detention, but has delegated its very legislative capacity so that the executive has defined the limits of its own powers by statutory instrument or regulation.[13]

It was not until the twentieth century when the technique of delegated legislation was used that the executive was given the kind of

---

[8] *R.* v. *Boyle* (1868) 4 P.R. 256 (Ont.). In one case, it was even said that a prisoner could be bailed, notwithstanding the act, if he was gravely ill: *Harvey of Comb's Case* (1715) 10 Mod. 334.

[9] See, e.g., 41 Geo. III, c.66.

[10] Dicey, *Introduction to the Study of the Law of the Constitution* (10th ed. 1959 by E.C.S. Wade), 236.

[11] *Wright* v. *Fitzgerald* (1798) 27 St. Tr. 759; but cf. O'Higgins, 'Wright v. Fitzgerald Revisited' (1962) 25 Mod. L.R. 413, suggesting that the decision has been qualified.

[12] Dicey, op. cit. 236.

[13] Subject, of course, to the requirement that the instrument be laid before Parliament: see now Statutory Instruments Act 1946, ss.4–7.

emergency powers of detention reminiscent of those claimed by the Stuarts. There is, of course, the important difference that Parliament must be seen to delegate such powers to the executive. However, during the 1914–18 war, the courts were willing to slide over this requirement and to imply the extreme power to enact a scheme of internment by regulation from general statutory language which made no specific reference to detention at all.

(*i*) *War-Time Regulation and Internment—1914–1918 War.* By the Defence of the Realm Act 1914, Parliament delegated to the King in Council the power to regulate generally for the safety of the realm. The Act made no mention of internment, but the executive did establish an internment scheme by statutory instrument. Under these regulations, the Secretary of State for Home Affairs was given the power, on the recommendation of a specified naval or military authority, where it appeared to the Minister 'that for securing the public safety or the defence of the Realm it is expedient in view of the hostile origin or associations...' to order the internment of any person.[14]

In the case of *R. v. Halliday*,[15] the legality of this internment scheme was challenged. An internee brought an application for habeas corpus alleging that his detention was illegal since the whole scheme of internment was *ultra vires*. The general power to act for the security of the realm, it was argued, could not be taken to have conferred the power to abridge personal liberty without more specific provision. The House of Lords rejected the contention and held that the danger to the public safety had reached such proportions that internment could reasonably be said to fall within the general regulatory competence to act for the safety of the realm.

According to the House of Lords, Parliament had intended to give a broad discretionary power to do what was required for the safety of the realm, and had intended that the executive be the judge of what was necessary. The impugned regulation had been adopted for the purpose of providing for the safety of the realm, and the powers in the Act had not, therefore, been exceeded. Lord Atkinson, in one brief passage, articulated the reason for the decision: 'However precious the personal liberty of the subject may be, there is something for which it may well be, to some extent, sacrificed by legal enactment, namely, national success in the war, or escape from national plunder or enslavement.'[16]

---

[14] Defence of the Realm Regulations, 14B   [15] [1917] A.C. 260.   [16] Ibid. at 271.

Lord Shaw argued cogently in his dissenting opinion that the scheme was a 'violent exercise of arbitrary power'[17] and that the power to establish such a scheme should only rest on specific statutory language. To infer the power from the general language of the Defence of the Realm Act, said Lord Shaw, was to infer the repeal of fundamental constitutional principles, and this he was not prepared to do, even in time of crisis.

The powers granted were admittedly broad, but it was surely stretching the language of the Act to its limit to imply the sweeping power of internment. It was later held that regulatory schemes for the expropriation of property, established at the same time and under the same general power, were *ultra vires*.[18] This shows that the language of the Act did not take away all choice from the judges. It demonstrates the extent to which the *Halliday* decision indicates a marked judicial reluctance in time of crisis to guard the supposedly favoured right to personal liberty when that right must be balanced against claims of public safety.

(*ii*) *1939–1945 War.* During the 1939–45 war, Parliament left no doubt and expressly provided that regulations could be made 'for the detention of persons whose detention appears to the Secretary of State to be expedient in the interests of the public safety or the defence of the realm'.[19]

While the legality of internment itself could not be questioned, the courts were asked, on habeas corpus, to review the exercise of the internment power, and the issue of review will be examined after some more general aspects of internment have been dealt with.

(*iii*) *Duration of the Power to Intern.* Unlike the 'Habeas Corpus Suspension Acts', war-time measures have not been specifically limited in duration. Clearly it is the continued existence of the emergency of war which politically justifies the existence of these extreme measures,[20] but they have not been worded so as to expire

---

[17] Ibid. at 277.

[18] *Newcastle Breweries* v. *The King* [1920] 1 K.B. 854. See also *Chester* v. *Bateson* [1920] 1 K.B. 829 (regulation forbidding court action to eject certain persons as tenants held to be ultra vires); *China Mutual Steamship Navigation Co. Ltd.* v. *MacLay* [1918] 1K.B. 33; *The Zamora* [1916] 2 A.C. 77; *A.G.* v. *De Keyser's Royal Hotel* [1920] A.C. 508; *A.G.* v. *Wilts United Dairies* (1922) 91 L.J.K.B. 897 (H.L.), for cases asserting some control over executive action during the war.

[19] Emergency Powers (Defence) Act 1939, s.1(2)(a).

[20] In *R.* v. *Halliday* [1917] A.C. 260 at 265, 272, 305, it was stressed that the life of the scheme was limited by the duration of the war.

automatically at the end of the emergency. It is still open to the courts
to determine whether the powers under such legislation are being
exercised for the proper purpose contemplated by Parliament, but
even here, the courts were reluctant to interfere. It was held as late as
1920 that there still existed the power to intern under the 1914–18 war
regulations[21] and that it did not matter that the impugned internment
order had been made in response to the situation in Ireland, another
emergency altogether different from that of the war. In other words,
the court in effect allowed the executive to decide for itself that the
Irish situation was within the circumstances contemplated by Parliament for the valid exercise of the statutory power.[22] This somewhat
unnoticed decision surely represents a virtual abdication by the courts
to the idea that if circumstances seem to require a course of action, the
law should be made to conform with what has happened. Even in time
of peril, it is submitted that the courts should closely examine the
situation to see whether the power to intern is being exercised for the
purposes intended by the act. In this case, the analysis was based on
the technical ground that by statute, a state of open war continued.[23] It
was said that as the troubles in Ireland would weaken the national
effort to face the enemy, the power had been properly exercised under
the war-time legislation. In fact, there was no enemy and the court's
reasoning is, to say the least, unconvincing.

A more positive approach was taken in the *O'Brien* case in 1923[24]
after the establishment of the Irish Free State. The Home Secretary
had made an internment order under the Restoration of Order in
Ireland Act and had surrendered the internee to the Irish authorities.
It was held that although the Act had not been repealed, the
establishment of the Irish Free State rendered the exercise of powers
under the Act improper. This was, perhaps, an easier case but it does
demonstrate that the courts may intervene where a statutory power is
exercised for an improper purpose.

[21] *R.* v. *Governor of Wormwood Scrubs Prison* [1920] 2 K.B. 305.

[22] For other cases where the courts have declined to decide on whether a state of
emergency existed, see two Indian cases where the Privy Council held that the
Governor's decision to invoke emergency powers was not justiciable: *Bhagat Singh* v.
King-Emperor (1931) L.R. 58 I.A. 169; *King-Emperor* v. *Benoari Lal Sarma* [1945] A.C.
14. Cf. the more recent case from Malaysia where it was said that the question was a
difficult one: *Ningkan* v. *Government of Malaysia* [1970] A.C. 379 at 392; and cf. the
martial law cases, *infra*, pp. 110–15.

[23] Present War (Definition) Act 1918.

[24] *R.* v. *Secretary of State for Home Affairs, ex p. O'Brien* [1923] 2 K.B. 361 (aff'd [1923]
A.C. 603), discussed further *infra*, pp. 176–7.

(iv) Internment and the Suspension of Habeas Corpus. The regulations conferring the power to intern have quite properly been construed so as not actually to suspend the remedy of habeas corpus.[25] Clearly, a broadly worded power to intern will make the chances of success minimal, but the person interned is still free to attempt to impugn the legality of the internment. In the 1939 regulations, for example, there was included the provision that 'any person detained in pursuance of these Regulations shall be deemed to be in lawful custody...',[26] but it has been consistently held that such a phrase does not preclude the courts from determining whether the power to intern has been properly exercised and whether the Minister has acted within the powers conferred in the particular case.[27]

3. REVIEW OF THE EXERCISE OF THE POWER TO DETAIN

The review of the actual exercise of the power to intern is an exercise in the review of discretion. On the surface, this is very much a matter of statutory interpretation, but underneath, very much a matter of judicial attitude. The language of the legislation conferring the power is clearly important. If the discretion is broadly defined, there will be a stronger inclination to leave the minister or officer a broad range of

[25] *R. v. Halliday* [1917] A.C. 260; cases cited *infra*, n. 27. Cf. Lord Shaw's scathing comment in the *Halliday* case at 294: 'Formally in this case the writ of habeas corpus was allowed. It is now being tried. But what has been done by the Courts below is to give due formal respect to the procedure of the remedy, but to deny the remedy itself by inferring the repeal of those very fundamental rights which the remedy was meant to secure. This is to allow the subjects of the King by law to enter the fortress of their liberties only after that fortress has been by law destroyed.'
[26] Defence (General) Regulations, s.18B(8).
[27] *Greene* v. *Secretary of State for Home Affairs* [1942] 1 K.B. 87 at 116 (C.A.). See also *Ex p. Sacksteder* [1918] 1 K.B. 578 at 584, for a similar interpretation of a similar provision in the Aliens Order 1914. Cf. however the Canadian War Measures Act R.S.C. 1985 c.W-2 [invoked in 1970: (Public Order Regulations 1970 S.O.R./70–444), and upheld on habeas corpus: *R. v. Gagnon and Valieres* (1971) 14 C.R.N.S. 321 (Que. C.A.)]. S.5 of the Act provides that no person held under the Act or regulations thereunder 'shall be released upon bail or otherwise discharged or tried, without the consent of the Minister of Justice.' The section has been given broad interpretation in the cases and held to deprive the court of jurisdiction to release the prisoner: *Re Beranek* (1915) 33 O.L.R. 139 (H.C.); *Re Gottesman* (1918) 29 C.C.C. 439 (Ont. H.C.); *Re Gusetu* (1915) 24 C.C.C. 427 (Que. S.C.); *Re Sullivan* (1941) 75 C.C.C. 70 (Ont. H.C.). Such a result is intolerable. The reasoning used to evade the effect of privative clauses should be used. If the power has been exceeded, strictly speaking, the prisoner would not be a person 'held under this Act' and the section would have no application.

choices within which he is free to act. Clearly, however, the statutory language is not all. Broadly worded powers will often be narrowed where it is thought that the minister has come to the wrong decision or acted unfairly. Equally, as the war-time cases show, even where the power is defined in terms which would ordinarily make its exercise justiciable, the courts may hesitate to do more than see that the minister has acted in good faith and 'within the four corners of the act'. In practical terms, this usually means there will be no review at all.[28]

The choice lies in characterizing such a power as being exercisable according to either an objective or a subjective standard. In other words, is the power validly exercised only when the proper conditions actually exist, or is it enough that the Minister honestly believes them to exist? If the former, then it is for the court to decide whether or not those conditions were present, and if it finds that they did not exist, there has been an improper use of the power and the prisoner is entitled to be released. If the latter, then the only issue for the court is the minister's state of mind: did he or she act in good faith?

The characterization of the standard will depend upon the particular language of the legislative instrument conferring the power, and while this lessens the predictive value of decisions on different provisions, the cases do indicate the approach which the courts might be expected to take.

(a) *The 1939–1945 War: Regulation 18B*[29]

During the 1939–45 war, the Secretary of State for Home Affairs was empowered by the Defence (General) Regulations 1939, (pursuant the Emergency Powers (Defence) Act 1939) to order internment in the following terms:[30]

[28] *Supra*, p. 86.
[29] General discussions of the Reg. 18B internment scheme and the cases are: Carr, 'A Regulated Liberty' (1942) 42 Col. L.R. 339: Cotter, 'Emergency Detention in Wartime: The British Experience' (1954) 6 Stanford L.R. 238; Allen, *Law and Orders* (3rd ed. 1965) Appendix 1, p. 364. Comments on the *Liversidge* case in particular are: Goodhart (1942) 58 L.Q.R. 3; Holdsworth (1942) 58 L.Q.R. 1; Keeton (1941) 5 Mod. L.R. 162; and Heuston, '*Liversidge* v. *Anderson* in Retrospect' (1970) 86 L.Q.R. 33 and 87 L.Q.R. 161. Lewis, *Lord Atkin* (1983) 132–57 provides a lively account of the background to the House of Lords' decision. Simpson, 'Detention without Trial in the Second World War: Comparing the British and American Experiences' (1988) 16 Florida State L.R. 225 provides a good account of the historical context. For a discussion of the review of emergency powers in general, see Schwartz, *Law and the Executive in Britain* (1949), 305–63, with comparative American material.
[30] The Home Secretary was also given the power to intern persons who he had reasonable cause to believe were members of foreign or disaffected organizations (Reg.

18B. (1) If the Secretary of State has reasonable cause to believe any person to be of hostile origin or associations, or to have been recently concerned in acts prejudicial to the public safety or the defence of the realm, or in the preparation or instigation of such acts, and that by reason thereof it is necessary to exercise control over him, he may make an order against that person directing that he be detained.

The crucial cases came before the House of Lords in 1942. Up to that time, there had been judicial reluctance to define the standard to be applied in a way which would have precluded review of the merits of the decision. In at least one case an internee had obtained an order of release on the grounds, *inter alia*, that the Home Secretary had failed to demonstrate reasonable grounds to support a belief of the requisite matters.[31] In another case the judges suggested that more was required to justify the detention than an internment order valid on its face, and that habeas corpus could open a review of the Minister's decision.[32]

However, in *Liversidge* v. *Anderson*[33] and *Greene* v. *The Secretary of State for Home Affairs*[34] the House of Lords held that an entirely subjective standard had been intended, thereby effectively precluding review of the Home Secretary's decision to intern. Once there was produced an order valid on its face, the court could only go behind that order in the (entirely unlikely) event that the prisoner could show lack of *bona fides*.

18B 1A) or suspected persons in strategically important areas (Reg. 18B 1B). The regulations had to be approved by Parliament, and it has been suggested that a change in the wording from 'If the Secretary of State is satisfied' to 'If the Secretary of State has reasonable cause to believe' may have been indicative of Parliament's intention that a justiciable standard was imposed. This is discussed by Carr (1942) 42 Col. L.R. 339, 346; C.K. Allen, *Law and Orders* (1st ed. 1945) 337–40. Heuston (1970) 86 L.Q.R. 33, 60–2, reviews what went on when the wording was changed; some weight was attached to the change by Lord Atkin in his dissent in *Liversidge* v. *Anderson* [1942] A.C. 206 at 237.

[31] *Ex p. Budd (No. 1)* (unreported), cited in *Ex p. Budd (No. 2)* [1941] 2 All E.R. 749 at 751. In the second *Budd* case, the re-imprisonment of the applicant was upheld but Stable J. delivered a powerful dissent, *inter alia*, on the basis that an objective, justiciable standard was intended. See also *R.* v. *Halliday* [1917] A.C. 260 at 308 per Lord Wrenbury: 'If [the applicant's] case were that he had neither hostile origin nor associations he could have his writ of habeas corpus on the ground that that was so, and if he established the fact he would be discharged'; and *Ex p. Howsin* (1917) 33 T.L.R. 527 at 528 (C.A.), where it was suggested that the decision to intern could be reviewed on the grounds of 'no evidence'.

[32] *Ex p. Lees* [1941] 1 K.B. 72.

[33] [1942] A.C. 206 (action for false imprisonment).

[34] [1942] A.C. 284 (habeas corpus).

The order would be bad only if the Home Secretary lacked a reasonable belief on the relevant points, and according to the House of Lords, the Home Secretary could judge what was reasonable. So long as the *bona fides* of the order was not attacked by evidence, the validity of the order was unaffected and the Home Secretary could not be required to file affidavits supporting the action taken.[35]

In many respects, the Home Secretary's order of internment was given the same respect accorded to the record of a superior court.[36] It was said that habeas corpus merely required the production of the immediate legal cause for the prisoner's detention, and that if the order were regular on its face, the application had to be refused. By merely saying, 'I have no idea why the Home Secretary thinks I should be interned', the prisoner was not showing that the order was bad. Clearly, by this acceptance of the bald statement on the face of the order, the judges effectively precluded an applicant from ever succeeding.

The characterization in *Liversidge* and in *Greene* of the Home Secretary's power under Reg. 18B as being subjective, rested on several arguments. It was said that the minister was not required to have legally admissible evidence to act; that there was an advisory committee established to review the ministerial findings; that the information upon which the minister acted was confidential and that its disclosure could be avoided claiming crown privilege;[37] that the power was given to a minister responsible to Parliament and not to a minor official; and that these factors all pointed to a subjective, non-reviewable discretion. Such arguments could, of course, be made in many cases where it was sought to review ministerial action, and they certainly would not always be successful. The real basis of the decision lies beyond the words of the statute and in the circumstances of the war.

In *Liversidge* v. *Anderson*, Lord Atkin delivered a notable dissenting opinion which also applied to the *Greene* case.[38] He demonstrated that

---

[35] *Infra*, pp. 104–5. The issue of burden of proof, discussed in *Greene*, is dealt with in detail, *supra* pp. 86–7.

[36] See especially per Visc. Maugham, [1942] A.C. 284 at 294–6.

[37] The question of crown privilege in habeas corpus cases is discussed in detail *infra*, pp. 123–6.

[38] It will be noted, however, that even allowing for the broader scope of review, Lord Atkin would have found the Home Secretary's decision in *Greene* to have been reasonable: [1942] A.C. 206 at 246–7. It was possible to judge the grounds for the Home Secretary's belief as affidavits giving the grounds for internment had been filed by the Home Secretary before the Court held them to be unnecessary: *infra*, p. 104.

the majority had taken the unconvincing position of saying that 'if the Secretary has reasonable cause to believe' meant the same thing as 'if the Secretary thinks he has reasonable cause to believe'. Clearly, the majority had ignored the accepted construction of the phrase 'reasonable cause to believe' which had always been thought to delimit a justiciable power validly exercised only when certain objective conditions were found to exist.[39] Lord Atkin's dissent has since been accepted as the correct view, and it has been held by the House of Lords that the construction of these words by the majority in *Liversidge* and *Greene* would not now be followed.[40]

There was something more involved than the question of how a familiar phrase should be interpreted in law. At stake was the issue of the appropriateness of judicial interference with the executive in time of war. The protection to be given to the liberty of the subject had to be balanced against a real fear (possibly misguided) that there were people who presented a significant internal threat to the state. One Lord of Appeal went so far as to suggest that in such circumstances, the rule that legislation restricting the liberty of the subject should be construed in favour of the subject had '... no relevance in dealing with an executive measure by way of preventing a public danger'[41] and another added that 'the courts should... prefer that construction which is the least likely to imperil the safety of this country'.[42] The House of Lords simply felt that there was a real danger from internal subversion, and that this could be dealt with only by unchecked executive power. Lord Finlay's dictum from the *Halliday* case in the 1914–18 war was echoed by the House of Lords in *Liversidge*: 'It seems obvious that no tribunal for investigating the question whether circumstances of suspicion exist warranting some restraint can be imagined less appropriate than a court of law.'[43]

---

[39] See the authorities collected in Lord Atkin's dissent in *Liversidge* v. *Anderson* [1942] A.C. 206 at 227–32.

[40] In *Nakkuda Ali* v. *Jayaratne* [1951] A.C. 66, the Judicial Committee of the Privy Council (while refusing relief on other grounds) held that 'reasonable grounds to believe' in a Ceylonese enactment defined a justiciable standard and required that the court be satisfied that reasonable grounds did actually exist. In *Ridge* v. *Baldwin* [1964] A.C. 40 at 73, Lord Reid described *Liversidge* as a 'very peculiar decision.' The decisions were finally repudiated in *Inland Revenue Commissioners* v. *Rossminster Ltd* [1980] A.C. 952 at 1011, 1025 and *Khawaja* v. *Secretary of State for the Home Department* [1984] A.C. 74.

[41] Per Visc. Maugham [1942] A.C. 206 at 218–19, adopting the language of Lord Finlay in *R.* v. *Halliday* [1917] A.C. 260 at 270.

[42] Per Lord Romer, [1942] A.C. 206 at 280.

[43] [1917] A.C. 260 at 269, quoted by Lord MacMillan at [1942] A.C. 206 at 253–4.

It has been argued[44] that in coming to the conclusion that the Minister should be given a free rein, the judges accurately gauged what had been intended by Parliament, namely, a power to be exercised by the Minister personally, and not to be reviewable in the courts. Clearly, there is something to be said for this view. An advisory committee was established to review individual cases, and the Home Secretary was required to report regularly to Parliament on the operation of the scheme. There is undoubtedly a tendency in difficult times to view it as appropriate to entrust a Minister of the Crown with extraordinary powers and to expect that the exercise of such power will be controlled in Parliament.[45]

On the other hand, it is submitted that this analysis tends to assume that what was sought in *Greene* was an appeal from the minister's decision.[46] It should be remembered that Lord Atkin did not dissent from the actual result in *Greene*, but found, on the basis of the material which the Home Secretary had filed by affidavit, that it could be said that reasonable grounds existed.[47] The question was not whether the judges necessarily agreed with the minister, but simply whether, on the facts, the case was within the range of circumstances in which the power to intern could be properly exercised. Indeed, Lord Atkin was able to come to this conclusion because the Home Secretary had filed an affidavit stating his grounds. It was the House of Lords which held that the minister need do no more than produce a bald order, something the Home Secretary had not even claimed himself. It is submitted that in going this far, the judges stretched the statutory language, even in the context of the war-time emergency. While each statute falls to be interpreted on its own language and in its own context, the interpretation can only take place in the broader context of the principles of constitutional and administrative law. Those principles were asserted by Lord Atkin, but ignored by the majority.

---

[44] Heuston, *Essays in Constitutional Law* (2nd ed. 1964), 171–7; (1970) 86 L.Q.R. 64–5.

[45] See e.g. Report of the Committee of Privy Councillors Appointed to Consider Authorized Procedures for the Interrogation of Persons Suspected of Terrorism, (1972: Cmnd. 4901) para. 37–8; Brownlie, (1972) 35 Mod. L.R. 501, 505–6.

[46] See Heuston (1970) 86 L.Q.R. 65: '... the establishment of the advisory committee makes sense only on the assumption that no appeal to the court was being granted.' Cf. Lord Atkin in *Liversidge* v. *Anderson* [1942] A.C. 206 at 239: 'It is said that it could never have been intended to substitute the decision of judges for the decision of the minister, or, as has been said, to give an appeal from the minister to the courts. But no one proposes either a substitution or an appeal.'

[47] [1942] A.C. 206 at 246–7.

It seems wrong in retrospect that the protection of personal liberty should be so completely abandoned in favour of security. It cannot be doubted that even if some dangerous subversives are interned, many other innocent people are locked up for insubstantial reasons.[48] If such a sacrifice is to be made to the public safety, then Parliament should say so in the clearest and most unequivocal language. If Parliament does not make it clear that it intends to confer a very substantial discretion, then the courts should be slow to imply it from milder language.[49]

The extent to which the courts would review orders of internment on habeas corpus, should such circumstances arise again, would of course depend very much upon the language of the legislative instrument. The courts would have the advantage of the post-war experience of closely controlling executive powers, and if there is left any room for interpretation of the power, it is to be hoped that the majority view taken in *Liversidge* should be rejected in favour of Lord Atkin's famous statement:

In this country, amid the clash of arms, the laws are not silent. They may be changed, but they speak the same language in war as in peace. It has always been one of the pillars of freedom, one of the principles of liberty for which on recent authority we are now fighting, that the judges are no respectors of persons and stand between the subject and any attempted encroachments on his liberty by the executive, alert to see that any coercive action is justified in law.[50]

---

[48] In one action, *Knight* v. *Borough of Guildford* (1942), as reported in C.K. Allen, *Law and Orders* (1st ed. 1945), Appendix 6, p. 343, an internee brought an action against his employer for wrongful dismissal when he had been fired for being disloyal upon his internment. All the facts were brought out, and a disturbing lack of substance to the charges against the internee upon which the Home Secretary had acted was shown. The action succeeded. See also Report of the Commission to Consider Legal Procedures to Deal with Terrorist Activities in Northern Ireland (1972: Cmnd. 5185); para. 32: 'It is only natural that occasional errors of judgment may be made as to the probative strength of the material inculpating a particular suspect.'

[49] Even language such as 'if the minister is satisfied' has been held not to confer an absolute, unreviewable discretion: *Secretary of State for Education and Science* v. *Tameside Metropolitan Borough Council* [1977] A.C. 1014; *A.G. of St. Christopher, Nevis and Anguilla* v. *Reynolds* [1980] A.C. 637 (J.C.P.C.); Rawlings, 'Habeas Corpus and Preventive Detention in Singapore and Malaysia' (1983) 25 Malaya L.R. 324.

[50] [1942] A.C. 206 at 244. Heuston, '*Liversidge* v. *Anderson* in Retrospect' (1970) 86 L.Q.R. 33, 66–8, credits Lord Atkin's dissent with significant influence on post-war administrative law and suggests that in another emergency 'judicial attitude will be strongly influenced by Lord Atkin's approach'.

In *Khawaja*,[51] albeit a peace-time case, the House of Lords stated that the dissenting opinion of Lord Atkin was the correct view, and that the factual basis for an executive detention order was always subject to review on habeas corpus, absent a clear statement to the contrary from Parliament.

The courts of Canada[52] and Australia[53] were faced with the same problem of interpreting powers of internment on habeas corpus, and they interpreted them just as broadly as did the House of Lords. The case for effective judicial review in Canada would now be fortified by the express constitutional guarantees of the right to habeas corpus[54] and the right not to be arbitrarily detained or imprisoned.[55] In Ireland, it was held in one case,[56] partly but not solely on account of the Irish Constitution, that the exercise of the power of internment, based on a provision very similar in language to Reg. 18B, was quasi-judicial and reviewable.

In Commonwealth countries which have experienced emergency powers of internment or preventive detention since the war,[57] the courts have for the most part followed the reasoning of *Liversidge* and of *Greene*.[58]

(b) *Procedural Irregularities*

As well as being asked to review the decision to intern, the courts

---

[51] [1984] A.C. 74

[52] *Re Beranek* (1915) 33 O.L.R. 139 (H.C.); *Re Lawson; Re Steele* (1942) 77 C.C.C. 307 (Ont. H.C.); *Ex p. Sullivan* (1941) 75 C.C.C. 70 (Ont. H.C.); *Re Carriere* (1942) 79 C.C.C. 329 (Que. S.C.). See generally Marx, 'The Emergency Power and Civil Liberties in Canada' (1970) 16 McGill L.J. 39.

[53] *Lloyd* v. *Wallach* (1915) 20 C.L.R. 299; *Ex p. Paino* (1940) 42 W.A.L.R. 16; *Ex p. Walsh* [1942] A.L.R. 359; *Ex p. Stephenson* (1942) 59 W.N. (N.S.W.) 118; *Little* v. *Commonwealth* (1947) 75 C.L.R. 94.

[54] Charter of Rights and Freedoms, s.10(c).

[55] Ibid., s.9.

[56] *The State (Burke)* v. *Lennon and the Attorney General* [1940] I.R. 136. Amending legislation was immediately brought forth and tested in the courts: see *Re Art. 26 and the Offences Against the State (Amendment) Bill 1940* [1940] I.R. 470.

[57] See: Holland, 'Emergency Legislation in the Commonwealth' (1960) 13 *Current Legal Problems* 148; Aihe, 'Preventive Detention in Nigeria' (1972) 9 I.C.J. Rev. 68; Ghosh, *The Law of Preventive Detention in India* (1969); Alexander, 'The Illusory Protection of Human Rights by National Courts During Periods of Emergency' (1984) 5 Human Rights L.J. 1.

[58] Rawlings, 'Habeas Corpus and Preventive Detention in Singapore and Malaysia' (1983) 25 Malaya L.R. 324; Mureinik, '*Liversidge* in Decay' (1985) 102 South Africa L.J. 77; cf. *A.G. of St. Christopher, Nevis and Anguilla* v. *Reynolds* [1980] A.C. 637 (J.C.P.C.). In *Re Benn* (1964) 6 W.I.R. 500, it was held that habeas corpus did not lie against the Governor of a colony. This is clearly wrong. Cf. *Charles* v. *Phillips and Sealey* (1967) 10 W.I.R. 423, where emergency regulations were held to be ultra vires.

may be required to interpret the statutory procedures which are laid down, and to determine whether there has been a breach of the procedural requirements which entitles the internee to be released. This is illustrated by a case from Northern Ireland where an internee was released for no other reason than that he had not been arrested and notified of the cause of his detention in the required manner.[59] In 1941, an internee was similarly released where he had not been given a document setting out the correct grounds for his internment as required by the regulation.[60]

However, in the *Greene* case,[61] it was held by the House of Lords that a procedural error of this nature did not affect the validity of the internment order. The provision requiring delivery to the internee of a document setting out the grounds for his internment was said to be merely a concession to facilitate making representations to the advisory committee which could recommend release to the minister. Non-compliance with the provision did not, it was said, reflect back upon the internment order. On habeas corpus, only the internment order was challenged and what happened after it had been made did not affect its validity.

A distinction has been made, therefore, between procedural requirements which bear directly upon the order of internment and those which do not. The distinction is that made between 'directory' provisions and those which are 'mandatory'. The line is a difficult one to draw,[62] and the characterization of the requirement in the *Greene* case as being non-essential and directory only was probably coloured by the emergency of the war.

Following *Greene*, the courts upheld an order directed against 300 people, all the while acknowledging that the minister had to give consideration to each individual case.[63] In another case,[64] the minister was allowed to depose that he had formed the requisite belief where the order was bad on its face for failing to make this assertion. In other

[59] *Re McElduff* (1971) 23 N.I.L.Q. 112, discussed in more detail, *infra*, p. 109.

[60] *Ex p. Budd (No. 1)* (unreported) cited in *Ex p. Budd (No. 2)* [1941] 2 All E.R. 749 at 751. As a result of the *Greene* decision, *infra*, it was held in a subsequent action for false imprisonment based on the same situation that the court had been wrong to grant habeas corpus: *Budd* v. *Anderson* [1943] K.B. 642.

[61] [1942] A.C. 284

[62] See de Smith, *Judicial Review*, 142: 'The law relating to the effect of failure to comply with procedural requirements resembles an inextricable tangle of loose ends.'

[63] *Stuart* v. *Anderson and Morrison* [1941] 2 All E.R. 665 (an action for false imprisonment).

[64] *R.* v. *Governor of Brixton Prison, ex p. Pitt-Rivers* [1942] 1 All E.R. 207.

words, while the courts acknowledged in these cases that failure to comply with the requisite procedures would be fatal to the legality of the internment, they gave every possible benefit of doubt to the Home Secretary.

It should be noted that even where a prisoner is released on a procedural irregularity, he or she may well be liable to re-arrest and internment if the proper procedure is followed the second time.[65]

(c) *Present-Day Emergency Powers*

The continuing source of British experience with emergency powers is the Irish situation where extraordinary powers of detention have been resorted to on several occasions in modern times.[66] There are few reported cases challenging orders of internment under the legislation enacted in response to this unrest. In 1922, the Court of Appeal held that a person could be interned in England under the powers of the Restoration of Order in Ireland Act.[67] In the same year, the Northern Ireland King's Bench gave broad interpretation to a regulatory internment scheme under the Special Powers Act, and refused to review whether there had been 'reasonable grounds for suspecting' the applicant, holding that it was 'not within our province to express an

---

[65] *Ex p. Budd (No. 2)* [1941] 2 All E.R. 749 (aff'd [1942] 2 K.B. 14), and see *infra*, pp. 213–17.

[66] Walker, *Prevention of Terrorism in British Law* (1986); Bonner, *Emergency Powers in Peacetime* (1985); Lee, *Emergency Powers* (1984); Lowry, 'Internment in Northern Ireland' (1976) 8 Toledo L.R. 169; O'Boyle, 'Emergency Situations and the Protection of Human Rights; A Model Derogation Provision for a Northern Ireland Bill of Rights' (1977) 28 N.I.L.Q. 160; Walker, 'Arrest and Rearrest' (1984) 35 N.I.L.Q. 1; Finnie, 'Rights of Detained Persons Detained Under the Anti-Terrorist Legislation' (1982) 45 Mod. L.R. 215; Spjut, 'Internment and Detention Without Trial in Northern Ireland 1971–1975: Ministerial Policy and Practice' (1986) 49 Mod. L.R. 712; Jackson, 'The Northern Ireland (Emergency Provisions) Act 1987' (1988) 39 N.I.L.Q. 235. For the type of measure used in the nineteenth century, see the 'Coercion Act' of 1881 (44 Vict. c.4), which allowed for the arrest and detention on the Lord Lieutenant's warrant of any person reasonably suspected of being guilty of treason or any crime of violence or intimidation tending to interfere with the maintenance of law and order. Such person was to be held without bail and not to be tried or discharged without the Lord Lieutenant's consent. The warrant was to be deemed to be conclusive of all matters contained, including the jurisdiction for its issue. The act excluded virtually any possibility of review on habeas corpus. For discussion of the use of special powers in the Republic, see Kelly, *Fundamental Rights in the Irish Law and Constitution* (2nd ed. 1967), 77–88; and in Northern Ireland, see Calvert, *Constitutional Law in Northern Ireland* (1968), 380–9; Edwards, 'Special Powers in Northern Ireland' [1956] Crim. L.R. 7. See also the discussion of martial law, *infra*, pp. 110–15.

[67] *R. v. Cannon Row Police Station (Inspector), ex p. Brady* (1922) 91 L.J.K.B. 98 (C.A.). Cf. the *O'Brien* case, *supra*, p. 98.

opinion on the facts', and that the court had 'nothing to do with the consideration of whether there is any evidence against him.'[68]

The invocation of the Special Powers Act in the early 1970s produced two decisions which, perhaps, show a certain change in approach. In the first,[69] it was held on habeas corpus that the power to intern was improperly exercised where the applicant had been improperly arrested. The court admitted that the regulations only allowed an inquiry into the *bona fides* of the existence of the suspicion of the arresting officer, but held that an arrest without a warrant is only valid when reasonable steps are taken to inform the party of the legal authority for the arrest and of the general nature of the suspicion leading to the arrest. The internment order was contingent upon a proper arrest and, therefore, it was held, the applicant should be released. In the second case,[70] the Northern Ireland court held on mandamus that an internee was entitled to a statement of the material on which the internment order was based (excluding information which would endanger public safety or the work of the security forces) so that representations could be made to the advisory committee constituted to review individual cases and advise the Minister. It was also suggested that natural justice might require that the internee be allowed legal representation before the advisory committee, but the court considered this unnecessary in the circumstances.

These cases, perhaps, mark a cautious advance, and may indicate that while powers will still be broadly interpreted in time of crisis, the post-war activism in administrative law will not be entirely forgotten.[71]

(*i*) *European Convention for the Protection of Human Rights and Freedoms.*
Proceedings were brought before the European Court of Human Rights alleging that the internment scheme under the Special Powers Act and other acts of the security forces were not justifiable under the Convention.[72] Article 15 permits derogation from certain obligations if there is 'an emergency threatening the life of the nation', and the Court found that the requirements of that article had been met so as to

---

[68] *R. (O'Hanlan)* v. *Governor of Belfast Prison* (1922) 56 I.L.T.R. 170.
[69] *Re McElduff* (1971) 23 N.I.L.Q. 112; see also comment by Boyle, ibid. at 334.
[70] *Re Mackey* (1972) 23 N.I.L.Q. 113; see also comment by de Smith, ibid. at 331.
[71] Cf. however, *McKee* v. *Chief Constable for Northern Ireland* [1984] 1 W.L.R. 1358 (H.L.); *Murray* v. *Ministry of Defence* [1988] 1 WL.R. 692 (H.L.). For a general review of emergency powers, see Lee, *Emergency Powers* (1984).
[72] *Ireland* v. *United Kingdom* (1978) 2 E.H.R.R. 25. See also: *McVeigh, O'Neill and Evans* v. *United Kingdom* (1981) 5 E.H.R.R. 71 (Commission); *Lyttle* v. *United Kingdom* (1987) 9 E.H.R.R. 381 (Commission).

allow for extra-judicial deprivation of liberty. On the other hand, certain practices of the security forces were found to amount to inhuman treatment in violation of Article 3. In a subsequent case,[73] the Court held that detention of suspected terrorists for more than four days without being charged and brought before a court violated Article 5(3) of the Convention, which requires that 'everyone arrested or detained... shall be brought promptly before a judge or other officer authorized by law to exercise judicial power...' It is clear that the statement of standards in the Convention is becoming a matter to be reckoned with in the definition of emergency powers, even in the domestic sphere.[74]

(d) *Martial Law*[75]

The question of the extent to which the remedy of habeas corpus is suspended in time of martial law has arisen on several occasions in cases before the Irish and colonial courts but has not been conclusively decided in English law. While most of the cases dealing with martial law have arisen on habeas corpus, the issue to be faced is really the broader one of the propriety of the courts reviewing action taken by the military in time of civil war, insurrection, or invasion.

It is to be remembered that the topic under discussion is martial law under the common law. It is, perhaps, unlikely that the authorities would deal with a protracted conflict without emergency legislation or regulation, but it is still useful to analyse the common law background.[76]

---

[73] *Brogan, Coyle, McFadden and Tracey* v. *United Kingdom* (29 November 1988).
[74] See e.g. Commission to Consider Legal Procedures to Deal with Terrorist Activities in Northern Ireland (1972: Cmnd. 5185), para. 12.
[75] Reference may be made to the following: a series of articles in (1902) 18 L.Q.R. 117–58; O'Sullivan, *Military Law and the Supremacy of the Civil Courts* (1921); Minattur, *Martial Law in India, Pakistan and Ceylon* (1962); Wiener, *Civilians under Military Justice* (1967) 219–26; Heuston, *Essays in Constitutional Law* (2nd ed. 1964), 150–63; Marx, 'The Emergency Power and Civil Liberties in Canada' (1970) 16 McGill L.J. 39 at 43–56; Keir and Lawson, *Cases in Constitutional Law* (6th ed. 1979), 217–50; 1 Stephen, op. cit. 207–16; Wade and Phillips, *Constitutional Law* (8th ed. 1970), 408–12; Schwartz, *Law and the Executive in Britain* (1949), 305–14; Hopwood, 'Martial Law' (1866) 3 Papers of the Judicial Society 219; Dicey, op. cit. 284–94; Forsyth, op. cit. 188–216; *Manual of Military Law*, Part II, Section V.
[76] In *Egan* v. *Macready* [1921] 1 I.R. 265, it was held that where emergency legislation is passed, the common law doctrine of martial law is superseded and cannot be used to justify extraordinary acts. The decision, however, rests on the assumption that martial law stems from the prerogative and, therefore, following the principle of *A.G.* v. *De Keyser's Royal Hotel* [1920] A.C. 508, is superseded by legislation. Keir and Lawson, op. cit. points out that martial law does not properly rest on the prerogative and that the

(*i*) *The Meaning of 'Martial Law'*. 'Martial law', the common law principle which allows for the suppression of armed attack or rebellion, is to be distinguished from the particular set of rules applicable to members of the forces (more usually known as 'military law'), and from the powers which may be exercised by a general in command of his army in hostile territory. The source of martial law is necessity, and it is no more than the application of the principle that acts which would otherwise be illegal may be regarded as legitimate if they were necessary to defend the state from armed attack or overthrow by violence. This was admirably explained by Cockburn C.J. in his charge to the grand jury in 1867 in a case arising from the Jamaica rebellion:[77]

... the only justification of [martial law] is founded upon the assumption of an absolute necessity—a necessity paramount to all law, and which, lest the commonwealth should perish, authorizes this arbitrary and despotic mode of proceeding.

[Martial law] is simply the application of a universally acknowledged principle; namely, that where illegal force is resorted to for the purpose of crime, you may meet that illegal force by force, and may repress and prevent it by any amount of force that may be necessary for the purpose, even if that necessity should involve the death of the offender.

In circumstances where the principles of martial law apply, the legal rules and rights normally secured are abrogated only to the extent required by the overriding consideration of preserving the state. As Hale put it, '[martial law] is in truth and reality not a law, but something indulged, rather than allowed, as a law',[78] or, in the words of a modern text, martial law 'is not law in the sense of a code of rules, but a condition of affairs'.[79]

(*ii*) *Martial Law and the Courts*. The justification for extraordinary acts is founded upon the situation itself, and not by reason of an executive proclamation of martial law.[80] It is well established that it is for the courts to decide for themselves on the evidence whether or not

---

common law principle may well permit resort to martial law principles as justification for extraordinary acts any time that statutory powers prove insufficient.

[77] *R.* v. *Nelson and Brand* (1867) Special Report, 29, 84–5.
[78] *History of the Common Law* (4th ed. 1779), 34.
[79] Wade and Phillips, op. cit. 410.
[80] *Tilonko* v. *A.G. of the Colony of Natal* [1907] A.C. 93; Forsyth, op. cit. 198 (Opinion of Campbell & Rolfe); *Re Clifford and O'Sullivan* [1921] 2 A.C. 570 at 581.

the emergency constitutes a state of war.[81] It is difficult to define a situation which justifies the application of martial law principles, but the test adopted by the Irish courts would seem to be a good one: 'Is the forcible resistance to authority so widespread, so continuous, so formidable, of such duration that the help of an army must be invoked, not merely in one or two instances, but habitually or constantly, lest the state shall perish.' [82]

The possibility of recourse to the courts supposes a delicate state of affairs short of full scale war so that the courts can still function, but unsettling enough to require military intervention.[83] After the termination of hostilities, and in the absence of an act of indemnity, there can be little doubt that the courts will entertain an action which disputes the necessity of military activity.[84]

More difficult, and more to the point so far as habeas corpus is concerned, is the question of direct judicial interference with military activity. The leading decision is *Marais* v. *General Officer and A.G. of the Colony*[85] a case arising from the Cape of Good Hope colony during the Boer War, in which the petitioner asked for an order for immediate release from military custody, the relief analogous to habeas corpus under the law of the colony. Lord Halsbury, on behalf of the Judicial Committee of the Privy Council, held that 'no doubt has ever existed that where war actually prevails the ordinary courts have no jurisdiction over the action of the military authorities.'[86] *Marais* was followed by the Irish courts during the insurrection of the 1920s,[87] and in a

---

[81] *R. (Garde)* v. *Strickland* [1921] 2 I.R. 317; and esp. *R. (O'Brien)* v. *Military Governor North Dublin Union Internment Camp* [1924] I.R. 32 (C.A.), where habeas corpus was granted and the release of a military prisoner ordered where the court was not satisfied that a state of war existed.

[82] *Johnstone* v. *O'Sullivan* [1923] 2 I.R. 13 at 25 (C.A.). See also *R. (O'Brien)* v. *Military Governor North Dublin Union Internment Camp* [1924] I.R. 32. Cf. the old common law test, *infra*, pp. 113–14.

[83] It may be difficult to know when the courts are actually functioning: See e.g. *R. (Childers)* v. *Commanding Officer and Adjutant-General* [1923] 1 I.R. 5 at 15, per O'Connor M.R.: 'Can the Court be said to be freely functioning when it requires the protection of a military guard, when the circuits of the Judges are interfered with, and when some of the County Court Judges dare not enter their districts? . . . The truth is that the Courts are just struggling for continued existence in the state of war which is now prevailing. They are not functioning as in times of peace.'

[84] *Higgins* v. *Willis* [1921] 2 I.R. 386; Dicey, op. cit. 290–1.

[85] [1902] A.C. 109 (P.C.).   [86] Ibid. at 115.

[87] *R.* v. *Allen* [1921] 2 I.R. 241; *R. (Garde)* v. *Strickland* [1921] 2 I.R. 317; *R. (Royayne & Mulcahy)* v. *Strickland* [1921] 2 I.R. 333; *R. (Childers)* v. *Commanding Officer & Adjutant-General* [1923] 1 I.R. 5 (C.A.); *R. (O'Brien)* v. *Military Governor North Dublin Union Internment Camp* [1924] 1 I.R. 32 (C.A.).

Ceylonese case in 1915,[88] and the prevailing view clearly is that habeas corpus is not available to question the acts of the military authority.[89]

However, it has been held with equal consistency that the question of the existence of a state of war is one for the court to decide for itself.[90] Even *Marais* made this clear,[91] and in one Irish case it was held on habeas corpus that the prisoner should be released since it had not been shown to the court's satisfaction that a state of war existed.[92] The rule of law has been preserved at least to this extent.

The position reached is, then, that while it is open to the court to decide for itself whether or not a state of war exists, once it is shown that there is such a situation, the courts have no power to review the legality or necessity of the detention.

It should be remembered, however, that neither *Marais* nor the Irish cases are actually binding on the English courts. In another case reaching the House of Lords from Ireland, the question of the availability of habeas corpus was expressly left open.[93] It cannot be said that the issue is an entirely settled one in English law.

It can be argued that the *Marais* case is wrong in holding that military acts are not justiciable. In his decision, Lord Halsbury relied on an old Privy Council decision which dealt not with the power of the court to review military activity in a rebellion, but with the very different proposition of the immunity of an occupying army in a hostile land.[94] Moreover, his statement that 'where war actually prevails the ordinary courts have no jurisdiction over the action of the military authorities'[95] seems to ignore the old common law authorities which had said that so long as the Courts at Westminster were sitting, there could be no resort to martial law.[96] The Privy Council may have been right in rejecting this rather artificial test of when circumstances allowed for acts of necessity. There may, however, still be scope for the

---

[88] *Re De Silva* (1915) 18 N.L.R. 277.

[89] Cf. *Egan* v. *Macready* [1921] 1 I.R. 265, discussed *supra*, n. 76, p. 110. Two Cape of Good Hope cases decided before *Marais* came to the same result as did the Privy Council in *Marais: Re Fourie* (1900) 17 S.C.R. 173; *R.* v. *Gildenhuys* (1900) 17 S.C.R. 266.

[90] *Supra*, pp. 111–12.   [91] [1902] A.C. 109 at 115.   [92] *Supra*, n. 81, p. 112.

[93] *Re Clifford & O'Sullivan* [1921] 2 A.C. 570 at 584–5, 591.

[94] *Elphinstone* v. *Bedreechund* (1830) 1 Knapp P.C. 316.

[95] *Supra*, n. 86, p. 112.

[96] Hale, *History of the Common Law*, 35; 1 Bl. *Comm.*, 413; 3 Rushworth *Historical Collections* II App., pp. 79, 81 (Coke and Rolle); *R.* v. *Nelson and Brand* (1867) Special Report 69; Forsyth, op. cit. 192 (Hargrave's Opinion), 198 (Campbell and Rolfe's Opinion). It is noted in Forsyth, op. cit. 207, that some of the old authorities may well

principle behind that rule, namely, that even acts taken in times of national peril should be subject to judicial scrutiny so long as there are still courts of law sitting. There is, in other words, a middle ground which has not really been explored by the cases or the commentators. The *Marais* case did, it is submitted, break new ground, and it may be asked whether it should be followed. It has been supported[97] on the ground that the military campaign should not be at all hampered if the rebellion is to be quashed quickly and effectively. The certainty of obedience to orders and unity of command, it is said, could be threatened if it is admitted that the courts can interfere during the period of rebellion.

However, it must always be of the utmost importance to maintain, so far as possible, those essential rights which are secured by the legal order which is being defended. Again, to quote Cockburn C.J. in his charge to the Grand Jury in a case arising from the Jamaica rebellion where the accused were charged for their part in the summary trial and execution of an alleged conspirator:

> But it is said that, as the necessity of suppressing rebellion is what justifies the exercise of martial law, and as to this end, the example of immediate punishment is essential, the exhibition of martial law in its most summary and terrible form is indispensible... There are considerations more important even than the shortening of the temporary duration of an insurrection. Among them are the eternal and immutable principles of justice, principles which never can be violated without lasting detriment to the true interests and well-being of a civilized community.[98]

refer to the law applicable to soldiers and before the Mutiny Acts, even soldiers could only be tried in the civil courts while they were sitting.
In the case of *Wolfe Tone* (1798) 27 St. Tr. 614, the Irish King's Bench granted the writ to bring up a rebel who had been sentenced to death by an *ad hoc* military court. Dicey, op. cit. 294, said of the case: 'no more splendid assertion of the supremacy of the law can be found.' The prisoner died before the return could be made, and in *R.* v. *Allen* [1921] 1 I.R. 241, the case was said not to have actually decided anything since no final order was made.

[97] Heuston, *Essays*, 161–2. See also Lt. Col. Tovey, *Martial Law and the Custom of War* (1886), 73: 'Practically, in England and the United States, the essence of Martial Law is the suspension of the privilege of the writ of habeas corpus—that is, the withdrawal of a particular person, or of a particular place or district or county from the authority of the civil tribunals. A mere declaration of Martial Law would be utterly useless, unless accompanied by a suspension of the privileges of the writ of habeas corpus; for, if the local civil authorities were permitted, in such a case to enforce this writ, they might, and some probably would, render the military powerless to provide for the public safety.'
[98] *R.* v. *Nelson and Brand* (1867) Special Report 108.

It may be unlikely that on habeas corpus the court would find that without undue danger to the proper prosecution of the war it could order the release of a person detained by the military. It is submitted, however, that it is most important to maintain that review is possible. There is no reason to suspect that the judges would fail to give liberal interpretation to the justification of necessity. It is surely better to err on the side of too much rather than too little judicial interference even if in times of real peril, the possibility of interference is remote.

(e) *Alien Enemies and Prisoners of War*

An alien who is the subject of an enemy power has, *prima facie*, no right of access to English courts.[99] An alien does, however, have full right of access when 'in protection' or when enjoying the revocable licence of the crown to maintain civil capacity.[100] Alien enemies may be considered to be 'in protection' when they have registered under an alien restriction order.[101] Prisoners of war are considered to be living under protection without any registration, and they enjoy full civil and procedural capacity in English law.[102]

These general rules are, however, said to be subject to the exception that a prisoner of war has no standing to apply for the writ of habeas corpus.[103] This has been said to deprive not only combatants taken as prisoner of the benefit of the writ, but also any alien enemy interned pursuant to the prerogative power of the crown over such individuals in time of war.[104]

There has, however, been no careful examination of this proposition in the cases, and it may be asked whether this exception to the civil capacity of prisoners of war, and to the general availability of habeas corpus, should be so readily accepted.

It is submitted that while the cases ostensibly support the proposition that prisoners of war lack capacity to apply, a close reading indicates that the courts do not really decide the cases on that basis.

---

[99] 39 Hals. (3rd), 34.
[100] McNair and Watts, *The Legal Effects of War* (4th ed. 1966), 79.
[101] Ibid.
[102] Ibid. 93; *Sparenburg* v. *Bannatyne* (1797) 1 Bos. & B. 163; *Schaffenius* v. *Goldberg* [1916] 1 K.B. 284 (C.A.).
[103] *Three Spanish Sailors Case* (1779) 2 W. Bl. 1324; *R.* v. *Schriever* (1759) 2 Burr. 765; *Furley* v. *Newnham* (1780) 2 Dougl. 419 (habeas corpus ad testificandum); *R.* v. *Vine St. Police Supt.*, *ex p. Liebman* [1916] 1 K.B. 268; *Ex p. Weber* [1916] 1 K.B. 280n (aff'd [1916] A.C. 421); *R.* v. *Home Secretary*, *ex p. L.* [1945] K.B. 7; *R.* v. *Bottrill*, *ex p. Kuechenmeister* [1946] 2 All E.R. 434 (C.A.).
[104] *R.* v. *Bottrill*, *ex p. Kuechenmeister* [1946] 2 All E.R. 434 (C.A.).

The crown does appear to have the power, quite apart from statute, to detain prisoners of war (including non-combatant alien enemies) as part of the prerogative under which it wages war.[105] This means that if an applicant is detained in a prisoner-of-war camp, and is properly considered a prisoner of war, he or she will have no right to be liberated. This is the rule which the courts have applied and it is not to say that such a person lacks capacity to apply for the writ. A more appropriate phrasing of the result would be: where someone held applies for habeas corpus, a complete answer to the writ will be that the applicant is both in fact and in law a prisoner of war detained by authority of the Crown. The application discloses no cause for the writ to issue, and it will be dismissed on that basis. If, however, it appears that the applicant may have been improperly detained as a prisoner of war, or is a prisoner of war on licence and detained for some other cause, the court will investigate the propriety of the detention.[106] Capacity to apply has nothing to do with the matter: it is purely a question of whether a case can be made out for the remedy.

This formulation is not only more satisfactory in principle, but it would seem to reflect more accurately what the courts do in practice. In one case, the applicant alleged that as the war was over, he could no longer be held as a prisoner of war.[107] In the end, the court refused to discharge him, accepting a ministerial certificate that a state of war still existed. In proceeding to that stage, the reasoning of the court suggests that the basis for refusal was not lack of capacity. In other cases,[108] the courts have entertained the argument that the prisoner is not in law a citizen of the enemy state. Again, the applications failed, and again the formula of 'lack of capacity' was uttered, but by entertaining the question, in one case all the way to the House of Lords,[109] the action

---

[105] McNair and Watts, op. cit. 95, 98.

[106] Tucker L.J.'s dictum in the *Kuechenmeister* case, [1946] 2 All E.R. 434 at 438, tends to support this analysis: '...the real objection is that an alien enemy cannot be heard to complain against the Crown or its officers in respect of acts done under and within the limits of the prerogative, whereas the preliminary objection based on the status of prisoner of war appears to me to be open to doubt, and, moreover, to suggest that as a prisoner of war he could not even have habeas corpus against a private citizen who was imprisoning him without any pretence of authority from the Crown.'

[107] *R. v. Bottrill, ex p. Kuechenmeister* [1946] 2 All E.R. 434 (C.A.). At one time, it was feared that Napoleon would apply for habeas corpus on the grounds that there was no authority in English law to hold him after the termination of war. Special legislation was passed: see Bellot, 'The Detention of Napoleon Buonaparte' (1923) 39 L.Q.R. 170.

[108] *R. v. Vine St. Police Supt., ex p. Liebman* [1916] 1 K.B. 268; *Ex p. Weber* [1916] 1 A.C. 421; *R. v. Home Secretary, ex p. L.* [1945] K.B. 7.

[109] *Ex p. Weber* [1916] 1 A.C. 421 (aff'g [1916] 1 K.B. 280n). In the Court of Appeal,

of the courts made it clear that 'lack of capacity' is a misleading description of the grounds for the decision.

The danger in saying that a prisoner of war cannot apply for the writ is that it makes it appear that merely by being placed in an internment camp, the legality of the detention of an alleged alien enemy is conclusively determined. While the result may well be the same in the vast majority of cases, the proposed statement of the rule is theoretically more sound, and also removes doubts about the capacity of an alien enemy to use habeas corpus to contest the legality of the detention at the hands of a private citizen, or even to use habeas corpus to gain the custody of a child.[110] The lack-of-capacity rule could have the effect of discouraging an applicant who may be entitled to relief from applying, and in the interests of clarity, it should be abandoned.

4. EXECUTIVE DETENTION ORDERS IN PEACE-TIME

The vast majority of habeas corpus cases dealing with challenges to the exercise of executive power have arisen in war-time and the reasoning in those cases is plainly coloured by the circumstances. There are few situations in peace-time where the executive is given discretionary power to order detention, but there are habeas corpus cases which have arisen, and these cases reflect judicial attitudes quite different from those observed in the war-time cases.

(a) *Examples of Judicial Interference with an Executive Power to Detain*

One of the best examples of effective review by way of habeas corpus of executive action is, perhaps, the *Eshugbayi Eleko* case.[111] This was a decision of the Privy Council in 1931 on appeal from Nigeria. The Governor of the colony was empowered to order the deportation and detention of certain specified individuals in certain specified circumstances. Unlike the language of Reg. 18B, the ordinance giving this power read, 'If facts A, B, and C exist, then the Governor may make an

reference was made to the *locus standi* argument, but the House of Lords does not even appear to have dealt with it.

[110] *Supra*, n. 106, p. 116, per Tucker L.J. See *R.* v. *DeManneville* (1804) 5 East 221, where an alien enemy was given custody of a child on habeas corpus, without the point being argued.

[111] *Eshugbayi Eleko* v. *Officer Administering the Government of Nigeria* [1931] A.C. 662 (P.C.).

order.'[112] It will be remembered that Reg. 18B allowed the minister to act where he or she had 'reasonable cause to believe'[113] that the requisite circumstances were present, wording which more easily lent itself to the subjective interpretation.

As in the war-time cases, the applicant in the Nigerian case alleged that none of the circumstances were present. The Governor's reply was that the decision on these points was not open to question, but was to be respected as if it were the order of a superior court, and that habeas corpus did not open an attack which allowed for judicial investigation of the facts. This was the same argument which was to be made in *Liversidge* and in *Greene*, but in the Nigerian case, the Privy Council held that the valid exercise of the power was contingent on the objective existence of the facts contemplated by the ordinance, and that once the applicant alleged that those conditions did not exist, it was for the court to see for itself that they did.

Lord Atkin cogently explained the basis for judicial review in the following language:

As the executive he [the Governor] can only act in pursuance of the powers given to him by law. In accordance with British jurisprudence no member of the executive can interfere with the liberty or property of a British subject except on the condition that he can support the legality of his action before a court of justice. And it is the tradition of British justice that judges should not shrink from deciding such issues in the face of the executive.[114]

There can be little doubt that it was easier to apply an objective standard in the Nigerian case than it would have been in the war-time cases, simply because the facts in question were more readily determinable. Still, there can be little doubt that the war-time cases marked a departure from the ordinary rule of reviewability of executive acts and that the departure may be explained by the emergency circumstances of the war.

The principle of reviewability which is illustrated by the Nigerian case was extended in 1969 by the decision of the Divisional Court in *Ahsan*,[115] already discussed in detail with respect to the problem of burden of proof.[116] There, the court held that not only could it review

---

[112] Deposed Chiefs Removal Ordinance, allowing the Governor to make an order with respect to a deposed native chief where native law and custom required the deposed chief to leave the area over which he exercised jurisdiction if the Governor was satisfied that this was necessary for the re-establishment of peace, order, and good government.

[113] *Supra*, p. 100.   [114] [1931] A.C. 662 at 670.

[115] *R.* v. *Governor of Brixton Prison, ex p. Ahsan* [1969] 2 Q.B. 222.

[116] *Supra*, pp. 86–91.

an immigration officer's decision to order the detention of the applicant for having allegedly illegally entered the country, but that the burden of proving that the proper circumstances existed for the power to be exercised rested with the officer. This principle now enjoys the support of the House of Lords in *Khawaja* v. *Secretary of State for the Home Department*,[117] overruling a series of cases[118] which had departed from *Ahsan*. Both *Ahsan* and *Khawaja* explicitly reject the reasoning which deprived the war-time detainees of an effective means to challenge the legality of their incarceration. As soon as the applicant casts some doubt on the validity of what has been done, on the principle established by these decisions, it rests with the officer to justify the detention. Not only is the standard objective, but the applicant is relieved of the difficulty of collecting enough evidence to convince the court.

Indeed, habeas corpus has proved to be an important remedy in the law of immigration, and there are many cases which show that it will lie to test the legality of acts which lead to the immigrant's detention. If it does not appear that the immigrant falls within the class of persons against whom an order can be made,[119] or even if the authorities act unfairly the remedy of habeas corpus will be available.[120] In most of these cases, a clear issue of law, usually one of statutory interpretation, is presented and such an issue is plainly open on habeas corpus.

In the next group of immigration cases to be examined, those dealing with ministerial deportation orders, the discussion returns to the problem of the review of a broadly worded discretionary power where the possibilities for review are more tenuous.

(b) *The Deportation Cases*

The deportation cases provide another instance of habeas corpus being used to challenge an executive order made pursuant to a broad discretionary power given by statute. They present a curious mixture of emergency and peace-time factors. The definition of the power to

---

[117] [1984] A.C. 74.

[118] *Supra*, nn. 50 and 51, p. 74.

[119] *R.* v. *Governor of Pentonville Prison ex p. Azam* [1973] 2 W.L.R. 949 (aff'd [1974] A.C. 18); *Samejina* v. *R.* [1932] S.C.R. 640 at 646: 'It is established law that jurisdiction on the part of an official will not be presumed. Where jurisdiction is conditioned upon the existence of certain things, their exercise must be clearly established before jurisdiction can be exercised.' per Lamont J.

[120] *Re H.K. (An Infant)* [1967] 2 Q.B. 617. *R.* v. *Governor of Richmond Remand Centre, ex p. Asghar* [1971] 1 W.L.R. 129.

deport is of war-time vintage, and while the courts do not appear ever to have upset an order, the cases are full of dicta threatening to do just that.

Until 1971, the deportation of aliens was governed by the Aliens Order[121] which began as an emergency measure during the 1914–18 war. It gave the Home Secretary the power to order deportation and detention pending deportation in a number of specified instances, including where 'he deems it to be conducive to the public good to make a deportation order against the alien.'[122] At present, the matter is governed by the Immigration Act 1971, which allows for the review of most deportation orders by appeal tribunals constituted under the Act.[123] However, the Secretary of State still may deport an alien if the Secretary 'deems his deportation to be conducive to the public good',[124] and there is no administrative appeal 'if the ground of the decision was that his deportation is conducive to the public good as being in the interests of national security or of the relations between the United Kingdom and any other country or for other reasons of a political nature'.[125] No appeal is given against a refusal of leave to enter if the Secretary of State certifies that the person's exclusion has been directed as being 'conducive to the public good'.[126] Moreover, there is no appeal at all in certain cases until the person affected leaves the United Kingdom.[127]

There still exists, then, an executive power to order the detention and deportation of an alien, and habeas corpus will be an appropriate remedy where it is alleged that the power has been exercised unlawfully.[128] Originally, this power was thought to be one of those regrettable but unavoidable incidents 'happen[ing] in time of war which would, in truth, shock the majority of persons in this country in

---

[121] Aliens Order 1953 (S.I. 1953 No. 1671), pursuant to the Aliens Restriction Act 1914, as amended by the Aliens Restriction (Amendment) Act, 1919 (repealed by Immigration Act 1971, s.34, sched. 6). For the history of immigration control and deportation see Thornberry, 'Dr. Soblen and the Alien Law of the United Kingdom' (1963) 12 I.C.L.Q. 414, 416 *et seq.*
[122] Art. 20(2)(6).
[123] ss.12–21. For a list of the cases in which there is no appeal, see Evans, *Immigration Law* (2nd ed. 1983) at 333–41.
[124] s.3(5).
[125] ss.13(3), 15(3).
[126] s.13(5). There is, however, a special non-statutory appeal procedure in these cases under which representations are heard by three advisors: [1972] Public Law 74.
[127] ss.13(3), 15(5), 16(2).
[128] Macdonald, *Immigration Law and Practice* (1983) at 400–26 discusses the availability of habeas corpus.

time of peace'.[129] The provision was introduced during the first war but was not withdrawn at the end of the war, and has now even survived, to the extent outlined, the remaking of the law of deportation and is firmly established in the current legislation.

Perhaps because of the war-time origins and phrasing of the power, the courts have been hesitant, and at times wholly unwilling, to interfere with its exercise. It has been consistently held that there can be no review of the merits of the decision to deport, and 'review of the merits' has been broadly construed.[130] Especially in the early cases, the power is described by such phrases as an 'unlimited discretion' with which 'it is impossible for any court of law to interfere.'[131]

On the other hand, the judges have been wary of the possibility of an abuse of such a wide power, and have consistently maintained that, on habeas corpus, the court could go behind a deportation and detention order if it were shown that the minister had acted outside the proper ambit of the legislation. There appears to be no case where the courts have actually gone behind the order, but there can be little doubt that they have power to do so if a proper case is made out. In the first reported case of a challenge to an order under the Aliens Order, it was pointed out that an applicant for habeas corpus would not necessarily be foreclosed by the production of an order which was good on its face:

I do not agree that if the executive were to come into this court and simply say 'A person is in our custody, and therefore the writ of habeas corpus does not apply because the custody is at the moment technically legal,' the Court would

---

[129] *R. v. Governor of Brixton Prison, ex p. Sarno* [1916] 2 K.B . 742 at 750, per Earl of Reading C.J. The argument that the continued validity of the order was contingent on the continued state of emergency, was rejected in *R. v. Brixton Prison (Governor), ex p. Soblen* [1962] 3 All E.R. 641 at 649–50.

[130] See, e.g., cases cited *infra*, n. 131; *R. v. Brixton Prison (Governor), ex p. Bloom* [1920] All E.R. 153; *R. v. Inspector of Leman Street Police Station, ex p. Venicoff* [1920] 3 K.B. 72, holding that the audi alterem partem rule had no application in deportation proceedings. See also the decision of Stephenson J. in *R. v. Brixton Prison (Governor), ex p. Soblen* [1962] 3 All E.R. 641 at 657: '... what the Aliens Acts and Orders give the Secretary of State are emergency powers conferred at a time, and only for a time when the legislature considered that the executive, in its treatment of aliens, should be almost out of reach of the control of the judiciary, and the judiciary was unwilling and unable to interfere with the executive's treatment of aliens... Counsel for the applicant's argument that the arm of the law should be extended further to protect aliens in peace than it was in the two wars, and that in peace the alien and not the Secretary of State should be allowed to choose the place to which he will go if deported, is one which should be addressed, not to the court, but to Parliament.'

[131] *R. v. Home Secretary, ex p. Chateau Thierry* [1917] 1 K.B. 922 at 935 per Bankes L.J., quoted in *R. v. Home Secretary, ex p. Bressler* (1924) 131 L.T. 386 at 387 (C.A.).

have. no power to consider the matter and, if necessary, deal with the application for the writ. In my judgment that answer from the Crown in reply to an application for the writ would not be sufficient if this court were satisfied that what was really in contemplation was the exercise of an abuse of power. The arm of the law in this country would have grown very short, and the power of this court very feeble, if it were subject to such a restriction in the exercise of its power to protect the liberty of the subject as that proposition involves.[132]

This same principle of reviewability was again enunciated in the important case of *Soblen*[133] in 1962, a decision which amply illustrates the contrast between a stated willingness to intervene on the one hand, and a queasiness about actually giving relief on the other. The argument was that the Home Secretary was using the power to order deportation for an improper purpose, to wit, extraditing the applicant for a non-extraditable offence. A request had been made by the American government for the surrender of the applicant, and clearly, if the Home Secretary had made the deportation order for that purpose alone, the power had been unlawfully exercised. Lord Denning left no doubt that the court could '... always go behind the face of the deportation order in order to see whether the powers entrusted by Parliament have been exercised lawfully or no'.[134]

While the application of the doctrine of crown privilege precluded the applicant from getting the facts needed to make out an iron-clad case,[135] even on the evidence presented, the action of the Home Secretary was open to grave suspicion.[136] The judges went to some length to emphasize their power to interfere if the power had been exercised for this improper purpose, but in the end, held that while the Home Secretary's action had the effect of extraditing Soblen, the true purpose all along had been a valid exercise of the power to deport.[137]

The case makes it clear that in practical terms, it is difficult for the applicant to show that such a power has been improperly exercised. The court was quick to point to its power to give relief against an

---

[132] *R.* v. *Governor of Brixton Prison, ex p. Sarno* [1916] 2 K.B. 742 at 752 per Low J. See also *Ex p. Sacksteader* [1918] 1 K.B. 578 at 586, 589 (C.A.).
[133] *R.* v. *Brixton Prison (Governor), ex p. Soblen* [1962] 3 All E.R. 641 (C.A.).
[134] Ibid. at 661.   [135] *Infra*, pp. 124–5.
[136] See Thornberry, 'Dr. Soblen and the Alien Law of the United Kingdom' (1963) 12 I.C.L.Q. 414 for a detailed review of the facts: and also O'Higgins, 'Disguised Extradition: The *Soblen* Case' (1964) 27 Mod. L.R. 521.
[137] See also *Znaty* v. *Minister of State for Immigration* (1972) 126 C.L.R. 1. It is suggested by de Smith, *Judicial Review*, 331, that a 'dominant purpose' test would have been more appropriate. This would require the court to focus on the primary reason for the action, and could well have made all the difference in this case.

improper use of the power, but seemed reluctant to actually use it. These cases on deportation provide something of a bridge between the war-time and peace-time cases. The executive power under scrutiny was defined in time of emergency, and its exercise has been contested in cases full of political overtone. The language of the judges suggests a greater willingness to assert control over the exercise of the power than in the emergency cases, but in the end, there has been a failure to carry out the threat. Admittedly, the terms of the statute are broad, and the element of public interest to be considered influences the court to shy away from intervention.

5. A NOTE ON CROWN PRIVILEGE

An important element in several cases involving executive orders has been crown privilege. In the war-time cases, considerable importance was placed on the supposedly unchallengeable privilege of a minister of the crown to refuse to disclose information where disclosure is deemed to be harmful to interests of state.[138] One reason given by the courts for characterizing the minister's power to intern as being wholly subjective was that the decision was based on information for which privilege could always be claimed, and that the court could not, therefore, examine the reasonableness of the action taken.

Since the war, the rules regarding the determination of the propriety of a claim of privilege have changed, and a ministerial certificate that disclosure of the information would be contrary to the public interest is no longer conclusive.[139] It is now possible for the court to examine the documents for which privilege is claimed and to decide whether or not the ministerial claim should be upheld, balancing the public interest to have the evidence withheld against the frustration of justice which occurs when relevant information is kept from the court's consideration.

There are, however, more fundamental reasons to reconsider what was said and assumed by the courts in the internment cases with

---

[138] See esp. *Ex p. Lees* [1941] 1 K.B. 72 at 78–9 (C.A.); *Greene* v. *Secretary of State* [1942] A.C. 284 at 296; *Liversidge* v. *Anderson* [1942] A.C. 206 at 254.

[139] *Conway* v. *Rimmer* [1968] A.C. 910; *D.* v. *National Society for the Prevention of Cruelty to Children* [1978] A.C. 171; *Burmah Oil Co. Ltd.* v. *Bank of England* [1980] A.C. 1090; *Air Canada* v. *Secretary of State for Trade* [1983] 2 A.C. 394; *Carey* v. *The Queen in Right of Ontario* [1986] 2 S.C.R. 637. Cf. *Duncan* v. *Cammell Laird and Co. Ltd.* [1942] A.C. 624 for the old rule.

regard to crown privilege. It is a grave error, it is submitted, to suppose that crown privilege has anything at all to do with whether or not the minister has justified the detention of a subject on habeas corpus. Crown privilege is a reason on the basis of public policy for the exclusion of relevant evidence where the reception or disclosure of that evidence would be contrary to the public interest. Such a claim may be made in an action between two private parties or in an action between the state and a private party. If the claim is successfully made out, it may well deprive a party of the evidence required either to make out an unanswerable claim or to set up a complete defence, but it does not absolve anyone from satisfying the burden of proof. It does not mean, for example, that in a civil action where the onus of proving a certain fact is cast upon the crown, the onus can be discharged simply by claiming privilege.

The issue of the burden of proof in habeas corpus cases has already been examined. It has been suggested that once the applicant overcomes the initial burden of adducing evidence which casts doubt upon the propriety of his detention, the legal burden of proof is cast upon the party detaining.[140] In the internment cases, the intolerable suggestion was made that a claim of crown privilege went some of the way to excuse the minister from supporting his decision to intern.[141]

While the court may be reluctant to force the minister to supply the applicant with the facts needed to support the case,[142] if the applicant has surmounted the initial hurdle and established *prima facie* grounds for doubting the validity of the detention, there can be no place at all for a claim of privilege. If the minister chooses not to disclose the basis for the order, the prisoner must be released.

In the *Soblen* case,[143] the application of the doctrine of crown privilege probably deprived the applicant of the facts required to raise a real doubt about the propriety of the deportation order. It is submitted, however, that while the case is a regrettable example of the application of crown privilege at this stage, there are dicta in the case which indicate that crown privilege should not be confounded with burden of proof, and that where the applicant is able to cast a real doubt on what

[140] *Supra*, pp. 85–91.

[141] *Supra*, p. 102; *Lloyd* v. *Wallach* (1915) 20 C.L.R. 299.

[142] Note, however, that discovery may be possible on judicial review: *R.* v. *Secretary of State for the Home Department, ex p. Herbage (No. 2)* [1987] Q.B. 1077 (C.A.). It may be possible for the applicant to get the necessary facts by ordinary subpoena: *R.* v. *Brixton Prison (Governor), ex p. Soblen* [1962] 3 Al E.R. 641 at 648.

[143] [1962] 3 All E.R. 641.

has been done, the respondent will not be able to justify the detention simply by claiming crown privilege.

Donovan L.J. noted that where information is withheld, the applicant's task is made more difficult, and he went on:

[The applicant] will be left to do his best without such assistance, and in the nature of things, therefore, he will seldom be able to do more than raise a *prima facie* case, or alternatively to sow such substantial and disquieting doubts in the mind of the court about the bona fides of the order he is challenging that the court will consider that some answer is called for. If that answer is withheld, or being furnished is found unsatisfactory, then, in my view, the order challenged ought not to be upheld, for otherwise there would be virtually no protection for the subject against some illegal order which had been clothed with the garment of legality simply for the sake of appearances and where discovery was resisted on the ground of privilege.[144]

Similarly, Denning L.J. explained:

The court cannot compel the Home Secretary to disclose the materials on which he has acted, but if there is evidence on which it could be reasonably supposed that the Home Secretary was using the power of deportation for an ulterior purpose, then the court could call on the Home Secretary for an answer: and if he fails to give it, it can upset his order.[145]

Indeed, it might be added that anything short of this analysis would defeat the whole basis of habeas corpus. The internment cases should be distinguished on the basis that all the courts meant to say was that until the internee showed something to suggest that the detention was illegal, the Home Secretary was not required to supply any information or justification.

Finally, it should be pointed out that the suggested limitation on crown privilege in habeas corpus cases is really a bare minimum, and that an argument can be made for its exclusion altogether.[146] An analogy may be found in the criminal law where it is the established practice that no claim of privilege on the grounds of state interest should be made.[147] An exception is made for the names of informers

---

[144] Ibid. at 664. See also at 666.   [145] Ibid. at 661.

[146] Cf. the remarks of Stephenson J. in *Soblen* [1962] 3 All E.R. 641 at 652.

[147] This is a rule of practice, established by the Lord Chancellor in 1956, rather than a rule of law: see 'Crime and Crown Privilege' [1959] Crim. L.R. 10. In *Duncan* v. *Cammell Laird and Co. Ltd.* [1942] A.C. 624, Visc. Simon L.C. observed at 633: '. . . the practice, as applied in criminal trials where an individual's life or liberty may be at stake, is not necessarily the same.' See also 'Crown Privilege in Criminal Cases' [1971] Crim. L.R. 675, 682; and cf. *R.* v. *Lewes JJ., ex p. Home Secretary* [1973] A.C. 388.

which need not be disclosed on the grounds of public interest, but even this exception appears to be overridden where the name of the informer is necessary to show the prisoner's innocence.[148] The reason for the virtual exclusion of claims for non-disclosure in the name of public interest is undoubtedly that the liberty of the subject is at stake: '...one public policy is in conflict with another public policy, and that which says that an innocent man is not to be condemned when his innocence can be proved is the policy that must prevail.'[149]

Such reasoning clearly applies equally to habeas corpus cases. It may be hoped that now that the courts can examine the evidence and balance for themselves the public interest against the interest of the party seeking justice, information which is helpful to the prisoner will never be withheld.

6. CONCLUSION

This review of the authorities demonstrates that habeas corpus can be an effective remedy to control the exercise of discretionary power, but that policy considerations may often make the courts reluctant to act. There are several habeas corpus cases which illustrate the ordinary rule of the reviewability of executive action and most recently, the law of immigration has provided examples. On the other hand, it is submitted that the cases which involve emergency powers indicate a reluctance on the part of the courts to use the remedy of habeas corpus to its full potential. Judicial innovation would not have been required to justify intervention in *Halliday* or in *Greene* and in *Liversidge* v. *Anderson*. In each case, accepted principles of constitutional and administrative law were available and applicable. In *Halliday*, and almost certainly in *Greene* and in *Liversidge* v. *Anderson*, the legal arguments weighed against the result reached, and the judges acted on policy grounds.

In neither of the two wars did Parliament clearly stipulate that personal liberty had to be sacrificed to the public good to the extent claimed by the executive and allowed by the courts. If personal liberty is to be so sacrificed, it is for Parliament to say so and not for the courts to imply. In jurisdictions such as Canada having constitutionally

---

[148] *Marks* v. *Beyfus* (1890) 25 Q.B.D. 494 at 498 (C.A.); *R.* v. *Lewes JJ.*, *ex p. Home Secretary* [1973] A.C. 388 at 407.

[149] *Marks* v. *Beyfus* (1890) 25 Q.B.D. 494 at 498 per Lord Esher M.R.

entrenched charters of rights, even powers expressly conferred by the legislature will be subject to judicial scrutiny. Where executive action interferes with personal liberty, the courts should be prepared to scrutinize its legality carefully and to check its exercise unless Parliament has clearly granted the power. The use of habeas corpus in *Eshugbayi Eleko* and in the immigration cases provides a point of comparison. These cases demonstrate that the techniques for judicial interference are readily available if the courts want to use them.

It cannot be repeated too often that in the law of judicial review the negative war-time approach has been abandoned and the courts have recently shown a determined and innovative capacity for controlling administrative action. While it may be unrealistic to suppose that these powers of review would be as vigorously exercised in time of emergency, it is unlikely that this experience would be entirely forgotten.

5

Habeas Corpus in Criminal Law

1. REVIEW OF PRE-TRIAL PROCEEDINGS AND BAIL

(a) *Historical Background*

From the seventeenth century to the nineteenth century, habeas corpus was an important aspect of day-to-day criminal procedure. It was the accepted method by which a person committed by the local justices could appeal to the general power of the King's Bench to grant bail, and it generally provided a method of review over pre-trial proceedings. It was, and still is, thought to provide a measure of protection against arrest and detention unauthorized by the ordinary criminal process.

Habeas corpus provided a remedy where pre-trial proceedings had been defective. When an accused person was arrested, in the normal course, he or she was brought before a justice of the peace.[1] The justice had to decide whether to discharge, commit or bail the prisoner according to the facts and according to the applicable legal principles.[2] The justice was required to take in writing the examination of the accused and of the other witnesses.[3] Before a statutory change in 1848,[4] this early form of the preliminary inquiry had a distinctly inquisitorial character. The justice set out to collect evidence. He examined the accused about the offence,[5] and took the depositions of

---

[1] Before the office of justice of the peace developed the local administration of criminal justice, including the power to bail, was in the hands of the sheriff: 2 Hale *P.C.*, 136; Petersdorff, *Law of Bail* (1824), 476–82. In cases of homicide, the coroner's inquest has always played an important preliminary role: 1 Stephen, *History of the Criminal Law of England* (1883), 216–19.

[2] See 2 Hale *P.C.*, 120–4, 127–40 for the rules governing justices and their powers to grant bail.

[3] (1554) 1 & 2 Phil. & Mary, c.13; (1555) 2 & 3 Phil. & Mary, c.10. 1 Stephen, op. cit. 219 suggests that these statutes may have been a codification of early practice.

[4] 11 & 12 Vict. c.42; 1 Stephen, op. cit. 220–1. Preliminary hearings are now governed by Magistrates' Court Act 1980, ss.4–8.

[5] It is pointed out in Coleridge's note, 4 Bl. *Comm.* (16th ed. 1825), 296–7, that the accused was not compelled to answer, and that the prudent magistrate would so warn him.

the witnesses in the accused's absence.[6] The proceedings were designed to prepare the prosecution's case for trial and not as a judicial process to determine whether or not, on the evidence, a full trial was warranted.[7]

While an accused person was committed for trial without preliminary proceedings of a judicial character, habeas corpus did provide a method of judicial review of the case at an early stage. The prisoner could argue that the justice had wrongfully refused bail, that the evidence was too weak to warrant pre-trial detention or that the charges were deficient in law.

In the first place, the court looked at the legal sufficiency of the charges against the accused. As Hale explained, when discussing the requisites of a good warrant of committal:

It must contain the certainty of the cause, and therefore if it be for felony, it ought not to be generally *pro felonia*, but it must contain the especial nature of the felony briefly ... and the reason is, because it may appear to the judges of the King's Bench upon an habeas corpus, whether it be felony or not.[8]

While it was sometimes said that a warrant of committal for safe custody pending trial needed to be less explicit than a warrant in execution,[9] there were many cases where the court either bailed or discharged the prisoner on account of insufficient charges in law.[10] It is quite clear, however, that the court went far beyond the question of the sufficiency of the committal. The depositions taken by the justices were brought before the court, and in many cases, however good or bad the committal, the court decided for itself whether the evidence warranted putting the accused on trial.[11]

---

[6] 1 Stephen, op. cit. 221.   [7] Ibid.   [8] 2 Hale *P.C.*, 122.

[9] *R. v. Jacobi & Hillier* (1881) 46 L.T. 595. Cf. *R. v. Hawkins* (1715) Fort. 272, where it was said that after conviction, the warrant need not be so particular as the conviction itself could be relied on, whereas before, full particulars were necessary.

[10] 2 Hale *P.C.*, 111; *R. v. Kendal & Roe* (1700) 1 Salk. 347; *R. v. Judd* (1788) 2 T.R. 255; *R. v. Remnant* (1793) 5 T.R. 169.

[11] *R. v. Horner* (1783) 1 Leach 270–1: 'The practice of this court is, and upon reference to the officers of the Crown Office we find it to have been long established, that even where the commitment is regular, the Court will look into the depositions to see if there be a sufficient ground laid to detain the party in custody; and if there be not, they will bail him. So also, where the commitment is irregular, if it appear that a serious offence has been committed, they will not discharge or bail the prisoner without first looking into the depositions, to see whether there is sufficient evidence to detain him in custody.' See also: *Mohun* (1698) 1 Salk. 104; *Anon.* (1704) 1 Salk. 104; *R. v. Dalton* (1731) 2 Str. 911; *R. v. Judd* (1788) 2 T.R. 255; *R. v. Gittus* (1824) 3 L.J.O.S.K.B. 55; *R. v. Manning* (1888) 5 T.L.R. 139; Chitty, *Criminal Law* (1816), vol. 1, 113, 129; Petersdorff, *Law of Bail* (1824), 520.

If it was found that the committal was bad, but that on the facts disclosed by the depositions an offence had been made out, the court would remand the prisoner for trial.[12] In such a case, the judges of the King's Bench were acting within their inherent powers as conservators of the peace. Technically, the prisoner was not remanded to the former custody, but was committed for trial simply on the authority of the court. A good example of this is one case[13] where the prisoner, suspected of murder, had not been brought before a magistrate or even formally charged, but held for some time in custody on board a ship of war. The court held that the officers of the ship had acted reasonably in the circumstances, and on its own authority the court committed the prisoner to the custody of its prison to be further dealt with according to law.

In other cases, the court found that the committal was perfectly good, but that the evidence was weak and did not warrant holding the prisoner.[14] In this situation the accused would be bailed or even discharged, whatever the offence. The court did, on occasion, allow the complainant to attend to give identification evidence,[15] and would admit affidavits on the prisoner's behalf showing why bail should not be granted,[16] for example, where the affidavits showed the complaint to be a case of malicious prosecution.[17] There was, in other words, a very full review of the proceedings before the justice, as well as an opportunity to present collateral evidence. The line was drawn, however, at entering upon the ultimate question of guilt or innocence, an inquiry which would have been considered a usurpation of the function of the jury.[18] The court would not look at an alibi[19] or other excuse,[20] but simply looked to see whether or not there was a prima facie case for the prisoner to meet at trial.

(b) *Present-Day Use*

(i) *Review of Committals for Trial.* For reasons which are not apparent, habeas corpus does not appear to have been used in England since the nineteenth century to review committals for trial. As the

[12] *R. v. Marks* (1802) 3 East 157; *supra,* n. 11, p. 129.
[13] *Ex p. Krans* (1823) 1 B. & C. 258.
[14] *Supra,* n. 11, p. 129.
[15] *R. v. Greenwood* (1739) 2 Str. 1138.
[16] See e.g. *Farington* (1682) T. Jones 222; *Kirk* (1704) 5 Mod. 454.
[17] *Barney* (1701) 5 Mod. 323.
[18] *Anon.* (1704) 1 Salk. 104.
[19] *R. v. Greenwood* (1739) 2 Str. 1138.
[20] *R. v. Acton* (1729) 2 Str. 851, refusing to consider a plea of double jeopardy.

preceding few pages show, there is ample authority for the court to review committal proceedings freely. It is submitted that the law should provide a remedy for someone who has been improperly committed. Very often, an accused person may unnecessarily be put to the expense, embarrassment and worry of a full trial. Where committal proceedings are defective, or where the evidence does not meet the requisite standard, there is really no reason why habeas corpus could not be used. There are dicta in decisions of the House of Lords saying that a committal for trial cannot be reviewed on habeas corpus,[21] but it is submitted that this is unwarranted by the authorities, and an unnecessary denial of a remedy where a remedy is needed.

The Canadian courts have continued to review committals for trial on habeas corpus. The sufficiency of evidence is examined, and the accused discharged if, on the facts disclosed, the trial judge would be justified in withdrawing the case from the jury.[22] It has been held, however, that there is jurisdiction to quash the committal but refuse to discharge the applicant and remit the case for further hearing to give the Crown the opportunity to adduce further evidence, although this appears to be done only where the offence is a serious one and the issue is the gravity of the offence for which the accused should be committed.[23]

In Ontario, it is thought that a pre-Confederation statute gives the courts the power to review committals.[24] In other provinces where the

[21] *Armah* v. *Government of Ghana* [1968] A.C. 192 at 235 per Lord Reid; *Atkinson* v. *U.S. Government* [1971] A.C. 197 at 241–2 per Lord Morris of Borth-y-Gest. See also *R.* v. *Collins* [1969] 3 All E.R. 1562 at 1564 (C.C.A.). Committals are sometimes challenged on certiorari: see e.g. *R.* v. *Epping and Harlow Justices, ex p. Massaro* [1973] Q.B. 433; *R.* v. *Oxford City Justices, ex p. Berry* [1988] Q.B. 507; *Re Skogman* v. *The Queen* [1984] 2 S.C.R. 93; *Dubois* v. *The Queen* [1986] 1 S.C.R. 366; *infra*, n. 22; prohibition: *R.* v. *Aubrey-Fletcher, ex p. Ross-Monro* [1968] 1 All E.R. 99; cf. *Ex p. Coffey* [1971] 1 N.S.W.L.R. 434; mandamus has also been used: *R.* v. *Herts JJ., ex p. Larsen* (1926) 86 J.P. 205; *R.* v. *Norfolk Quarter Sessions, ex p. Brunson* [1953] 1 All E.R. 346. An invalid committal may afford grounds for appeal following conviction: see e.g. *R.* v. *Gee Bibby and Dunscombe* [1936] 2 All E.R. 89 (C.C.A.).

[22] *R.* v. *Cowden* (1947) 90 C.C.C. 101 (Ont. H.C.). In *Re Martin, Simard, and Desjardins and The Queen* (1977) 41 C.C.C. 308 at 340 (Ont. C.A.) per Estey C.J.O. it was said that the test for review of a committal on certiorari was whether there was 'an entire absence of proper material as a basis for the formation of a judicial opinion that the evidence was sufficient to put the accused on trial' rather than 'whether in the opinion of the reviewing tribunal there was evidence upon which a properly instructed jury acting judicially could convict.' The Supreme Court of Canada affirmed, *Martin* v. *The Queen* [1978] 2 S.C.R. 511, and held that the same test applied on habeas corpus.

[23] *Re Demerais and The Queen* (1978) 42 C.C.C. (2d) 287 (Ont. C.A.), overruling on this point *Re Joly and The Queen* (1978) 41 C.C.C. (2d) 538 (Ont. H.C.).

[24] *Ex p. Page* (1923) 41 C.C.C. 59 (Ont. C.A.).

statute does not apply, committals are reviewed with the same thoroughness, the courts saying that technical justification for the review is given by issuing certiorari-in-aid.[25] Whatever the technical reason, it is clear that the Canadian courts are simply following a tradition which seems to have been forgotten in England.

As well as weighing the evidence, the Canadian courts grant relief where the accused's procedural rights have been violated,[26] or where the charges are legally defective.[27]

In England, the courts regularly review extradition committals which take exactly the form of committals in domestic cases, and the practice could readily be extended. It is entirely likely that the broad powers of review which are exercised in the extradition cases stem from the old practice with respect to domestic committals.[28]

(ii) Review of Unlawful Police Practices. Quite apart from the question of using habeas corpus to review preliminary proceedings before the magistrates, there is the important matter of its use to control police practices in arresting, detaining, and questioning suspects. In this area, habeas corpus is, and probably always has been, much more a threat than a remedy which is actively used. Unfortunately, at times, a threat which is not regularly used may not be effective.

A person detained by the police can theoretically apply for habeas corpus from the moment detention begins.[29] A detainee may complain that the arrest was improper, that he or she has been improperly arrested, held for an unreasonable length of time without being charged,[30] or that the authorities have failed to bring the matter before a magistrate with due dispatch.[31] If such a case is made out, there can

---

[25] *R. v. Thompson* (1950) 99 C.C.C. 89 (B.C.S.C.); cf. *Re Barnes and Witter and The Queen* (1977) 35 C.C.C. (2d) 329 (B.C.S.C.); *Re Shumiatcher* [1962] S.C.R. 38, refusing to review a committal where there was no certiorari-in-aid. The authority of these cases seems suspect now that it is clear that the test for review is the same whether on habeas corpus or on certiorari: *supra*, n. 22, p. 131.

[26] *R. v. Churchman and Durham* (1954) 110 C.C.C. 382 (Ont. H.C.); *R. v. Feener* (1960) 129 C.C.C. 314 (Ont. H.C.); *Ex p. Burke* (1896) 2 R. de Jur. 151 (Que.). In these cases, however, the Canadian courts often act on a special statutory provision which allows them to refuse to discharge the prisoner pending further proceedings: *supra*, n. 179, p. 56.

[27] *R. v. McDearmid* (1899) 19 Can. L.T. 329 (N.S.); *R. v. Gallagher* [1925] 3 W.W.R. 757 (B.C.S.C.).

[28] *Supra*, pp. 82–3.

[29] *Re Isbell* (1929) 52 C.C.C. 170 at 173 (S.C.C.).

[30] Police and Criminal Evidence Act 1984, s.40 provides for the review of pre- and post-charge detention at various intervals by senior police officers.

[31] The common law requires that a suspected person be brought as soon as is

be no doubt that habeas corpus is an appropriate remedy. The practical problem is, of course, that a suspect who is being unlawfully held will rarely be given the opportunity to contact a solicitor or a friend. It is possible for a third party to launch proceedings on behalf of such a prisoner,[32] but this is only likely to happen in a case of extreme abuse.

The Police and Criminal Evidence Act 1984 does accord an arrested person the right to contact and be advised personally by a solicitor,[33] but there is an enormous, and it is submitted unacceptable, exception which permits the police to deny this right for up to thirty-six hours in the case of a serious arrestable offence,[34] and up to forty-eight hours where the individual is suspected of terrorism.[35] In Canada, the right on arrest or detention 'to retain and instruct counsel without delay and to be informed of that right' now has constitutional force[36] and 'detention' has been given a liberal construction.[37]

When habeas corpus proceedings are actually threatened, the likely effect is to cause the police to proceed according to law before the application actually comes before the court. Once things are put back on course, the prisoner is left to a civil action for redress and will not be able to get relief on habeas corpus.[38] This may appear to deprive the writ of significant effect as it is purely remedial and carries no preventative or deterrent force. However, the courts have condemned police practices which ignore the legal requirement to bring a prisoner promptly before the court, and in one case the police were required to pay the costs of an application which prompted them to regularize the

---

reasonably possible before a magistrate: *Wright* v. *Court* (1825) 4 B. & C. 596; Street, *Torts* (5th ed. 1972), 92. See now Police and Criminal Evidence Act 1984, s.46, which stipulates in detail when a detainee is to be brought before the court. The Canadian Criminal Code, s.503(1) provides that a suspect must be brought before a justice at least within twenty-four hours, or, where a justice is not available within twenty-four hours, then as soon as possible. In *Drouin* v. *Detention Officer of Montreal Police Headquarters* (1979) 16 C.R. (3d) 383 (Que. S.C.) a prisoner who had been detained for a week without being brought before a justice was discharged. Cf. *Ex p. Venlerberghe* (1973) 13 C.C.C. (2d) 84 (B.C.S.C.), refusing habeas corpus although the accused had been held beyond the statutory limit on the ground that he had subsequently been brought before a justice and that failure to observe the statutory limit did not deprive the court of jurisdiction.

[32] *Infra*, p. 222.·   [33] s.58(1).   [34] s.56(6).   [35] s.58(13).

[36] Charter of Rights and Freedoms, s.10(b); see also *Thornhill* v. *A.G. of Trinidad and Tobago* [1981] A.C. 61 (J.C.P.C.), interpreting a similar provision in the Constitution of Trinidad and Tobago.

[37] *R.* v. *Therens* [1985] 1 S.C.R. 613.

[38] *Infra*, pp. 180–1, 186–7.

situation by laying charges and having the prisoner released on bail.[39] Donaldson L.J. emphasized that habeas corpus is alive and well and that 'all should know that the writ of habeas corpus has not fallen into disuse, but is ... a real and available remedy', adding that 'habeas corpus is a remedy for abuse of power and it should rarely be necessary to invoke it.'[40]

(iii) Habeas Corpus to Obtain Bail. It has already been seen that, as the principal method of obtaining bail, habeas corpus once was an essential aspect of criminal procedure. It was sometimes said that habeas corpus and the Act of 1679 absolutely entitled persons charged with misdemeanour to be bailed:[41] it is more accurate to say that the remedy of habeas corpus merely ensured that there was a quick and readily accessible channel for bail applications where the justices had acted improperly.[42]

Once the usual and accepted method of applying for bail, habeas corpus gradually gave way during the nineteenth century to a summary chambers application which dispensed with the need to have the prisoner brought before the court.[43] This sort of distinct summary procedure, designed particularly for the purpose of bail and which is now used in most jurisdictions,[44] is undoubtedly an offspring of habeas corpus.[45] It is really nothing more than a simplified habeas corpus application, and in a sense, all bail applications are rooted in the law of habeas corpus.

The rules of the Supreme Court now provide that 'every application to the High Court in respect of bail in any criminal proceeding ... must be made by a summons before a judge in chambers ...'[46] It may be, however, that the rules are not intended to preclude habeas corpus in certain exceptional circumstances and there is an inherent power in

---

[39] *R.* v. *Holmes, ex p. Sherman* [1981] 2 All E.R. 612.

[40] Ibid. at 616.

[41] *R.* v. *Judd* (1788) 2 T.R. 255; *Re Frost* (1888) 4 T.L.R. 757; *R.* v. *Larkin* (1913) 48 I.L.T. 95.

[42] See *R.* v. *Phillips* (1922) 86 J.P. 188, where the cases cited *supra*, n. 41, were not followed.

[43] Short and Mellor, *Crown Practice* (2nd ed. 1908), 284. Two early examples are *R.* v. *Massey* (1817) 6 M. & S. 108; *R.* v. *Jones* (1817) 1 B. & Ald. 208, where the applications for habeas corpus were altered by the court to save the prisoner the expense of being brought up.

[44] The English procedure is laid down by the Rules of the Supreme Court, Ord. 79, r.9.

[45] *Supra*, n. 43.

[46] Ord. 79, r.9(1).

the High Court to grant bail.[47] It has been held in Canada, for example, that bail may be secured by way of habeas corpus on behalf of a prisoner appealing a court martial conviction in the absence of any statutory scheme,[48] or where held under immigration legislation[49] or for extradition.[50]

Before 1967, the High Court clearly could grant bail where it had been refused, but its power to vary bail set by a magistrate was dubious.[51] It was held, however, that where there had been imposed excessive bail, so as to contravene the Bill of Rights 1688, an application for habeas corpus could be made to the Divisional Court on the grounds that the detention was unlawful.[52] There seems to have been no other effective remedy against excessive bail[53] until the Criminal Justice Act 1967, which expressly empowered the High Court on the ordinary summons proceeding to vary the conditions of bail set by the magistrate.[54] While the provision of the statutory remedy will render recourse to habeas corpus unnecessary in the first instance, attempts have been made to use the writ to get to the Divisional Court when the chambers application fails,[55] as there is no

---

[47] *R. v. Secretary of State for the Home Department, ex p. Turkoglu* [1988] Q.B. 398 (C.A.); *Re Di Stefano* (1976) 30 C.C.C. (2d) 310 (N.W.T.S.C.); *Re Reddekopp and The Queen* (1983) 6 C.C.C. (3d) 241 (Ont. H.C.); *Dunstan v. Crown Solicitor* (1980) 24 S.A.S.R. 64; *Tobin v. Minister for Correctional Services* (1980) 24 S.A.S.R. 389; but cf. *R. v. Rademeyer* [1985] 1 N.S.W.L.R. 285.

[48] *R. v. Hicks* (1981) 63 C.C.C. (2d) 547 (Alta. C.A.).

[49] *Ex p. Augustin* (1976) 31 C.C.C. (2d) 160 (Que. C.A.).

[50] *Re Lawrence and the United States of America and The Queen* (1980) 54 C.C.C. (2d) 551 (Man. C.A.); *Re Meier and Warden of the Lower Mainland Detention Centre* (1982) 3 C.C.C. (3d) 472 (B.C.S.C.); cf. *Sowa v. R.* (1982) 18 Man. R. (2d) 4 (C.A.) (no jurisdiction to grant judicial interim release on habeas corpus pending parole board hearing).

[51] The doubts seemed to have been based on *Ex p. Speculand* [1946] K.B. 48, which, however, perhaps was distinguishable as it dealt with the case of a convicted prisoner who had lodged an appeal.

[52] *Ex p. Thomas* [1956] Crim. L.R. 119; for a similarly based application which failed on the merits, see *Ex p. Goswani* [1967] Crim. L.R. 234. See also *Dunstan v. Crown Solicitor* (1980) 24 S.A.S.R. 64 at 66: 'where the conditions of bail are so unrealistic as to be tantamount to an abdication of the power to exercise the discretion to grant bail ... habeas corpus would lie.'

[53] Cf. *Linford v. Fitzroy* (1849) 13 Q.B. 240 for the possibility of an action in trespass where the magistrate acted with malice, and *R. v. Badger* (1843) 4 Q.B. 468, holding that the refusal to accept sufficient sureties could amount to a criminal offence. Judicial review may be available in certain cases: see *R. v. Nottingham Justices, ex p. Davies* [1981] Q.B. 38.

[54] s.22(1).

[55] Cf. Hampton, *Criminal Procedure* (3rd ed. 1982), 61: 'Applying for habeas corpus as an indirect application for bail is not approved.'

appeal from an order on a bail application.[56] Such a habeas corpus application was attempted in 1965 in a case where bail had been refused by the magistrate and by a High Court judge.[57] While the court did refuse the application on the merits, Lord Parker C.J. made it clear that he was doubtful about the court's jurisdiction. He suspected that since bail applications on summons were essentially applications for habeas corpus, the statutory prohibition against successive applications[58] ruled out the possibility of bringing the matter before the Divisional Court. In the same case, the extraordinary step was taken of a further habeas corpus application to the Lord Chancellor.[59] Gardiner L.C. held that whatever the nature of his jurisdiction to grant habeas corpus, the application was precluded by the prohibition of successive applications.

It is now provided by the Rules of Court that: 'If an applicant to the High Court in any criminal proceeding is refused bail by a judge in chambers, the applicant shall not be entitled to make a fresh application for bail to any other judge or to a Divisional Court.'[60] The question remains whether an 'application for bail' is the same as an application for habeas corpus to get bail. It could be argued that if the two were the same, a successive bail application would have been barred by the rule against successive applications and made the provision unnecessary. It can only be said that the question has not been conclusively determined. In a case where both the magistrate and judge at chambers set bail at an excessive amount, the Divisional Court might find it possible to put the matter right on habeas corpus, but the court could very well identify a bail application with an application for habeas corpus so as to preclude relief.

2. HABEAS CORPUS AND DELAY IN TRIAL

Perhaps the most neglected aspect of habeas corpus has been its use as a device to secure the right of accused persons, detained pending their

---

[56] *R.* v. *Foote* (1883) 10 Q.B.D. 378.
[57] *R.* v. *Kray* (1965) *The Times*, 17 Feb.
[58] Administration of Justice Act 1960, s.14, discussed in detail *infra*, pp. 207–10. Successive applications for bail are allowed in some jurisdictions; *R.* v. *Quinby* [1967] 2 C.C.C. 186 (Alta. S.C.); *R.* v. *Higgs* [1962] N.S.W.R. 34; *contra Re Johnson* (1958) 122 C.C.C. 144 (Sask. Q.B.).
[59] *Re Kray, Kray and Smith* [1965] 1 All E.R. 710.
[60] Ord. 79, r.9(12). *In the Application of Harrod* [1978] 1 N.S.W.L.R. 331 holds that habeas corpus does not lie to challenge a bail order by a superior court.

trial, to be either tried quickly or released. One of the most important provisions of the celebrated Habeas Corpus Act 1679, s.6 (now repealed)[61] gave a prisoner the right to be either indicted within one term or session after commitment, or bailed and to be either tried within two terms or sessions or discharged. The section provided as follows:

Provided alwayes . . . that if any person or persons shall be committed for high treason or felony, plainely and specially expressed in the warrant of committment upon his prayer or petition in open court the first weeke of the terme or first day of the sessions of oyer and terminer or generall goale delivery to be brought to his tryall shall not be indicted sometime in the next terme sessions of oyer and terminer or generall goale delivery after such committment it shall and may be lawful to and for the judges of the Court of Kings Bench and justices of oyer and terminer or generall goale delivery and they are hereby required upon motion to them made in open court the last day of the terme sessions or goale-delivery either by the prisoner or any one in his behalfe to sett at liberty the prisoner upon baile unlesse it appeare to the judges and justices upon oath made that the witnesses for the King could not be produced the same terme sessions or generall goale-delivery. And if any person or persons committed as aforesaid upon his prayer or petition in open court the first weeke of the terme or first day of the sessions of oyer and terminer or generall goale delivery to be brought to his tryall shall not be indicted and tryed the second terme sessions of oyer and terminer or generalle goale delivery after his committment or upon his tryall shall be acquitted he shall be discharged from his imprisonment.

From the seventeenth century to the present, judges have considered this section to be the very hub of the design of the Habeas Corpus Act 1679. Lord Holt's words in 1694: '. . . the design of the Act was to prevent a man's lying under an accusation of treason, &c. above two terms',[62] were echoed by Abbott C.J. in 1825: 'The object of the Habeas Corpus Act . . . was to provide against delays in bringing persons to trial, who were committed for criminal matters'[63] and by Parker C.J. in 1959: 'The Act of 1679 was a procedural Act . . . and was directed specifically to the abuse of detaining persons in prison without bail and without bringing them to trial.'[64] As Dicey pointed

---

[61] Courts Act 1971, s.56(4), Sched. 11, Pt. IV.
[62] *Crosby's Case* (1694) 12 Mod. 66.
[63] *Ex p. Beeching* (1825) 6 D. & R. 209.
[64] *In re Hastings (No. 2)* [1959] 1 Q.B. 358 at 369. The purpose of the Act to avoid delays in trial is also discussed in *R. v. M'Cartie* (1859) 11 Ir. C.L.R. 188, and in Dicey, op. cit. 217–19. See also Chitty, *Criminal Law* (1816), vol. 1, 130–1: 'But the principal ground for bailing upon habeas corpus, and indeed the evil the writ was chiefly intended to remedy, is the neglect of the accuser to prosecute in due time.'

out,[65] the section gave habeas corpus an important dual purpose. As a result, an accused person was able to test the validity of the warrant and charges from the moment of incarceration, but if these preliminary grounds for detention were found to be sufficient, the accused was then able to demand to be either brought quickly to trial or bailed or released.

In view of the importance of the principles at stake, it is surprising to find so little discussion of the section in the modern cases. Indeed, this once-important provision was unceremoniously repealed by the Courts Act 1971.[66] It had undoubtedly become difficult to apply s.6 because of its archaic language[67] but the principle it established, namely, the guarantee of a remedy to ensure speedy trial, should have been continued.

Indeed, once it is accepted that in certain circumstances detention pending trial is justified, then habeas corpus protection is defective unless there is some limit on the time a person may be held without trial. Justification for pre-trial detention is plainly conditional upon having the prisoner brought to trial as quickly as possible. The principle of ensuring that every detention is justified in law would be violated if accused persons were held for unlimited periods of time without trial and without remedy. The right to be either tried according to law or released is really the right that habeas corpus is supposed to secure.

In place of the provision in the Act of 1679, the Courts Act contains a rather toothless provision which stipulates that accused persons are to be tried within the time fixed by the rules of the Crown Court 'unless a judge of the Crown Court otherwise orders.'[68] The period

[65] Dicey, op. cit. 218.

[66] Courts Act 1971, s.56(4), Sched. 11, Pt. IV.

[67] See *R.* v. *Campbell* [1959] 2 All E.R. 557 at 559–60: 'It may be that in the conditions of today it is difficult, if not impossible, to comply with the requirements of the statute. That may be an argument of validity and force for amending or reconstructing the law of habeas corpus, but today I must construe the Act 1679 as it is' (per Judge Laski, Liverpool Crown Court). In *Clarkson* v. *Director-General of Corrections* [1986] V.R. 425 (Full Ct.) it was held after a detailed review that the guarantee of s.6, although not repealed, could no longer be applied in the face of modern legislation in Victoria. Cf., however, the dictum of Lord Goddard C.J. in *R.* v. *Oliver* (1957) 42 Cr. App. R. 27 at 32, where he referred to the 'stringent provisions' of the section as still being an effective guarantee. See also the comment made by Lord Devlin in *The Criminal Prosecution in England* (1960), 84: 'What guarantee is there that the accused will be tried and the case disposed of at the Assizes or Sessions to which he is committed? The guarantee is contained in the Habeas Corpus Act 1679, s.6. Although the letter of the Act may be a little obscure, the spirit of it still governs criminal procedure.'

[68] Supreme Court Act 1981, s.77(2)(b).

fixed by the rules is eight weeks after the committal.[69] The Act fails to provide a sanction in the event of delay beyond the period specified and there is nothing to indicate appropriate grounds for an order extending the time.

There have been several studies which have shown that a significant proportion of cases take an unacceptable length of time to come to trial.[70] The Habeas Corpus Act 1679 extended a positive protection rather than an administrative direction, and it may be asked whether the example of the Act should not be followed today.

In several Commonwealth jurisdictions, the Act and s.6 are still in force,[71] and there is, therefore, practical as well as historical justification for looking at the way the section actually worked, and at the nature of the protection it provided.

(i) Protection Extended by the Section. It is provided that the prosecution may have a legitimate excuse for not indicting the prisoner within the first term or session where the cause of the delay is the unavailability of witnesses. There are several cases of prisoners being bailed pursuant to the section where an indictment was not preferred within one term or session.[72] There is, however, no exception whatsoever to the prosecution's obligation to bring the accused to trial within two

[69] Crown Court Rules 1982 (S.I. 1982, 1109), r.24(b).

[70] Gibson, *Time Spent Awaiting Trial* (1960: Home Office Research Unit Project); *Report of the Interdepartmental Committee on the Business of the Criminal Courts* (1961: Cmnd. 1289); *Royal Commission on Assizes and Quarter Sessions*, 1966–9 (1971: Cmnd. 4153). Vennard, 'Court Delay and Speedy Trial Provisions' [1985] Crim. L.R. 73; Osborne, 'Delay in the Administration of Criminal Justice: Commonwealth Developments and Experience' (1980), Commonwealth Secretariat. The problem has been the subject of judicial comment: *R. v. Lawrence* [1982] A.C. 510 at 514 per Lord Hailsham; *R. v. Governor of Brixton Prison, ex p. Walsh* [1985] 1 A.C. 154 at 166–7 per Lord Fraser of Tullybelton.

[71] The Act was applied in Canada in *R. v. Chapman and Currie* (1971) 2 C.C.C. (2d) 237 (Ont. D.C.) (aff'd at 252n.), discussed in detail in my note in (1972) 14 Crim. L.Q. 399 (which contains much of the material used here). For other Canadian cases discussing the section, see *R. v. Keeler* (1877) 7 P.R. 117 (Ont.); *R. v. Cameron* (1897) 1 C.C.C. 169 (Que. Q.B.); *R. v. Dean* (1913) 21 C.C.C. 310 (B.C.S.C.). S.6 was held to have been superseded in effect by modern legislation in *Clarkson v. Director-General of Corrections* [1986] V.R. 425 (Full Ct.). The Irish Habeas Corpus Act 1782, s.6 contains a similar protection. For an unsuccessful attempt to have it applied see *R. (O'Reilly) v. A.G. of Irish Free State* [1928] 1 I.R. 83. See also *Re Singer* (1960) 97 I.L.T.R. 130, upholding on habeas corpus the right of the prisoner to be tried before the first 'available court'. The operation of the 1679 Act in Jamaica is discussed in the decision of Fox J. in *R. v. Shirley Chen See* [1972] Jamaica Law Journal 13.

[72] See e.g. *Fitz-Patrick's Case* (1700) 1 Salk. 103; *Barney's Case* (1701) 5 Mod. 323; *R. v. Bell and his wife* (1737) Andr. 64.

Habeas Corpus in Criminal Law

terms or sessions. The section requires the court to discharge the accused, whatever reason may be offered for the delay.[73]

(*ii*) *The Time within which the Accused Must be Tried.* The actual effect of the Act's guarantee of a speedy trial varied, depending upon where the prisoner was to be tried. At common law, persons charged with treason or felony could be tried by the Court of King's Bench at Westminster, although it was never very common for ordinary criminal cases to be tried there.[74] Commissioners of oyer and terminer and gaol delivery could try treason or felony. These commissions were issued by the Crown, as the practice developed, so that there would be commissioners in each country of the kingdom at regular intervals.[75] The commission of oyer and terminer, 'to hear and determine', empowered its holder only to try indictments found at the same assizes, but the commission of gaol delivery permitted the justice to try and deliver every prisoner in gaol in the circuit town, however that person had been committed and for whatever crime.[76] It became established practice that the judges of assize would also hold these two commissions, and this was one way of ensuring that every person detained for a criminal offence would be tried within the time of the next assizes, even before the Habeas Corpus Act.[77]

Sessions of oyer and terminer and gaol delivery at Blackstone's time were held twice every year in each county, except in the four northern counties where they were held only once a year, and in London and Middlesex, where such sessions were held eight times each year.[78] The court year at Westminster was divided into four terms. The

[73] Cf., however, *R. v. Bowen* (1840) 9 C. & P. 509, where the Crown's request for a postponement of the trial to the next assize was countered by an argument based on the 1679 Act, since the accused had already waited two terms. Williams J., at p. 512, granted the postponement, holding that the Act 'is human law and must be humanly interpreted' and the prisoner's trial 'must be subject to human contingency'. This is not, however, a case within the section, since it does not appear that a prayer was entered, and the application was made by the prosecution. Cf., also, *Bernardi's Case* (1728) 10 Har. St. Tr. Appendix 63, where the prisoner, charged with treason in 1696, died after forty years in Newgate without trial, having brought unsuccessful habeas corpus applications in the intervals between the various bills of attainder against him.
[74] 1 Holdsworth, op. cit. 212–13.
[75] Ibid. 280–1; 4 Bl. *Comm.*, 269–70.
[76] 4 *Inst.*, 164, 168; 4 Bl. *Comm.*, 270.
[77] 4 Bl. *Comm.*, 270. In one case, before the Act, bail was granted to a prisoner brought out of Wales on the grounds that there had been no gaol delivery: *Anon.* (1654) Style 418. Section 8 of the Act provides that no prisoner is to be removed from the circuit town while the justices of assize are in attendance.
[78] 4 Bl. *Comm.*, 268–9.

protection of s.6 varied greatly, therefore, depending upon where the prisoner was committed.[79] At about the time the Act was passed, the period within which the prisoner would have to have been tried or discharged was up to three months in London and Middlesex before the sessions, up to six months before the King's Bench, up to one year in a southern county, and up to two years in one of the northern counties.

(*iii*) *The Prayer for Trial.*   It is clear that the prisoner had to make a prayer or petition, either in person or by counsel, to be tried in order to gain the benefit of the section.[80] The purpose of requiring the prayer was probably to excite the vigilance of the prosecutor, and to prevent the authorities from being caught off-guard by a forgotten prisoner.[81] The prayer had to be entered within the appropriate period,[82] and before the court where the prisoner ought to be tried.[83] Attempts were made to get around this last-mentioned rule because the assizes in some of the more remote counties were infrequent, but a prayer entered elsewhere than the place where the trial should be held did not suffice, notwithstanding this unfairness.[84]

The courts refused to bend these statutory requirements, but relied upon their inherent common law power to grant bail in certain cases where the Act was not complied with.[85] Bail in treason and felony matters before the Act was purely a matter for the court's discretion, and one of the grounds for granting bail had been want of

---

[79] This is discussed further, *infra*, n. 84.

[80] *Anon.* (1680) 1 Vent. 346; *R.* v. *Campbell* [1959] 2 All E.R. 557.

[81] This is suggested in *R.* v. *M'Cartie* (1859) 2 Ir. C.L.R. 188 at 194.

[82] *Lord Aylesbury's Case* (1701) 1 Salk. 103. The same case held that where the Act had been suspended, the prayer need only be entered at the first opportunity after the suspension's expiry.

[83] *R.* v. *Delamere* (1685) Comb. 6; *R.* v. *Leason & Edwards* (1700) 1 Ld. Raym. 61; *R.* v. *Yates* (1691) 1 Show. 190.

[84] In *R.* v. *Yates* (1691) 1 Show. 190 at 191, the prisoner had been committed for high treason at Hull, and his counsel moved to enter his prayer at Westminster, and reports his argument as follows: 'I urged the privilege of this Act, the liberty of the subject, the inconveniences on the other side, that then a Secretary of State might send a man to Hull or Canterbury where assizes are rare, and he is certainly a prisoner for a year or two, which spoils the true intent of our law-makers, for then slavery would be as rife as before the making of the Act.' The argument was rejected, although the prisoner was bailed on other grounds.

[85] *Gage* 3 Vin. Abridg. 518; *Wyndham* (1715) 1 Str. 2; *Lord Aylesbury's Case* (1701) 1 Salk. 103. Cf. the suggestion made in *R.* v. *Delamere* (1685) Comb. 6, that within the period limited by the Statute 'the discretion of bailing, which the Court had before, is now restrained by that Act.'

prosecution.[86] Moreover, while there is no right to discharge outside the Act, it has been held that the court may stay proceedings on the ground of unreasonable delay where it considers the delay to constitute an abuse of its process.[87]

(iv) Persons Protected by s.6. The section covered only persons charged with treason or felony. Those charged with misdemeanours were not protected, probably because they were considered to have a right to be bailed pending trial.[88] Misdemeanants were finally given a similar protection by the Assizes Relief Act 1889,[89] a statute which seems to have been modelled on s.6 of the Habeas Corpus Act. When the distinction between felony and misdemeanour was abolished in 1967,[90] s.6 was significantly weakened by the repeal of the words 'or felony' so that from 1967 until 1971 when the section was repealed, only those charged with treason were protected.

(v) Accused Free on Bail. It is doubtful that the section was intended to extend to persons who had been bailed, but not tried, within two terms, and there is some old authority to the effect that 'a man bailed cannot make his prayer.'[91] In two Canadian cases,[92] relief was granted under s.6 to an accused who had been bailed, but this was refused in an Irish case.[93] While there can be little doubt about the propriety of giving preference to the trial of accused remanded in custody, delay may have serious consequences for someone on bail, and it is submitted that

[86] *Morgan* (1610) Bulst. 84; *Pye's Case* (1659) 2 Sid. 179; *Crofton* (1662) 1 Keble 305. In *Gage* 3 Vin. Abridg. 518, Holt C.J. said: '... there were many cases omitted out of the habeas act, and before this act there was a rule at common law, that persons in prison, in convenient time, must be bailed, and that trials for capital offences ought to be recent, and that the Court would consider of the circumstances, if the party were to be bailed.'
[87] *R.* v. *Campbell* [1959] 2 All E.R. 557 at 560: *infra*, n. 96, p. 144; *R.* v. *Robins* (1844) 1 Cox C.C. 114; *R.* v. *Brentford Justices, ex p. Wong* [1981] Q.B. 445; *R.* v. *Oxford City Justices, ex p. Smith* (1982) 75 Cr. App. R. 200; *R.* v. *Derby Crown Court, ex p. Brooks* (1985) 80 Cr. App. R. 164; *Bell* v. *D.P.P.* [1985] A.C. 937 at 950 (J.C.P.C.); *R.* v. *Bow St. Magistrates Court, ex p. Van Der Holst* (1985) 83 Cr. App. R. 114.
[88] Cf. also *Anon.* (1810) Russ. & Ry. C.C. 173. Commissioners of gaol delivery had a discretion, often exercised, to discharge anyone in custody where the assizes intervened before the quarter sessions to which the misdemeanant had been committed, as the accused ought to be tried by the first available court. See also *Re Singer* (1960) 97 I.L.T.R. 130.
[89] Repealed by the Courts Act 1971, s.56(4), Sched. 11, Pt. IV.
[90] Criminal Law Act 1967, s.10(2), Sched. 3, Pt. III.
[91] *R.* v. *Yates* (1691) 1 Show. 190; Gude, *Practice* 273. Cf. the broader issue of the restraint required to justify habeas corpus: *infra*, Chapter VII.
[92] *R.* v. *Cameron* (1897) 1 C.C.C. 169 (Que. Q.B.); *R.* v. *Chapman and Currie* (1971) 2 C.C.C. (2d) 237 (Ont. D.C.).
[93] *A.G.* v. *Blennerhasset* (1933) 67 I.L.T.R. 136.

some guarantee of speedy trial should be extended to such persons as well.

(*vi*) *Effect of an Order of Discharge.* S.6 is the only section of the 1679 Act to use the word 'discharge'. The Act was primarily designed to ensure that persons accused of crime could apply for and obtain bail pending trial. It was only where the prisoner had not been tried after two terms that the Act directed discharge. It would seem that the accused was discharged from custody and that the proceedings against him were brought to a halt. It is doubtful, however, that such an order of discharge would have operated as an absolute bar to further proceedings for the same offence. The prosecution would have to have been launched anew, and the accused would probably have had no protection against further proceedings as the substance of the charge had not been decided on the habeas corpus application.[94] It may be that a bar to further proceedings is the only iron-clad guarantee of speedy trial: it does not seem, however, that the 1679 Act had that effect.

(*vii*) *Conclusion.* It should not be supposed that a legal protection against delay in trial would solve the problem of slowness in the administration of justice. The solution lies in improved administration and added resources, but this is no reason to reject the idea of a statutory protection against delay. As the law of England now stands, there is very little offered in the way of protection.[95] It may be possible

[94] In *R. v. Hill* [1982] Tas R. 1, it was held that absent circumstances amounting to abuse of process, discharge pursuant to s.355 of the Criminal Code of Tasmania, a provision derived from s.6, did not bar further prosecution. An order of discharge on habeas corpus only operates to bar further proceedings where those proceedings would involve the potential re-litigation of the point at issue: see *infra*, pp. 213–17 for a detailed discussion.

[95] In *Edwards* (1975) 62 Cr. App. R. 166 it was held that r.19 of the Crown Court Rules 1971, requiring the trial to commence within 8 weeks of committal, was directory only and that failure to comply afforded no ground for appeal from conviction. Cf. the limitation on the length of time a prisoner may be held pending extradition under certain treaties: see e.g. *R. v. Governor of Ashford Remand Centre, ex p. Besse* [1973] 1 W.L.R. 969; *Government of the Federal Republic of Germany* v. *Sotiriadis* [1975] A.C. 1; *Government of Belgium* v. *Postlethwaite* [1987] 3 W.L.R. 365 (H.L.); *Ingram* v. *A.G. for the Commonwealth* [1980] 1 N.S.W.L.R. 190. Delay in proceedings may also be grounds for refusal to commit under the Fugitive Offenders Act: see e.g. *R. v. Governor of Brixton Prison, ex p. Campbell* [1956] Crim. L.R. 624; *Union of India* v. *Narang* [1978] A.C. 247; *Kakis* v. *Government of the Republic of Cyprus* [1978] 1 W.L.R. 779 (H.L.); *Oskar* v. *Government of the Commonwealth of Australia* [1988] A.C. 366. Cf. *Re Rojas and The Queen* (1978) 41 C.C.C. (2d) 566 (Ont. C.A.), holding that delay caused by difficulty in finding a country to accept a prisoner subject to a deportation order is not grounds for habeas corpus. See also *Re Lind and Sweden* (1987) 36 C.C.C. (3d) 327 (Ont. C.A.), holding that delay by the extraditing state is not grounds pursuant to s.7 of the Charter for habeas corpus.

to appeal to the court's power to prevent an abuse of its process in the case of a long delay,[96] but that sort of protection is, at best, uncertain. In a few cases, delay has been taken into account in determining sentence,[97] and it may afford grounds for bail in certain cases.[98] There have been applications under the European Convention for the Protection of Human Rights to the Commission, including some from England.[99]

The Canadian Criminal Code contains certain protections,[100] and the Charter of Rights and Freedoms guarantees 'any person charged with an offence ... the right to be tried within a reasonable time'.[101] This guarantee has produced a significant volume of case law.[102] It undoubtedly has s.6 of the Habeas Corpus Act as its source and inspiration.[103] While s.6 has been repealed in England, and will be applied only with difficulty in Commonwealth jurisdictions because of

---

[96] *Supra*, n. 87, p. 142; *R. v. K.* (1972) 5 C.C.C. (2d) 46 (B.C.S.C.); *A.G. for Saskatchewan v. McDougall* [1972] 2 W.W.R. 66 (Sask. D.C.); cf. *R. v. Myles (No. 2)* (1972) 17 C.R.N.S. 241 (N.S. Cty. Ct.) refusing relief where the delay emanated from the court itself. See also *R. v. Thompson (No. 1)* (1945) 86 C.C.C. 193 (H.C.), where relief was given against delay in court martial proceedings, but cf. *R. v. O/C Depot Battalion, R.A.S.C. Colchester, ex p. Elliot* [1949] 1 All E.R. 373.

[97] *Reynolds & Milne* [1956] Crim. L.R. 2, 290; *Bower v. R.* (1955) 113 C.C.C. 270 (Sask. C.A.).

[98] *Supra*, n. 86, p. 142; *R. v. Pascoe* [1960] N.S.W.R. 481.

[99] *X. v. U.K.* (1971) 37 Collection of Decisions 51; *X. v. United Kingdom* (1979) 3 E.H.R.R. 271.

[100] S.525 requires judicial review where an accused has been detained for more than ninety days pending trial. In *Ex p. Mitchell* (1975) 23 C.C.C. (2d) 473 (B.C.C.A.); *Ex p. Gioia* (1975) 24 C.C.C. (2d) 298 (B.C.S.C.); and *Ex p. Amos* (1975) 24 C.C.C. (2d) 552 (B.C.S.C.) it was held on habeas corpus that failure to observe this requirement constitutes grounds for release from custody. Cf., however, *Ex p. Gooden* (1975) 27 C.C.C. (2d) 161 (Ont. H.C.); *Ex p. Cordes* (1976) 31 C.C.C. (2d) 279 (Alta. C.A.); *Re Dass and The Queen* (1978) 39 C.C.C. (2d) 365 (Man. C.A.); *R. v. Johnson* (1980) 57 C.C.C. (2d) 49 (Ont. H.C.), holding that while habeas corpus would lie in a case of inordinate delay, failure to comply with the ninety-day rule does not render the detention unlawful and the appropriate remedy is mandamus to compel the review contemplated by the statute. In *Re Ferreira and The Queen* (1981) 58 C.C.C. (2d) 147 (B.C.C.A.) it was held that failure to comply with the ninety-day rule rendered the detention unlawful, but that the applicant could be remanded so that the appropriate hearing could be held.

[101] s.11(b).

[102] See e.g. *Mills v. The Queen* [1986] 1 S.C.R. 863 and *Rahey v. The Queen* [1987] 1 S.C.R. 588.

[103] Reference may be made as well to the stringent provisions adopted in some American jurisdictions, said to have s.6 of the 1679 act as their source: *Petition of Provoo* 17 F.R.D. 183 at 196–7 (1955). For surveys of the American provisions from a Commonwealth perspective, see Misner, 'Legislatively Mandated Speedy Trials' (1984) 8 Crim. L.J. 17; Vennard, 'Court Delay and Speedy Trial Provisions' [1985] Crim. L.R. 73. The United States Constitution guarantees the right to speedy trial; for interpretation, see *Barker v. Wingo* 407 U.S. 514 (1972); *U.S. v. MacDonald* 456 U.S. 1 (1982);

its archaic language, it provides an example and historical precedent for a protection against excessive delay in trial.

3. REVIEW OF CONVICTIONS

The English courts have a decided aversion to the review of convictions on habeas corpus.[104] As Lawton L.J. put it: 'A writ of habeas corpus is probably the most cherished sacred cow in the British constitution; but the law has never allowed it to graze in all legal pastures.'[105] Many aspects of this question have already been canvassed in the chapter dealing with the scope of review. It will be remembered that while there are cases from the nineteenth century in which summary convictions were reviewed, and while theoretically this still should be possible, there are no modern examples.[106] Convictions on indictment by courts of sessions, courts of assize, or the King's Bench have never been reviewed on habeas corpus, although it has been said that such review is theoretically possible where the court patently exceeds jurisdiction.[107]

The reason for the refusal of the English courts to allow habeas corpus to develop as a post-conviction remedy is undoubtedly a strong desire to preserve finality in the criminal process. Until modern times, it was not even always possible to appeal a criminal conviction,[108] and the judges saw no reason to depart from the view that trial by jury guaranteed fairness in criminal proceedings. Now that it is possible to appeal convictions, there is a marked desire to confine matters to the normal channels for appeal, and to stifle the development of any collateral method of attack.[109] If the appellate courts fail to remedy an

---

U.S. v. *Gouveia* 467 U.S. 190 (1984); *U.S.* v. *Loud Hawk* 106 S.Ct. 648 (1986). See also *Bell* v. *D.P.P.* [1985] 1 A.C. 937 (J.C.P.C.), interpreting the Jamaican constitutional guarantee to a trial within a reasonable time.

[104] *Re Featherstone* (1953) 37 Cr. App. R. 146; *Ex p. Corke* [1954] 2 All E.R. 440; *Re Philpot* [1960] 1 All E.R. 165; *Re Wring, Re Cook* [1960] 1 All E.R. 536; *Ex p. Hinds* [1961] 1 All E.R. 707.

[105] *Linnet* v. *Coles* [1987] Q.B. 555 at 561 (C.A.).

[106] *Supra*, pp. 31–2.

[107] *Supra*, pp. 49–51.

[108] The general right of appeal was first given by the Criminal Appeal Act 1907. It had been possible under the Crown Cases Act 1848 for the trial judge to state a case, for the Court of Crown Cases Reserved, but this was discretionary and rarely used: 1 Stephen, op. cit. 312. For common law remedies, see *supra*, pp. 46–7.

[109] See *Re Korponay* v. *Kulik* [1980] 2 S.C.R. 265, upholding the refusal of the Quebec courts to entertain a habeas corpus application challenging a conviction on

injustice, the matter is left to the discretion of the Home Secretary. This may even allow the matter to come again before the courts as the Home Secretary has the power to refer a case to the Court of Appeal.[110] This contrasts markedly with the use of habeas corpus in the United States. There, the principal use of the writ is as a post-conviction remedy. Habeas corpus provides a vehicle for prisoners convicted in the state courts to have the proceedings reviewed in the federal courts where a right guaranteed by the constitution has been violated.[111] It is apparently thought that a constitutional claim can best be weighed in a forum which is divorced from the guilt-finding process, and a forum which is able to establish uniform minimum national standards for the administration of criminal justice.[112] There is, however, by no means unanimity on the propriety of federal habeas corpus jurisdiction,[113] and this is understandable in view of the protracted litigation which may follow any criminal proceeding which gives rise to a constitutional claim. Although Canada has opted for an entrenched Charter of Rights, it is unlikely that habeas corpus will be permitted to be used to open a collateral method of attack upon convictions,[114] unless for some reason no other avenue is available to remedy the Charter violation.[115]

In any case, the American experience with habeas corpus significantly differs from that of the English. The writ transplanted has virtually

indictment where an appeal was available and where the Supreme Court of Canada had already granted leave to appeal the conviction. See also *A.G.B.C.* v. *Johnson* (1982) 31 C.R. (3d) 329 (B.C.C.A.); *Zamai* v. *R.* (1981) 24 C.R. (2d) 33 (B.C.S.C.). In *Re Kestle* [1980] 2 N.Z.L.R. 337, habeas corpus to challenge a conviction for murder was refused, but on the grounds that there was no jurisdictional error.

[110] Criminal Appeal Act 1968, s.17.

[111] *Brown* v. *Allen* 344 U.S. 443 (1953).

[112] For discussion, see 'Developments in the Law—Federal Habeas Corpus' (1970) 83 Harv. L.R. 1038; Wechsler, 'Habeas Corpus and the Supreme Court: Reconsidering the Reach of the Great Writ' (1988) 59 U. of Col. L.R. 167.

[113] See e.g. Friendly, 'Is Innocence Irrelevant? Collateral Attack on Criminal Judgments' (1970) 38 U. Chi. L.R. 142. Recent Supreme Court decisions have tended to restrict the availability of federal habeas corpus to review state convictions: see e.g. *Stone* v. *Powell* 428 U.S. 465 (1976); *Wainwright* v. *Sykes* 433 U.S. 72 (1977); *Sumner* v. *Mata* 449 U.S. 539 (1981); *Engle* v. *Isaac* 456 U.S. 107 (1982); *U.S.* v. *Frady* 456 U.S. 152 (1982).

[114] *Re Wilson and The Queen* (1987) 35 C.C.C. (3d) 316 (Man. C.A.).

[115] See especially *Gamble* v. *The Queen* [1988] 2 S.C.R. 595 at 642 per Wilson J.: '. . . courts should not allow habeas corpus applications to be used to circumvent the appropriate appeal process, but neither should they bind themselves by overly rigid rules about the availability of habeas corpus which may have the effect of denying applicants access to courts to obtain Charter relief.'

grown into a different strain altogether. The Americans have taken the writ's fundamental purpose of ensuring that every imprisonment is legally justifiable, and developed it fully according to their profound belief in the importance of broadly defined constitutional guarantees.

4. REVIEW OF SENTENCE

(a) *Habeas Corpus to Determine the Length of Sentence*

While the English courts are hesitant to allow convicted prisoners to apply for habeas corpus, there can be little doubt that it is the proper remedy where the applicant alleges that he or she is being detained longer than is legally warranted by the sentence.[116] It may be contended, for example, that a series of sentences was intended to run concurrently rather than consecutively,[117] that the prison authorities have incorrectly interpreted the legal effect of the sentence,[118] or simply that the sentence has expired.[119]

There are only a few reported English cases of habeas corpus to interpret a sentence of imprisonment,[120] but the practice is relatively common in Canada.[121] In a few cases, both English[122] and

---

[116] *R.* v. *Williams* (1909) 3 Cr. App. R. 2; *Re Featherstone* (1953) 37 Cr. App. R. 146; *Re Wring, Re Cook* [1960] 1 All E.R. 536; *Re Savundra* [1973] 3 All E.R. 606; *R.* v. *Governor of Blundeston Prison, ex p. Gaffney* [1982] All E.R. 492. For the procedure regarding applications by prisoners, see *infra*, pp. 224–7.

[117] *Ex p. Askew* [1963] Crim. L.R. 507; and see *R.* v. *Governor of Leeds Prison, ex p. Huntley* [1972] 1 W.L.R. 1016, where the prisoner argued (unsuccessfully) that a warrant of execution should have been executed so as to start the time under it running while he was held on remand for other charges. Cf. *Reid* v. *Hughes* (1982) 29 S.A.S.R. 207, where habeas corpus was granted in similar circumstances.

[118] *R.* v. *Governor of Leeds Prison, ex p. Stafford* [1964] 2 Q.B. 625, where, however, there was a question of remission which the court felt should be left to the Home Secretary.

[119] *R.* v. *Williams* (1909) 3 Cr. App. R. 2; *Re Featherstone* (1953) 37 Cr. App. R. 146.

[120] *Supra*, nn. 116–19.

[121] See e.g. *Re Ange* [1970] 5 C.C.C. 371 (Ont. C.A.); *Re McCaud* [1970] 1 C.C.C. 293 (Ont. H.C.); *Ex p. Simoneau* [1971] 2 O.R. 561 (Ont. C.A.); *Ex p. Kolot* (1973) 13 C.C.C. (2d) 417 (B.C.S.C.); *Ex p. Heinsworth* (1974) 21 C.C.C. (2d) 26 Ont. H.C.); *R.* v. *Foster* [1976] 4 W.W.R. 681 (B.C.S.C.); *Re MacDonald and Deputy Attorney General of Canada* (1981) 59 C.C.C. (2d) 202 (Ont. C.A.); *R.* v. *Law* (1981) 24 C.R. (3d) 332 (Ont. C.A.); *Re Hipke and The Queen* (1985) 20 C.C.C. (3d) 378 (Ont. H.C.). There are also some old Australian cases where habeas corpus was used in this way: *R.* v. *Murray* (1846) 1 Legge 287; *Re Court* (1871) 2 Q.S.C.R. 171.

[122] *Hancock* v. *Prison Commissioners* [1960] 1 Q.B. 117; *Silverman* v. *Prison Commissioners* [1955] Crim. L.R. 116 (aff'd [1956] Crim. L.R. 56).

Canadian,[123] prisoners have sued for a declaration as to the effect of their sentence. Such an action is undoubtedly well-founded: it may, however, be slower and more cumbersome than habeas corpus. It is seen in another chapter that there are problems encountered when it is sought to challenge a period of imprisonment under a sentence which has yet to commence, and in such cases, the action for a declaration has been used to avoid these technical problems.[124]

(b) *Improper Execution of Sentence*

Where the requisite statutory procedures are not carried out in the execution of a sentence, a prisoner may be entitled to discharge.[125] However, in *R. v. Mount*,[126] the Privy Council held that there was an inherent power to remand a convicted felon until the appropriate steps had been taken: 'The prisoners who had been convicted of felony, ought not to have been set at large during the term of their sentence, until it was clear that no lawful means of executing it could be found.'[127] It is clear from the *Mount* case that the courts will do everything they can to prevent a convicted person from being freed because of some procedural defect in the manner of execution of his sentence.

See Hague

(c) *Illegal Sentence*

A matter to be kept distinct from testing the period of imprisonment authorized by a sentence is that of questioning the legality of the sentence itself. In the latter situation, the courts have rather blindly applied the rules governing the impeachment of convictions on habeas corpus.[128] This has meant that the prisoner is able to base an application on a legal defect relating to the sentence where the

---

[123] *Sedore v. Commissioner of Penitentiaries* [1972] F.C. 898 (T.D.); *Re Ellis & The Queen* (1793) 9 C.C.C. (2d) 149 (Fed. Ct. T.D.).

[124] See *infra*, p. 184.

[125] *Re Allen* (1860) 30 L.J.Q.B. 38, where the place of confinement for a person convicted by a military court had not been specified by the proper official. In *Re Bell and Director of Springhill Medium Security Institution* (1977) 34 C.C.C. (2d) 303 (N.S.S.C.) the applicant had been illegally transferred to a prison and succeeded on habeas corpus in securing his return to the proper institution in his home province.

[126] (1875) L.R. 6 P.C. 283.

[127] Ibid. 305. See *supra*, pp. 56–7 for discussion of the approach taken by the courts where the prisoner relies on a technical defect.

[128] *Supra*, pp. 145–6. Cf., however, *Ex p. Risby* (1975) 24 C.C.C. (2d) 211 (B.C.S.C.), reviewing the legality of a sentence on the ground that there was error on the face of the committal.

sentence was imposed by an inferior court, but will be unable to complain [129] of an unlawful sentence handed down by a superior court or court of quarter sessions (now the Crown Court).[130]

It is submitted, however, that this situation is unsatisfactory. First of all, from a technical point of view, there is said to be an exception to the inviolability of superior court orders: where the process of the court itself demonstrates vitiating error, it is subject to attack.[131] If, for example, a court sentences someone to fourteen years where the maximum penalty for the offence is seven years,[132] the error of law must necessarily be apparent to the court on habeas corpus, and there is no question of going behind the record. This is an error relating to the imprisonment itself, not something which invalidates the proceedings behind the sentence, and for this reason, would seem appropriately subject to review on habeas corpus.

From the point of view of policy, it is difficult to imagine what interest is served by denying a remedy in such a case. While there may be good reason to foster an element of finality in the criminal law, and therefore, to protect convictions from collateral attack, it seems pointless to protect unlawful sentences. If the time for appeal has gone by, the law should provide another remedy. In some cases it is suggested that only an appeal to executive power to pardon is appropriate,[133] but it is submitted that where there is an unlawful deprivation of liberty, the matter should not be left to anyone's discretion.[134]

---

[129] See e.g. *Re Cavenett* [1926] N.Z.L.R. 755; *Re Skied and The Queen* (1975) 24 C.C.C. (2d) 93 (B.C.S.C.). Cf., however, *R. v. Carrachelo* (1958) 120 C.C.C. 401 (B.C.) where the court refused to allow such an application, incorrectly applying the rules relating to superior court orders to an inferior court.

[130] *Brenan & Galen's Case* (1847) 10 Q.B. 492; *Ex p. Plante* (1856) 6 L.C.R. 106 (Can.); *R. v. Kavanagh* (1902) 5 C.C.C. 507 (N.S.); *Ex p. Boucher* (1928) 50 C.C.C. 161 (Que. C.A.); *Re Millar* (1866) 3 W.W. & A'B (L.) 41 (Vict.); *R. v. Allen* (1868) S.A.L.R. 54; cf. cases cited *infra*, nn. 135–6, p. 150. In *Re Hass and The Queen* (1978) 40 C.C.C (2d) 202 at 208 (Ont. H.C.) it was said to be in accord with general principle to preclude habeas corpus to review the legality of a sentence imposed by any court of competent jurisdiction, the proper remedy being an appeal. This is qualified, however, by *Gamble* v. *The Queen* [1988] 2 S.C.R. 595, holding that if no other remedy is available, habeas corpus will lie to attack an illegal sentence.

[131] *Supra*, pp. 49–51.

[132] The cases cited *supra*, n. 130, all involved the plea that the legal maximum had been exceeded, or that the sentence was unlawful (e.g. hard labour).

[133] *Ex p. Plante* (1856) 6 L.C.R. 106 (Can.); *Ex p. Boucher* (1928) 50 C.C.C. 161 (Que. C.A.); *R. v. Allen* (1868) 2 S.A.L.R. 54, where one of the judges corresponded with the Governor of the Colony and had the unlawful part of the sentence pardoned.

[134] *Gamble* v. *The Queen* [1988] 2 S.C.R. 595.

There are a few Australian decisions[135] which do allow habeas corpus and the desirable approach is shown by an old English case where the applicants had been convicted on indictment at Quarter Sessions and given an illegal sentence.[136] It was argued that habeas corpus was inappropriate and that they should be left to take proceedings by writ of error. The court sensibly ordered the prisoners' discharge, adding: '... it would be very hard; that the defendants should continue in prison under the illegal part of this judgment, until they can obtain a reversal of those parts upon a writ of error.'[137]

(d) *Habeas Corpus and Parole*

The courts will not assume the role of the minister or board upon whom the discretion to grant parole has been conferred, and will only interfere on habeas corpus where that authority has acted unlawfully.[138] The Supreme Court of Canada has held that habeas corpus is not the appropriate remedy until the applicant attains the status of a parolee.[139] Hence, habeas corpus will not lie where the applicant was refused parole,[140] but will be available where parole was granted and for some reason the applicant was not released in accordance with the terms of the parole order,[141] or where the applicant was released and now challenges the termination of parole. Habeas corpus will, however, be granted to a prisoner unlawfully denied the right to apply for parole, even though the final authority for determining whether parole should be granted rests with the parole board.[142] Habeas corpus has frequently been granted in Canada to challenge the illegal revocation of parole,[143] where the prescribed

---

[135] *Re Price* (1885) 6 L.R.N.S.W. 140; *Re Forbes* (1887) 8 L.R. (N.S.W.) 68; *R*. v. *Governor of Metropolitan Gaol, ex p. Kimball* [1937] V.L.R. 279. Cf. *R.* v. *Allen* (1868) 2 S.A.L.R. 54. For discussion, see Lanham, 'The Reviewability of Superior Court Orders' (1988) 16 Melb. U.L.R. 603 at 613–16.

[136] *R.* v. *Collyer and Capon* (1752) Sayer 44.

[137] Ibid.

[138] *R.* v. *Governor of Leeds Prison, ex p. Stafford* [1964] 2 Q.B. 625; *Payne* v. *Lord Harris of Greenwich* [1981] 1 W.L.R. 754; *Mitchell* v. *The Queen* [1976] 2 S.C.R. 570; *Ex p. Carlson* (1975) 26 C.C.C. (2d) 65 (Ont. C.A.); *Re Munday and The Queen* (1982) 69 C.C.C. (2d) 436 (B.C.C.A.).

[139] *Dumas* v. *Director of Leclerc Institution of Laval* (1986) 30 C.C.C. (3d) 129 (S.C.C.).

[140] Although as noted in *Dumas, supra,* judicial review may be available.

[141] For an example of such a case, see *R.* v. *Acting Governor of Her Majesty's Prison, Pentridge, ex p. Butterly* [1974] V.R. 634.

[142] *Gamble* v. *The Queen* [1988] 2 S.C.R. 595.

[143] *Re Moore and The Queen* (1983) 4 C.C.C. (3d) 206 (Ont. C.A.) (aff'd S.C.C. ibid. at 216); *Truscott* v. *Director of Mountain Institution* (1983) 4 C.C.C. (3d) 199 (B.C.C.A.), both dealing with the practice of 'gating'.

statutory provisions were not followed,[144] or where the applicant's procedural rights guaranteed by the Charter have been infringed.[145]

5. HABEAS CORPUS TO CHALLENGE THE VALIDITY OF CONDITIONS OF IMPRISONMENT

The English authorities are meagre, but tend to say that habeas corpus cannot be used to test the validity of the conditions of confinement or of some added restraint with respect to someone who is admittedly legally incarcerated. In a case in 1843, an application was made for habeas corpus by a prisoner who alleged that he was being held in the wrong part of the prison, but Denman, C.J. refused the application: 'The object of the writ of habeas corpus is, generally, to restore a person to his liberty, not to pronounce a judgment as to the room or part of a prison in which a prisoner ought to be confined.'[146] This same view was more recently taken by Hilbery J., who held that the only question which could properly be taken on habeas corpus was whether or not the prisoner should be released.[147] In another case in 1848,[148] Wilde C.J. refused a similar application, but noted that if the prisoner was being improperly held under conditions more stringent

[144] *Re Rowling and The Queen* (1978) 45 C.C.C. (2d) 478 (Ont. H.C.). See also Cromwell, 'Parole Committals and Habeas Corpus' (1976) 8 Ottawa L.R. 560.

[145] *Re Cadeddu and The Queen* (1982) 4 C.C.C. (3d) 97 (Ont. H.C.) (appeal quashed ibid. at 112); *Re Conroy and The Queen* (1983) 5 C.C.C. (3d) 501; *Re Lowe and The Queen* (1983) 5 C.C.C. (3d) 535 (B.C.S.C.); *Re Doumoulin and The Queen* (1983) 6 C.C.C. (3d) 190 (Ont. H.C.); *Re Mason and The Queen* (1983) 7 C.C.C (3d) 426 (Ont. H.C.); *Re Swan and The Queen* (1983) 7 C.C.C. (3d) 130 (B.C.S.C.); *Re Martens and The Queen* (1983) 8 C.C.C. (3d) 336 (B.C.S.C.).

[146] *Ex p. Rogers* (1843) 7 Jur. 992. For a much earlier case where habeas corpus was refused to a convicted prisoner who complained of harsh treatment at the hands of the gaoler, see *Anon.* (1654) 1 Style 432. See also *Beaudin* v. *Landriault* (1921) 23 Que. P.R. 215 (S.C.), where a prisoner unsuccessfully sought complete discharge because he had been subjected to unauthorized forced labour.

[147] *R.* v. *Wandsworth Prison (Governor), ex p. Silverman* (1952) 96 Sol. Jo. 853, where the applicant claimed that the authorities had failed to make special rules for prisoners serving sentences of preventive detention, as required by Criminal Justice Act 1948, s.52. The prisoner also failed in a later action for declaration: *Silverman* v. *Prison Commissioners* [1955] Crim. L.R. 116 (aff'd [1956] Crim. L.R. 56). It may be that declaration is an appropriate remedy, although, in *Silverman*, it was refused on the grounds that the Prison Rules conferred no enforceable rights: see *infra*, p. 152. See also the dictum of Widgery C.J. in *R.* v. *Secretary of State for the Home Department, ex. p. Singh* [1976] 1 Q.B. 198 at 201: '... English law knows no partial habeas corpus—no right to habeas corpus for a particular purpose.'

[148] *Ex p. Cobbett* (1848) 5 C.B. 418.

than justified, 'the ordinary means of redress for the wrong are open.' This may have been a reference to the statutory right which then existed, whereby civil prisoners could petition the court for redress,[149] or even to the possibility of an action in tort.[150] This restrictive attitude towards the availability of habeas corpus mirrors a traditional reluctance on the part of the English courts to entertain proceedings which challenge the legality of prison conditions.[151] Actions in false imprisonment for breach of the Prison Rules have been rejected.[152] Until recently, judicial review was available only in exceptional cases. This attitude is changing, however. The propriety of judicial review to challenge prison disciplinary proceedings has been upheld by the House of Lords.[153] Judicial review will also lie to enforce the statutory duties of prison officials,[154]

[149] 2 Geo. II, c.22, s.6; 32 Geo. II, c.28, s.11, *Osborne* v. *Angle* (1835) 2 Scott 500; *Stead* v. *Anderson* (1850) 9 C.B. 262.   [150] *Infra*, n. 152.

[151] In *Hancock* v. *Prison Commissioners* [1960] 1 Q.B. 117 at 128, Winn J. said, obiter: '... it is manifest that the control of prisons and prisoners by the prison commissioners and the visiting justices should not be interfered with by the courts unless, in any particular case, there has been some departure from law and good administration amounting to an offence in law ...' See also *Morriss* v. *Winter* [1930] 1 K.B. 243; and *infra*, n. 152. For general discussion of prisoner's rights, see Zellick, 'Prisoner's Rights in England' (1974) 24 U.T.L.J. 331; Kaiser, 'The Inmate as Citizen' (1971) 1 Queen's L.J. 208; Jackson, 'Justice Behind Walls' (1974) 12 O.H.L.J. 1; Richardson, 'Time to Take Prisoner's Rights Seriously' (1984) 11 Journal of Law and Society 1; Zellick, 'Prison Discipline and Preventative Confinement' [1981] Crim. L.R. 218; Zellick, 'The Prison Rules and the Courts' [1981] Crim. L.R. 602; Zellick, 'Penalties for Disciplinary Offences in Prison' [1981] P.L. 228.

[152] *Arbon* v. *Anderson* [1943] K.B. 252; *Becker* v. *Home Office* [1972] 2 Q.B. 407 at 418 (C.A.) per Denning M.R.; *Williams* v. *Home Office (No. 2)* [1982] 2 All E.R. 564 (C.A.). Cf. the early cases holding that a prisoner unlawfully removed from one part of a prison to another or subjected to unlawful fetters can maintain an action in tort: *Cobbett* v. *Grey* (1850) 4 Exch. 729; *Yorke* v. *Chapman* (1839) 10 A. & E. 207; *Osborne* v. *Milman* (1886) 17 Q.B.D. 514 (rev'd on other grounds, 18 Q.B.D. 471); *Whittaker* v. *Roos and Bateman* [1912] S.A.L.R. (App. Div'n) 92.

[153] *Leech* v. *Deputy Governor of Parkhurst Prison* [1988] 2 W.L.R. 290, overruling *R.* v. *Deputy Governor of Camphill Prison, ex. p. King* [1985] Q.B. 735 (C.A.). See also *R.* v. *Secretary of State for the Home Department, ex p. McAvoy* [1984] 1 W.L.R. 1408; *R.* v. *Secretary of State for the Home Department, ex p. Herbage (No. 2)* [1987] Q.B. 1077 (C.A.). Certiorari is available in Canada to question the validity of prison disciplinary proceedings: *R.* v. *Institutional Head of Beaver Creek Correction Camp, ex p. MacCaud* [1969] 1 C.C.C. 371 (Ont. C.A.); *Martineau* v. *Matsqui Institution Disciplinary Board (No. 2)* [1980] 1 S.C.R. 602; *Re Howard and Presiding Officer of Inmate Disciplinary Court of Stony Mountain Institution* (1985) 19 C.C.C. (3d) 195 (Fed. C.A.). See also *Daemar* v. *Hall* [1978] 2 N.Z.L.R. 594.

[154] *R.* v. *Secretary of State for the Home Department, ex p. Herbage (No. 2)* [1987] Q.B. 1077 (C.A.). It has also been said that the transfer of an unconvicted prisoner from one prison to another is subject to review if the prisoner's rights are not taken into account: *R.* v. *Secretary of State for the Home Department, ex p. McAvoy* [1984] 1 W.L.R. 152.

and certiorari may be used to challenge the decisions of prison review boards.[155]

The Canadian courts have taken a liberal view of the availability of habeas corpus. The Supreme Court of Canada has held that habeas corpus is available to determine the validity of confinement within a prison in segregation or a special handling unit.[156] As LeDain J. put it:

a prisoner has the right not to be deprived unlawfully of the relative or residual liberty permitted to the general inmate population of an institution. Any significant deprivation of that liberty, such as that effected by confinement in a special handling unit meets the first of the traditional requirements for habeas corpus, that it must be directed against a deprivation of liberty.[157]

In England the visiting justices, now boards of visitors, play an important role in hearing prisoner complaints, and in certain cases, prisoners' complaints have even been scrutinized by the ombudsman.[158]

A considerable body of law has been developed under the European Convention for the Protection of Human Rights and Fundamental Freedoms with respect to the rights of prisoners,[159] and the case law includes successful applications from British prisoners.[160] While a

---

[155] *R. v. Hull Prison Board of Visitors, ex p. St. Germain* [1979] 1 All E.R. 701 (C.A.).
[156] *The Queen v. Miller* [1985] 2 S.C.R. 613; *Cardinal v. Director of Kent Institution* [1985] S.C.R. 643; *Morin v. National Special Handling Unit Review Committee* [1985] 2 S.C.R. 662; *R. v. Olson* (1987) 38 C.C.C. (3d) 534 (Ont. C.A.). The Irish courts have been cautious, but have not precluded habeas corpus to challenge conditions of confinement: see Byrne, 'Habeas Corpus and Conditions of Confinement in Prison' (1979) 14 Irish Jurist 109. Several actions have been brought in Canada for declaratory relief in relation to prison conditions based upon constitutional guarantees: *McCann v. The Queen* (1975) 29 C.C.C. (2d) 337 (Fed. Ct. T.D.); *Magrath v. The Queen* (1977) 38 C.C.C. (2d) 67 (Fed. Ct. T.D.); *Collin v. Kaplan* (1982) 1 C.C.C. (3d) 309 (Fed. Ct. T.D.); *Butler v. The Queen* (1983) 5 C.C.C. (3d) 356 (Fed. Ct. T.D.); *Piche et al. v. Solicitor General of Canada* (1984) 17 C.C.C. (3d) 1 (Fed. Ct. T.D.); *Re Soenen and Thomas* (1983) 8 C.C.C. (3d) 224 (Alta. Q.B.).
[157] *The Queen v. Miller, supra*, at 637.
[158] See Kaiser, op. cit. 277. In Canada, a Correctional Investigator has been appointed: see *Annual Report of the Correctional Investigator*, commencing 1973–4.
[159] Council of Europe, *Human Rights in Prison* (1971) sets out the work of the Commission in this regard.
[160] *Golder v. United Kingdom* (1975) 1 E.H.R.R. 524. See also *de Courcy* (1967) 10 Yearbook 368; *3868/68* (1970) 34 Collection of Decisions 10; *4220/69* (1971) 37 Collection of Decisions 51; *4451/70* (1971) 37 Collection of Decisions 124; *Knechtl*, discussed *infra*; *X v. United Kingdom* (1981) 4 E.H.R.R. 188; *X v. United Kingdom* (1982) 5 E.H.R.R. 162; *Silver v. United Kingdom* (1983) 5 E.H.R.R. 347; *Campbell and Fell v. United Kingdom* (1984) 7 E.H.R.R. 165.

petitioner must show some breach of the Convention and not just a breach of municipal law to get redress, the very fact that a British prisoner has the right to apply to this international body suggests that, as a matter of policy, steps should be taken to ensure a right of redress in the domestic courts with respect to domestic infringements.[161]

While the English courts have been reluctant to act in the past, it is submitted that the fact that a prisoner cannot be released altogether should be no reason to refuse relief on habeas corpus. If, for example, a prisoner is improperly put in solitary confinement (or, as the Prison Rules say, 'removed from association') there seems to be no reason why habeas corpus should not be available to secure release from that restraint. The situation may be seen as a 'prison within a prison'. This concept has been expressly adopted by the Supreme Court of Canada.[162] The applicant is simply released from the inner prison while being kept within the confines of the outer one. In several Canadian cases, habeas corpus has been granted where the effect of the order is to transfer the applicant from unlawful custody in one prison to the lawful place of confinement.[163] One of the evils remedied by the Habeas Corpus Act 1679 was the transfer of prisoners from one prison to another without lawful authority, and it hardly seems surprising that the modern writ should be used to the same effect.[164] In child custody cases, habeas corpus has been used to transfer rather than release from custody, and the same principle could be applied. From there, it might be possible to develop a more sophisticated approach which would allow anyone confined to contest the legality of

---

[161] In so far as rights secured by the convention itself are concerned, member states are required to 'secure to everyone within their jurisdiction the rights and freedoms defined': Art. 1. English practice with regard to legal proceedings by prisoners has been subject to scrutiny by the Commission: discussed further *infra*, p. 226.

[162] *The Queen* v. *Miller* [1985] 2 S.C.R. 613.

[163] *R.* v. *Tarchuk* (1928) 50 C.C.C. 423 (B.C.S.C.); *Re Bell and Director of Springhill Medium Security Institution* (1977) 34 C.C.C. (2d) 303 (N.S.S.C.); *Re Hass and The Queen* (1978) 40 C.C.C. (2d) 202 at 211 (Ont. H.C.); *Re Jollimore and The Queen* (1986) 27 C.C.C. (3d) 166 (N.S.S.C.). Cf. the following cases in which the availability of habeas corpus was assumed, but relief was refused on the merits: *Re Rowling and The Queen* (1980) 57 C.C.C. (2d) 169 (Ont. H.C.); *Re Morin and Director of Corrections for Saskatchewan* (1982) 70 C.C.C. (2d) 230 (Sask. C.A.); *Re F. and The Queen* (1985) 20 C.C.C. (3d) 56 (Ont. H.C.); *Balain* v. *Regional Transfer Board and Warden of Joyceville Institution* (1988) 62 C.R. (3d) 258 (Ont. H.C.). In *Re Hay and National Parole Board* (1985) 21 C.C.C. (3d) 408 (Fed. Ct. T.D.) certiorari and mandamus were granted to effect a transfer.

[164] See *Day* v. *The Queen* (1983) 153 C.L.R. 475, considering s.8 of the Habeas Corpus Act 1679.

the conditions of the confinement even where there is no complaint of some added physical restraint.

The important point is that if there is need for a judicial remedy, habeas corpus could be used effectively. The writ is nothing more than a command to the gaoler from the court to have the prisoner brought before it to justify the detention. It is but a small step to extend this to cases where a measure of restraint is unquestionably justified but where the prisoner contends that the conditions of imprisonment are improper, and requires the gaoler to justify the imposition of these conditions.[165]

It may be noted that while people in prison would be the principal beneficiaries of such a remedy, it could prove important to others as well. Patients held under the compulsory powers of the Mental Health Act are an obvious example.

The question is really not so much whether habeas corpus is an appropriate remedy: the writ has been moulded to meet new legal problems in the past.[166] The problem is whether the courts will deem it appropriate to become involved with such issues. In the past they have been reluctant to intervene directly, but have been content to give certain relief in damages after the violation of rights has ceased. If the legal system becomes more sensitive to the rights of prisoners and other people incarcerated, then habeas corpus could prove to be a significant remedy which would allow for more immediate relief.[167]

---

[165] *The Queen* v. *Miller, supra*, at 641 per LeDain J.: 'I do not say that habeas corpus should lie to challenge any and all conditions of confinement in a penitentiary or prison, including the loss of any privilege enjoyed by the general inmate population. But it should lie in my opinion to challenge the validity of a distinct form of confinement or detention in which the actual physical constraint or deprivation of liberty, as distinct from the mere loss of certain privileges, is more restrictive or severe than the normal one in an institution.'

[166] See e.g. *Re Faid and The Queen* (1978) 44 C.C.C (2d) 62 (Alta. S.C.), granting habeas corpus to afford the applicant proper facilities in which he could communicate with his lawyer.

[167] For the practice adopted with respect to habeas corpus applications from prisoners, see *infra*, pp. 224–7.

6

Review of Commitments for Compulsory Treatment

1. INTRODUCTION

The purpose of this brief chapter is to examine the use of habeas corpus as a remedy in cases of detention for treatment under compulsory powers. In principle, the grounds for review are the same as in any other situation. There are, however, a few special considerations which arise because of the purportedly therapeutic nature of the detention and because it is usually thought inappropriate to extend full legal rights to persons of unsound mind.

2. HABEAS CORPUS AND CIVIL COMMITTAL

The purpose of the Mental Health Act 1983, and of the modern legislation of many other jurisdictions, is to provide for a relatively informal procedure for admission and discharge of those who suffer from mental disorder and are deemed to require institutional care, but at the same time to protect the rights of patients by allowing for applications to a statutory review board. These review boards will often provide a remedy which would not have existed previously, and in other cases, simply take the place of an application for habeas corpus. There are, however, still situations where habeas corpus will be the most appropriate remedy, particularly where it is alleged that statutory procedural requirements have not been respected.[1]

There are many examples of the use of habeas corpus to test the propriety of mental illness committals in the cases which arose before

[1] Habeas corpus has been used in Canada to challenge successfully under the Charter of Rights and Freedoms the adequacy of provincial mental health legislation which failed to prescribe any objective criteria for involuntary committals for treatment: *Thwaites* v. *Health Sciences Centre Psychiatric Facility* (1988) 48 D.L.R. (4th) 338 (Man. C.A.). See also *Lussa* v. *Health Science Centre* (1983) 9 C.R.R. 350 (Man. Q.B.) Cf. *Re Procedures and the Mental Health Act* (1984) 5 D.L.R. (4th) 577 (P.E.I.S.C.).

the establishment of statutory review tribunals. In the first place, habeas corpus has often been used to test the sufficiency of the documents or proceedings which led to the patient's committal. Where the prescribed statutory procedures have not been followed,[2] or the statute misconstrued,[3] there are grounds for an application for habeas corpus.

However, the courts have, on occasion, taken a rather paternalist attitude in these cases and refused to order discharge unless it were also shown that the applicant was not actually dangerous to himself or herself or others.[4] The authority usually cited for this proposition is *Re Shuttleworth*[5] where Lord Denman C.J. said:

If the Court thought that a party, unlawfully received or detained, was a lunatic, we should still be betraying the common duties of members of society if we directed a discharge. But we have no power to set aside the order, only to discharge. And should we, as Judges or individuals, be justified in setting such a party at large? It is answered that there may be a fresh custody. But why so? Is it not better, if she be dangerous, that she should remain in custody till the Great Seal or the commissioners act? Therefore, being satisfied in my own mind that there would be danger in setting her at large, I am bound by the most general principles to abstain from so doing; and I should be abusing the name of liberty if I were to take off a restraint for which those who are most interested in the party ought to be the most thankful.

This means that the applicant has two hurdles; it must be shown that the committal was improper and that the applicant is not, in fact, dangerous. In the Canadian cases,[6] where a similar approach has been

---

[2] *R. v. Pinder, re Greenwood* (1855) 24 L.J.Q.B. 148; *R. v. Board of Control, East Ham Corp'n & Mordey, ex p. Winterflood* [1938] 1 K.B. 420; *Re Dell* (1891) 91 L.T.O.S. 375; *Re Avery* [1951] O.W.N. 810 (II.C.) *R. v. Rampton Institution Board of Control, ex p. Barker* [1957] Crim. L.R. 403; and cases cited *infra*, n. 18, p. 160.

[3] *Re Steneult* (1894) 29 L.Jo. 345; *Re Wilkinson* (1919) 83 J.P.Jo. 422; *R. v. Board of Control ex p. Rutty* [1956] 2 Q.B. 109, discussed in detail, *supra*, pp. 32–4.

[4] *Re Shuttleworth* (1846) 9 Q.B. 651; *Re Gregory* (1899) 25 V.L.R. 539 (leave to appeal refused [1901] A.C. 128); cases cited *infra*, n. 6. See also *R. v. Clarke* (1762) 3 Burr. 1362, where the time for submitting a return was extended to enable the respondent to get the proper authority for the detention where it appeared that the patient was insane. A similar course was taken in *Trenholm* v. *Attorney-General of Ontario* [1940] S.C.R. 301. It has also been suggested that a certain informality in the case of these committals may be tolerated: *R. v. Gourlay* (1828) 7 B. & C. 669; *Re Maltby* (1881) 7 Q.B.D. 18; *Re Fell* (1845) 15 L.J.M.C. 25; *Ex p. Wilson* (1870) 1 A.J.R. 100. Cf. *R. v. Pinder, re Greenwood* (1855) 24 L.J.Q.B. 148. See also *R. v. Martin* (1854) 2 N.S.R. 322, where the court held that notwithstanding the absence of statutory provision, there was a prerogative power to detain a person acquitted of murder by reason of insanity.

[5] (1846) 9 Q.B. 651 at 662.

[6] *Re Gibson* (1907) 15 O.L.R. 245 (C.A.) 245; *Re King* (1916) 30 D.L.R. 599 (Man.

taken, it has been held that the appropriate procedure is to direct the trial of an issue as to the patient's propensity to be dangerous.

On the other hand, there are cases where the court has simply discharged an applicant who has been illegally committed as a person of unsound mind apparently without inquiry into his or her actual mental state.[7] It is not apparent when the inherent power to refuse discharge will be exercised, and it may be that the courts are now less willing to use it. Even so, the same consideration may sway the court to construe an error in the committal as being non-vitiating.

The source of the power to refuse to discharge a person illegally committed simply because the court suspects he or she may be dangerous is not at all clear. It seems to be assumed that there is an inherent sort of *parens patriae* jurisdiction which is exercisable to protect the interests of the public and of the patient. It is worth noting that, in balancing individual rights against the public interest, this kind of reasoning has never been openly applied in criminal cases, where, very often, there is little doubt about the prisoner being dangerous. In mental illness cases, there is the added consideration of the patient's interest which may not always be seen to allow for release.

In addition to these cases which turn primarily on whether or not the authorities have properly pursued their statutory powers in committing the patient, there are a number of cases where the courts have allowed the issue of unsoundness of mind to be determined on habeas corpus. The argument that habeas corpus can be of no avail where the committal documents are in due form has, on occasion, been rejected, and means have been evolved for the court to determine the applicant's mental state.[8] It can be argued with some force that, however regular

K.B.); *Re Bowyer* (1930) 66 O.L.R. 378 (H.C.); *Re Carnochan* [1941] S.C.R. 470. See also the Irish case, *R. v. Riall* (1860) 2 L.T.N.S. 122.

[7] Most notably, the *Rutty* case [1956] 2 Q.B. 109, the result of which was the discharge of some 3000 other patients who had similarly been improperly committed: see Street, *Freedom, the Individual and the Law* (5th ed. 1982). E.C.S. Wade, Introduction to Dicey, *Law of the Constitution* (10th ed. 1959) comments at cxxxviii: 'Whether or not there was medical justification for the decision in *Rutty's case*, the requirement that no one can be deprived of their liberty except by due process of law was vindicated.' See also *R v. Rampton Institution Board of Control, ex p. Barker* [1957] Crim. L.R. 403; and *Re Callender* [1956] Crim. L.R. 617 at 618, where Goddard L.C.J. said: '... the mere fact that officials, or doctors, or anyone else, thought that it would be good for a child or young person, or any other person, to receive treatment, was no ground for putting into operation the procedure of the Children and Young Persons Act 1933, or of the Mental Deficiency Acts, or that of any other Act.'

[8] *Re Mineham* (1925) 28 O.W.N. 263 (H.C.); *Fawcett v. Attorney-General for Ontario* [1963] 3 C.C.C. 134 at 137 (H.C.), where Spence J. noted that the issue to be tried was

the original committal, the validity in law of the applicant's continued detention should be regarded as being contingent on the existence of the disability.[9] Indeed, it has been held by the European Court of Human Rights that to the extent that neither habeas corpus nor mental health legislation permits periodic review of the substantive justification for continued deprivation of liberty, there is a breach of Art. 5(4) of the Convention, which guarantees the right to have the lawfulness of any deprivation of liberty reviewed by a court.[10]

The practice of having the issue of sanity referred to an independent physician seems to have been initiated by Lord Mansfield,[11] and has been adopted in a few cases.[12] In several Canadian cases,[13] the courts have used the device of directing the trial of an issue so that the issue may be decided on the basis of evidence presented by both sides. While this practice does not appear to have been adopted by the English courts in cases dealing with mental illness, there is a dictum in a Privy Council decision which suggests that it would be possible.[14] Where an inquiry is directed, it is submitted that the burden to demonstrate a mental condition requiring confinement rests upon the hospital authorities.[15]

---

the applicant's present condition (aff'd on other grounds [1964] 1 C.C.C. 164; [1965] 2 C.C.C. 262); *Norris* v. *Seed* (1849) 3 Exch. 782 at 792; *R.* v. *Riall* (1860) 2 L.T.N.S. 122 (Ireland). Cf. *Ex p. Chidley* (1916) 33 W.N. (N.S.W.) 63, where the court refused to review the issue of insanity but where it appears that there was an alternate statutory remedy. *Re Procedures and the Mental Health Act* (1984) 5 D.L.R. (4th) 577 (P.E.I.S.C.) holds that habeas corpus does not lie unless there has been a failure to comply with the statutory requirements for committal.

[9] See *Winterwerp* v. *The Netherlands* (1979) 2 E.H.R.R. 387.

[10] *X* v. *United Kingdom* (1981) 4 E.H.R.R. 188; *B.* v. *United Kingdom* (1983) 6 E.H.R.R. 188.

[11] *R.* v. *Turlington* (1761) 2 Burr. 1115.

[12] *Re Dack* (1914) 5 (O.W.N.) 774 (H.C.); *Re O'Donnell* (1914) 7 O.W.N. 605 (H.C.); *Re Carnochan* [1941] S.C.R. 470.

[13] *Re Davidson* (1915) 8 O.W.N. 481 (H.C.); *Re Mineham* (1925) 28 O.W.N. 263 (H.C.); *Fawcett* v. *Attorney-General for Ontario* [1963] 3 C.C.C. 134 (H.C.) (aff'd on other grounds [1964] 1 C.C.C. 164; [1965] 2 C.C.C. 262). Cf. *Re Reid* (1953) 10 W.W.R. 383 (B.C.S.C.), holding that the court could only order the trial of an issue where it had been shown that there was something wrong with the committal itself.

[14] *Ex p. Gregory* [1901] A.C. 128 at 129: 'Under a habeas corpus the applicant is not entitled to have his sanity ascertained by a jury. The Court may come to a conclusion, as it has done in this case, that the applicant is lawfully detained upon the evidence before it. The Court is not bound to direct an issue to be tried by a jury. The Court can always direct such an issue if the Court is of the opinion that justice requires it.' For English cases where the trial of an issue has been directed in other contexts, see *supra*, pp. 78–9.

[15] *Supra*, pp. 85–91; *Re Procedures and the Mental Health Act* (1984) 5 D.L.R. (4th) 577 (P.E.I.S.C.).

There is no express provision in the Mental Health Act barring such an application, and habeas corpus should not be refused simply because there is an alternate remedy.[16] It might be expected, however, that the courts would treat such applications with circumspection. It would be possible for the court to evade the issue simply by relying on a valid detention order and avoid involvement beyond seeing that the statutory procedures had been observed.

A stronger case might be made out where the patient had no right to apply to the Mental Health Review Tribunal. In principle, the only justification for the detention of the patient is the continued existence of his mental disorder, and, perhaps, the continued treatment of that disorder, and it can be argued that if the patient cannot apply for discharge to the Review Tribunal, it should be possible to raise the issue on habeas corpus. Such an issue is not beyond the competence of the courts.[17]

(a) *Criminal Cases*

If there is some defect in the committal proceedings, habeas corpus is an appropriate remedy even where the committal is in a criminal case.[18] However, where it is argued that, although the prisoner was properly committed, his or her mental state no longer justifies the detention, criminal committals present difficulties. The detention order is made to be expressly subject to the pleasure of an executive officer. Since the matter of discharge is left to the exercise of executive

---

[16] *Supra*, p. 59. It is possible to appeal a decision of a Mental Health Review Tribunal on a question of law by case stated. See e.g. *Re V.E.* [1972] 3 All E.R. 374; *W.* v. *L.* [1973] 3 All E.R. 884 (C.A.). In some jurisdictions, there is a statutory right of review by the court in addition to recourse to the statutory tribunal: *Re Hoskins and Hislop* (1981) 121 D.L.R. (3d) 337 (B.C.S.C.).

[17] See the authorities cited *supra*, pp. 158–9, and also the cases dealing with the same question in actions for false imprisonment: *Hall* v. *Semple* (1862) 3 F. & F. 337; *Everett* v. *Griffiths* [1921] 1 A.C. 631; *De Freville* v. *Dill* [1927] All E.R. 205; all holding that a medical practitioner who negligently certifies someone as insane is liable to an action for false imprisonment. Cf. where the certification is incorrect but not negligent, no action will lie: *Williams* v. *Beaumont* (1894) 10 T.L.R. 543 (C.A.). Most Mental Health legislation extends some statutory protection to those purporting to act under it: see e.g. s.141(1) of the Mental Health Act which, however, still allows an action where there is want of reasonable care. See also the following cases where certiorari was used to quash medical certificates given under statutory authority: *R.* v. *Boycott, ex p. Keasly* [1939] 2 K.B. 651; *R.* v. *Kent Police Authority, ex p. Godden* [1971] 2 Q.B. 662 (C.A.).

[18] *Trenholm* v. *Attorney-General of Ontario* [1940] S.C.R. 301; *Laundry* v. *Legrand* (1949) 96 C.C.C. 303 (Que. C.A.); *Re Sommer* (1958) 27 C.R. 243 (Que. S.C.); *Ex p. Sayle* (1974) 18 C.C.C. (2d) 56 (B.C.S.C.); *R.* v. *Robson* [1977] 6 W.W.R. 565 (B.C.S.C.).

discretion, it will be difficult to challenge the continuing detention 'in the courts.[19] However, it has been held in Canada that declaratory relief can be granted where a review board has misconstrued the meaning of the statute, even though the power of the board is advisory.[20] Judicial review has also been granted on the basis of procedural error or breach of the duty to act fairly.[21]

It has been suggested in another Canadian case that habeas corpus could be granted where the executive decision refusing to release the prisoner was being exercised in an arbitrary way without proper medical evidence.[22] This, it is submitted, is the correct view.[23] It has been seen in the discussion of the review of executive detention orders that, however broad the discretion conferred, a decision which lacks *bona fides* or which was taken on unlawful considerations, can be questioned. It is, however, difficult to see how the executive officer could be forced to make a decision which could then be questioned.

3. CAPACITY OF PATIENTS TO TAKE PROCEEDINGS

While it has never been suggested that a person suffering from a mental disorder lacks the capacity to bring habeas corpus proceedings,[24] there

[19] *Delorme* v. *Soeurs de la Charite de Quebec* (1922) 40 C.C.C. 218 (Que. K.B.); *Larochelle* v. *Plouffe* (1941) 29 Que. S.C. 248; *Champagne* v. *Plouffe* (1941) 79 Que. S.C. 310; *R.* v. *Coleman* (1927) 47 C.C.C. 148 (N.S.S.C.); *Ex p. Kleinys* [1965] 3 C.C.C. 102 (B.C.S.C.). Sometimes an application will spur the authorities to review the case, even though the habeas corpus is not granted: see e.g. *Champagne* v. *Plouffe*, *supra*.

[20] *Lingley* v. *Hickman* [1972] F.C. 171 (T.D.). This may be possible in England: see *R.* v. *Criminal Injuries Compensation Board, ex p. Lain* [1967] 2 Q.B. 864. Cf. Wade, (1967) 83 L.Q.R. 486.

[21] *Re Lingley and New Brunswick Board of Review* (1975) 25 C.C.C. (2d) 81 (Fed. C.A.); *Re Abel and Advisory Review Board* (1980) 56 C.C.C. (2d) 153 (Ont. C.A.); *Re Egglestone and Mousseau and Advisory Review Board* (1983) 6 C.C.C. (3d) 1 (Ont. Div. Ct.); *Re Jollimore and The Queen* (1986) 27 C.C.C. (3d) 166 (N.S.S.C.).

[22] *Re Brooks' Detention* (1962) 38 W.W.R. 51 (Alta. S.C.) where Milvain J. refused the application for habeas corpus but stated, at 53: 'I am, however, firmly of the view that the lieutenant-governor cannot exercise his discretionary powers in any arbitrary fashion, and that unless proper evidence is produced to indicate that Mrs. Brooks' mental condition is such that it would be dangerous for her and the public for her to be at large, she should no longer be detained. If an arbitrary decision were made, I feel that the matter could then be reviewed by way of habeas corpus under the common law right of the court to intervene where the liberty of the subject is involved.'

[23] Cf. *Re McCann and The Queen* (1982) 67 C.C.C. (2d) 180 (B.C.C.A.), quashing an order for want of procedural fairness, but refusing release on habeas corpus.

[24] *Re Procedures and the Mental Health Act* (1984) 5 D.L.R (4th) 577 (P.E.I.S.C.) is unclear on this point. While the court suggested that such individuals lack capacity to bring habeas corpus proceedings (at 590), the court also held that they had a Charter right to the remedy. For discussion of capacity in general, see *infra*, p. 221.

is a delicate problem to be faced by a legal adviser consulted by a mentally ill patient. He or she must decide if the patient is capable of giving instructions. There has been some indication that a solicitor who sets the machinery in motion for habeas corpus may be responsible in costs if the court feels that he or she has acted without proper instructions.[25] Probably the courts will allow a certain amount of latitude in this regard so that solicitors are not discouraged from acting for these people. Some patients may find difficulty in persuading hospital authorities that they should be allowed to see a solicitor as some psychiatrists apparently consider it good policy to deprive a patient of information regarding legal rights lest the patient deny himself needed treatment.[26]

[25] Swadron, *Detention of the Mentally Disordered* (1964), 205; *Dack* (1914) 5 O.W.N. 774 (H.C.); *Avery* [1951] O.W.N. 810 (H.C.). See *Ex p. Child* (1854) 15 C.B. 238; *Re Carter* (1893) 95 L.T.O.S. 37; suggesting that costs should be awarded against a third party who unsuccessfully applied on behalf of a lunatic.

[26] Szasz, *Law, Liberty and Psychiatry* (1965), 67. Samuels (1973) 123 New L.J. 277 at 278, suggests that insufficient effort is made to inform patients of their legal rights. In *Lussa* v. *Health Science Centre* (1983) 9 C.R.R. 350 (Man. Q.B.) it was held that posting a sign in the ward advising patients of their rights was insufficient to satisfy the requirements of the Charter of Rights and Freedoms, s.10

7

Problems of Restraint and Time

1. RESTRAINT OF LIBERTY AS A BASIS FOR THE WRIT

Habeas corpus is a quick, efficient remedy which may be used at any stage of the legal process, and there âre many conceivable situations where a party who is not actually in a gaol cell may wish to seek relief of habeas corpus. A person's liberty can be curtailed, yet not completely taken away, and the person so restrained may wish to question the legality of the restraint, especially if no other remedy is available or appropriate.

The authorities do not define with precision the degree of confinement that will justify the issue of a writ of habeas corpus.[1] It has probably been assumed from the very nature of the remedy that there must be some form of physical restraint before the writ can issue.

In this chapter, the possibility of using habeas corpus to question the legality of a number of restraints less severe than actual custody is considered. It is argued that to avoid 'watering down' the remedy of habeas corpus, it should only be used where there is some significant curtailment of personal freedom. This, however, does not exclude the use of the writ where the applicant is not in actual custody: it merely requires the court to assess the nature of the control or restraint, and to quantify its gravity. If it appears to bear the weighty consideration of habeas corpus, then there is no reason to refuse to allow the writ to be used.

(a) *Quantitative Restraints*

A distinction may be drawn between two types of restraint, labelled here, for want of better expressions, quantitative and qualitative restraints. The first, quantitative restraint, signifies the confinement of a person within a given perimeter. The most obvious example is incarceration in gaol, where there can be no doubt that habeas corpus is appropriate. There have been several cases of habeas corpus being

---

[1] Similar problems arise under the European Human Rights Convention; see Fawcett, *The Application of the European Convention on Human Rights* (2nd ed. 1987), 68–74.

used to test the legality of a confinement on a ship,[2] in a hospital,[3] or in a camp.[4] In these situations there has been no doubt that habeas corpus is appropriate. It may be asked, however, whether the writ is only available to test a restraint of a relatively close nature. Beyond cases of confinement in a given room, vessel, or building, the person may be required to remain within a given city, territory, district or state. Several examples may be imagined. In an American case, a military person was required by orders to remain within the city of Washington.[5] During the war, emergency regulations were made which restricted movement out of or into certain parts of England.[6] If a passport is confiscated,[7] if the immigration authorities refuse the right of embarkation,[8] or even under the writ of *ne exeat regno*,[9] an individual may be effectively confined within the United Kingdom. In all these cases, the individual retains the freedom to move about within the defined area, but at the same time cannot go beyond its circumference, however large.

There has been very little discussion of whether habeas corpus may be used to test this sort of territorial restraint and the assessment here is, admittedly, speculative. The question was raised, however, by the *Mwenya* case in 1960,[10] where the writ was issued to determine the legality of the applicant's confinement within a district of 1,500 square miles. However, the point was not fully considered by the court since it was agreed by the parties not to argue the propriety of issuing the writ to test such a restraint,[11] and for that reason, the authority of the case on this point is weakened.

---

[2] *Sommersett's Case* (1772) 20 St. Tr. 1; case cited *infra*, n. 35, p. 222.

[3] See *supra*, Chapter 6.

[4] See the internment and alien enemy cases, cited *supra*, Chapter 4.

[5] *Wales* v. *Whitney* 114 U.S. 564 (1885): habeas corpus refused, but cf. *infra*, n. 54, p. 175.

[6] Reg. 14, pursuant to Defence of the Realm Acts 1914–15; Defence (General) Regulations, reg. 18(2), pursuant to Emergency Powers (Defence) Act 1939. Such an order was questioned (unsuccessfully) on certiorari in *Ronnfeldt* v. *Phillips* (1918) 35 T.L.R. 46 (C.A.) and in *R.* v. *Denison, ex p. Nagale* (1916) 85 L.J.Q.B. 1744.

[7] See *Ghani* v. *Jones* [1970] 1 Q.B. 693; discussed *infra*, p. 165.

[8] Immigration Act 1971, s.3(7); Sched. II s.3(2).

[9] For *ne exeat regno* see Bridge, 'The Case of the Rugby Football Team and the High Prerogative Writ' (1972) 88 L.Q.R. 83, commenting on *Parsons* v. *Burk* [1971] N.Z.L.R. 244; *Felton* v. *Callis* [1968] 3 All E.R. 673; *Glover* v. *Walters* (1950) 80 C.L.R. 172; *Al Nahkel for Contracting and Trading Ltd.* v. *Lowe* [1986] Q.B. 235; *Allied Arab Bank Ltd.* v. *Hajjar* [1988] 2 W.L.R. 942; Story, *Commentaries on Equity Jurisprudence* (3rd ed. 1920), 620–4.

[10] *Ex p. Mwenya* [1960] 1 Q.B. 241.

[11] Ibid. at 245–6.

It is submitted that it should not be automatically assumed that habeas corpus will only lie where the applicant is confined within a gaol or some other such close perimeter. A restraint within a broader circumference may very often be more than a trifling inconvenience. It may be seen as something of the order of a significant restraint on the liberty of the subject, and on that account, habeas corpus may be an appropriate remedy.

An example of judicial reaction to a restraint of this nature is provided by a case which involved a mandamus application to compel the police to return a confiscated passport.[12] Lord Denning M.R. called this a matter which involved restricting 'liberty of movement [which] is [something] regarded so highly by the law of England that it is not to be hindered or prevented except on the surest grounds.'[13] Placing the restriction at this level, it is submitted, may make the matter appropriate for review on habeas corpus.[14]

(b) *Qualitative Restraints*

As well as territorial restraints, the freedom of the individual may be curtailed in a more qualitative sense. This occurs where the individual's right to live and to come and go as he or she pleases is restricted even though there is no confinement within a given perimeter. Again, many examples may be imagined, and in fact, the appropriateness of testing the legality of this kind of restraint on habeas corpus has arisen more frequently[15] than has the issue of quantitative restraint.

(c) *Bail*

It seems that the English courts will allow an application where the applicant has been bailed. The usual practice is for the person concerned to surrender to his bail at the Royal Courts of Justice where the application is heard. The applicant is then either released or remanded

---

[12] *Ghani* v. *Jones* [1970] 1 Q.B. 693.   [13] Ibid. at 709.

[14] See also *Guzzardi* v. *Italy* (1980) 3 E.H.R.R. 333, holding that requiring the applicant to live on an island and within an area of 2.5 sq. km. constituted a deprivation of liberty within the meaning of Art. 5 of the European Convention on Human Rights.

[15] Cf. the law of false imprisonment, where it seems that there must be confinement within a certain boundary: 'Some confusion seems to me to arise from confounding imprisonment of the body with mere loss of freedom: it is one part of the definition of freedom to be able to go whithersoever one pleases; but imprisonment is something more than the mere loss of this power; it involves the notion of restraint within some limits defined by a will or power exterior to our own.' *Bird* v. *Jones* (1845) 7 Q.B. 742 at 744, per Coleridge J.

back to the custody of the person against whom the application is made. There does not appear to be any requirement for formal proof that the applicant is in custody at the time the application is heard.

It is not clear on the authorities whether the court will entertain an application for the writ by someone who remains free on bail.[16] A bail order may involve positive restrictions on movement, or impose other burdens and it can be argued that an applicant released on bail is still subject to a restraint, the legality of which can be questioned on habeas corpus.

It is clear that bail theoretically constitutes custody. The custody of the party bailed is said to be transferred from the gaoler to the sureties who become keepers with authority to imprison as they see fit: 'a man's bail are looked upon as his gaolers of his own choosing, and that person bailed is in the eye of the law, for many purposes, esteemed to be as much in the prison of the court by which he is bailed, as if he were in the actual custody of the proper gaoler.'[17]

In addition there is some early nineteenth-century authority which might be taken to suggest that the writ is available to an applicant who is free on bail. Habeas corpus 'cum causa' was used up to the mid nineteenth century to remove civil suits from inferior courts into the King's Bench,[18] since a defendant could, at this time, be imprisoned

---

[16] In *Re Amand* [1941] 2 K.B. 239 at 249 (aff'd [1943] A.C. 147), Visc. Caldecote C.J. noted that the applicant had been bailed, and added: 'this makes no difference and we have to deal with the application as if he were still detained in custody.' For other cases where applications have been entertained, but without discussion of the issue, see *R. v. Secretary of State for India in Council and Others, ex p. Ezekiel* [1941] 2 K.B. 169; *Re Caborn-Waterfield* [1960] 2 All E.R. 178 at 183; *R. v. Governor of Pentonville Prison, ex p. Khubchandani* (1980) 71 Cr. App. R. 241. See also *R. v. Spilsbury* [1898] 2 Q.B. 615 at 621, where Lord Russell C.J. said that the prisoner committed for extradition would still be able to apply for habeas corpus even though he had been bailed, relying especially on the statutory requirement that the defendant be advised of his right to challenge the extradition habeas corpus. In *Government of the United States of America v. Jennings* [1983] 1 A.C. 624 the applicant was committed for extradition but released 'on bail on her undertaking to apply for a writ of habeas corpus' (at 627).

[17] II Hawkins *P.C.*, 138–9. There is much authority to the same effect. See e.g. Highmore, *Digest of the Doctrine of Bail* (1783), p. xi: '... he is always accounted by the law, to be in their ward and custody for the time; and they may, if they will, hold him in ward or in prison till that time, or otherwise at their will: so that he who is bailed, shall not be said by the law to be at large, or at his own liberty.' Also, III Viner *Abridg.*, 438; II Hale *P.C.*, 124; *Foxall v. Barnett* (1853) 2 E. & B. 928; *R. v. Fortier* (1902) 6 C.C.C. 191 (Que. K.B.); *R. v. Lepicki* (1925) 44 C.C.C. 263 (Man. K.B.); *Anon.* (1704) 6 Mod. 231.

[18] Tidd, *Practice of the Courts of King's Bench and Common Pleas* (9th ed. 1828), vol. I, 397–418. For cases where habeas corpus was used, see *Anon.* (1665) 1 Sid. 231; *Highmore v. Barlow* (1750) Barnes 421. The use of habeas corpus for this purpose is discussed in *Goodright v. Dring* (1823) 2 D. & R. 401.

or held to bail in a civil cause. Civil practice permitted the plaintiff to attach the defendant's goods or person in certain cases in order to force the defendant to appear in the cause, but if the defendant could obtain bail, it was possible to have the goods released or to avoid being personally taken or held under the plaintiff's attachment.[19] Where the defendant was bailed and not in custody, habeas corpus could still be used to remove the cause.[20]

In these cases, the court was merely asserting its control over an inferior jurisdiction rather than actually making a determination on the legality of the applicant's confinement. But if this authority does anything, it suggests that habeas corpus is appropriate where the applicant has been bailed.

The issue has been discussed in greater detail in the Canadian cases where it has been held that the writ is only available where the applicant is in actual physical custody, and not when free on bail.[21] At the same time, however, the courts have had no difficulty in limiting the effect of this rule. In the case of an applicant free on bail, the practice is to surrender the applicant into the custody of the appropriate gaoler or sheriff on the day that application is to be heard.[22]

[19] See e.g. Petersdorff, *Law of Bail* (1824), 1–13.

[20] Tidd, op. cit. 403–4; *Mitchell* v. *Mitchinham* (1823) 2 D. & R. 722: 'When common bail is filed, still the party in the eye of the law is in custody, and in such case the habeas corpus may issue.' The writ was refused since the party had given no bail. The courts did look to the practice of the local court, and would only grant relief on habeas corpus where its use of bail involved some right of control over the body of the defendant: *Palmer* v. *Forsyth & Bell* (1825) 4 B. & C. 401.

[21] *Re Bartels* (1907) 13 C.C.C. 59 (Ont. H.C.); *Ex p. Seriesky* (1912) 21 C.C.C. 140 (N.B.S.C.); *Re Bhagwan Singh* (1914) 23 C.C.C. 5 (B.C.S.C.); *R.* v. *Keeper of Halifax County Jail, ex p. Simpson* (1918) 30 C.C.C. 334 (N.S.S.C.); *Verrault* v. *Lachance* [1929] 2 D.L.R. 900 (Que. S.C.); *Laberge* v. *Lachance* (1929) 32 Que. P.R. 85 (S.C.); *Re Isbell* (1929) 52 C.C.C. 171 (S.C.C.); *Re Kelly* (1939) 72 C.C.C. 401 (N.S. Cty. Ct.); *Masella* v. *Langlais* [1955] S.C.R. 263; *Ex p. Brent* [1955] O.R. 480 (Ont. C.A.) (aff'd, [1956] S.C.R. 318); *R.* v. *Pickett* (1975) 31 C.R.N.S. 239 (Ont. C.A.); *Re Chamakese and The Queen* (1978) 44 C.C.C. (2d) 361 (Sask. Q.B.). *Contra, R.* v. *Cameron* (1897) 1 C.C.C. 169 (Que. S.C.); *R.* v. *Duchaine* (1923) 34 Que. K.B. 479 (Que. C.A.); *de Bernonville* v. *Langlais* [1951] Que. S.C. 277.

[22] *Masella* v. *Langlais* [1955] S.C.R. 263 at 271, per Locke J.; *Re Shumiatcher* [1962] S.C.R. 38. *Ex p. Wortsman* (1970) 1 C.C.C. (2d) 316 (Ont. H.C.); *Ex p. Salajko* (1974) 19 C.C.C. (2nd) 368 (Ont. H.C.); Hart, 'Habeas Corpus and Certiorari in Criminal Cases', [1961] *Law Society of Upper Canada Special Lectures* 313, 316–17. Cf., however, *Ex p. McGinnis* [1971] 3 O.R. 783 (H.C.), where Wright J. expressed his displeasure with this 'artificial procedure' and dismissed the application on the grounds, *inter alia*, that the surrender into custody had not been proved by affidavit. *Re Martin, Simard and Desjardins and The Queen* (1977) 34 C.C.C. (2d) 453 (Ont. H.C.) (aff'd. (1977) 41 C.C.C. (2d) 308 (C.A.); [1978] 2 S.C.R. 511) holds that it is not sufficient for the applicant to have repudiated the recognizance entered to obtain judicial interim release

This is considered sufficient custody for the purposes of habeas corpus. It allows the applicant to use the writ where it is the accepted way to challenge the validity of the proceedings undergone, as for example, where it is sought to challenge a committal for trial.[23]

The result is that while the Canadian courts will continue to say that actual custody is a requisite to the exercise of habeas corpus jurisdiction, they will allow a person who is free on bail to apply for the remedy by following this bit of ritual on the day when his application is heard.

While the Canadian courts say one thing and do another in so far as bailed prisoners are concerned, it is still important to examine what they have said about the custody requirement. This will affect applicants not in actual custody and not in a position to surrender themselves into custody on the day of the application.[24]

It is submitted that the rationale given by the Canadian courts for the requirement of actual custody is unsatisfactory. In the leading case,[25] the Supreme Court merely relied on a supposed lack of authority in England, an American case holding that custody was required,[26] and principally, on the following dictum of Lord Watson in *Barnardo* v. *Ford*:

The remedy of habeas corpus is, in my opinion, intended to facilitate the release of persons actually detained in unlawful custody, and was not meant to afford the means of inflicting penalties upon those persons by whom they were at some time or other illegally detained. Accordingly, the writ invariably sets forth that the individual whose release is sought, whether adult or infant is taken and detained in the custody of the person to whom it is addressed, and rightly so, because it is the fact of detention, and nothing else, which gives the Court its jurisdiction.[27]

The *Barnardo* case will be more closely examined[28] and it will be shown that Lord Watson was dealing with another issue, namely, to

and be subject to immediate imprisonment—the applicant must be in actual custody. See also *Ex p. Gilbreath* (1974) 20 C.C.C. (2d) 393 (Ont. H.C.), discussed *infra*, n. 45, p. 173.

[23] *Supra*, pp. 130–2.

[24] As, for example, in the case of parole: see *Ex p. Hinks* [1972] 3 O.R. 182 (H.C.), where habeas corpus was refused to one on parole. The same application was later entertained as an action for an injunction and declaration: *Hinks* v. *National Parole Board* [1972] F.C. 925 (T.D.).

[25] *Masella* v. *Langlais* [1955] S.C.R. 263.

[26] *Wales* v. *Whitney* 114 U.S. 564 (1885). Cf. the more recent case of *Jones* v. *Cunningham* 371 U.S. 236 (1963), where habeas corpus was granted to a person released on parole.

[27] [1892] A.C. 326 at 333–4   [28] *Infra*, pp. 178–9.

whom the writ should be directed where the custody of the party sought has been improperly given up. The issue of the quantum of restraint which must exist for relief to be sought on habeas corpus was not before the court in the *Barnardo* case and the Supreme Court of Canada quoted this passage out of context.

Still, it might be argued from a technical standpoint that the applicant must be under sufficient control for the respondent to be able to bring him or her before the court on the return.[29] This reasoning is to be rejected: applicants are no longer brought before the court on a return to the writ and it will be seen that parties who are not in actual physical control of the applicant have been made respondent to the writ. Moreover, with respect to the control required to make someone a proper respondent, Atkin L.J. correctly pointed out, in the case of O'Brien, that: 'Actual physical custody is obviously not essential ... in testing the liability of the respondent to the writ the question is as to *de facto* control.'[30]

While the rationale given by the Canadian courts for the requirement of actual custody is unsatisfactory, the practice, followed in both England and Canada, permitting those on bail to have resort to habeas corpus by surrendering into custody for the hearing of the application is significant.

(d) *Parole, Probation, and Suspended Sentence*

There has been virtually no consideration of the appropriateness of habeas corpus to challenge the legality of parole, probation or suspended sentence controls. An individual who is subject to such controls may be restricted as to employment, place of residence, associates, and general daily habits.[31] Such an individual is not confined within a given precinct, but is subject to constant supervision and the threat of complete incarceration. While these restrictions differ from bail in that they do not involve custody in a technical sense, it is submitted that habeas corpus could still be an appropriate remedy.[32] It may well be that the writ should not be used in all

---

[29] See *Ex p. Seriesky* (1912) 21 C.C.C. 140 (N.B.S.C.), where the court refused habeas corpus to one on bail on the grounds that if the writ were granted it would require the sheriff to arrest the applicant. This reasoning is entirely unsatisfactory: if the court wanted to have the applicant physically present, it is doubtful that he would have refused to come in voluntarily.

[30] *R. v. Secretary of State for Home Affairs, ex p. O'Brien* [1923] 2 K.B. 361 at 398.

[31] Criminal Justice Act 1967, s.60(4); West (ed.), *The Future of Parole* (1972), 16, 86.

[32] Habeas corpus has been refused in Canada to an applicant free on parole: *supra*, n. 24, p. 168.

situations: the nature of the control over the applicant may vary from case to case. It would seem, however, that most controls of this nature would ordinarily be seen as a significant curtailment of personal freedom, if only because any breach of conditions of release usually carries the sanction of immediate incarceration.

(e) *Controls Under Mental Health Legislation*

One of the best examples of the English courts allowing habeas corpus to be used to question a qualitative restraint less severe than actual physical custody is provided by the *Rutty* case in 1956.[33] There, the applicant had previously been detained in a hospital under a magistrate's order pursuant to the Mental Deficiency Act 1913. At the time of the application, however, and for some considerable time before, she had been with her family on 'residential licence'. This provided that she should not be let out of the house alone, that she should not be allowed to form attachments with men, and that she was to be returned to the institution on written request by the medical superintendant.[34] The court ordered that the applicant be discharged without discussing the point of restraint, and the court seems to have treated the case just as if she had been held in the institution. It is submitted that the court correctly found this to be a proper case for habeas corpus. The applicant was not entirely confined within a building, but not to be allowed out unaccompanied must represent a significant curtailment of personal liberty. The threat of immediate incarceration without further proceedings itself entails a degree of control over the individual's habits and movements which is grave enough to warrant habeas corpus relief.

(f) *Indentures of Apprenticeship*

In at least three early cases, habeas corpus was granted to release an apprentice from indentures on the grounds of illegality or unjustified treatment.[35] There is no discussion of the sort of restraint that the apprentice was subjected to, but it is unlikely that it went beyond the controls to which such persons were ordinarily subjected. It would seem that habeas corpus was a convenient way to get both the master and the apprentice before the court so that the ground of complaint could be gone into. Again, the nature of the restraint was short of

---

[33] *R. v. Board of Control, ex p. Rutty* [1956] 2 Q.B. 109.   [34] Ibid. at 112.
[35] *Delaval* (1763) 3 Burr. 1434; *Davis* (1794) 5 T.R. 715; *Eden* (1813) 2 M. & S. 226; cf. *Gill* (1806) 7 East 376, where habeas corpus was refused to an apprentice.

actual incarceration, but nonetheless, of a pervasive nature, and one that seemed to satisfy the court as being appropriate for habeas corpus.[36]

(g) *Military Conscription*

Conscription into military service is another example of a restraint on freedom which involves less than actual incarceration, and yet which may allow for review on habeas corpus. Indeed, at one time, one of the principle uses of habeas corpus was to test the legality of impressment.[37] There may well have been a measure of restraint which approached actual incarceration and it may be that the courts did not give relief unless a restraint of that nature existed.[38] There are, however, instances of the writ being used in modern times where the restraint was much less severe. In an English case during the First War,[39] and in several Canadian cases,[40] habeas corpus has been issued where the only restraint on the applicant was ordinary military discipline.

Again, however, there has been little discussion of what was at stake. A Saskatchewan court explained simply that: 'The applicant . . . is now under command of [the] Lieutenant Colonel [and] of necessity his

---

[36] In *Jones* v. *Cunningham* 371 U.S. 236 at 238 (1963), discussed *infra*, n. 54, p. 175, the American Supreme Court placed special reliance on the fact that: 'English courts have long recognized the writ as a proper remedy even though the restraint is something less than close physical confinement.' The cases cited were *Delaval, supra,* n. 35, p. 170 and *Clarkson* (1720) 1 Str. 444 where the writ had been granted to determine whether a woman was being constrained by her guardians to stay away from her husband.

[37] *Opinion on the Writ of Habeas Corpus* Wilm. 86n.

[38] Ibid. 85n; 'When he was at liberty, with the regiment to which he was delivered, he could have no habeas corpus.' In *Reader* (1811) Gude, *Crown Practice* 286, where the applicant applied while free on leave, and Lord Ellenborough refused the writ: 'He is at large; therefore the writ cannot be granted. He must be in actual custody . . .' See also *R.* v. *Dawes* (1785) 1 Burr. 636; *R.* v. *Kessel* (1758) 1 Burr. 637; where the reporter's note reads: 'In both these cases, neither of them could have brought a habeas corpus: neither of them was in custody. Dawes had deserted and absconded: Kessel was made a corporal.'

[39] *R.* v. *Commanding Officer etc., ex p. Freyberger* [1917] 2 K.B. 129 (C.A.), where however, counsel expressly refrained from raising an objection on this point. Habeas corpus was also used in other cases to test the legality of conscription where there was no issue as to custody: see e.g. *R.* v. *Commanding officer of Morn Hill Camp, ex p. Ferguson* [1917] 1 K.B. 176; *R.* v. *Jones* [1917] 2 I.R. 7.

[40] *Arsenault* v. *Puise* (1916) 50 Que. S.C. 373; *Perlman* v. *Piche and the A.G. of Canada* (1918) 41 D.L.R. 147 (Que. S.C.); *Re Lewis* (1918) 41 D.L.R. 1 (Alta. C.A.); *Re Bien & Cooke* (1943) 81 C.C.C. 316 (Sask. K.B.); *Weiner* v. *Archambault* [1957] Que P.R. 13 (Q.B.); *Contra, Re Fournier* (1916) 26 C.C.C. 405 (Que S.C.); *Laflamme* v. *Renard* (1945) 84 C.C.C. 153 (Que. S.C.).

liberties are restricted in a way that would not be applicable if he were not in the army.'[41]

It is submitted that habeas corpus is properly allowed in such cases.

Admittedly, whether the applicant's liberties 'are restricted in a way that would not be applicable if he were not in the army' may not be a test of sufficient probative value for other cases. The extent of the restraint should be quantified: in the case of military service, the applicant may be confined to a camp, and will be subject to a peremptory disciplinary regime, liable to be immediately incarcerated if the limits of proper military conduct are transgressed. One's freedom to live, and to come and go as one pleases, is severely restricted and one is subjected to a substantial restraint which goes beyond mere inconvenience or the ordinary obligations of employment. It is the sort of restraint which may be challenged on habeas corpus without any risk of departure from the concept that it is a remedy to protect the personal liberty of the subject.

(h) *Immigration Cases*

A special problem has arisen in certain immigration cases where the applicant has been denied the right of entry, or ordered to be deported. The applicant for habeas corpus in such a case could gain immediate release by forgoing proceedings which impugn the order refusing entry, or by simply agreeing to go where he or she has been sent.[42] In the vast majority of cases, no objection is taken to the immigrant's resort to habeas corpus.[43] However, in the case of *Mughal*,[44] Widgery C.J. indicated that habeas corpus was inappropriate where the applicant was refused the right of re-entry following a holiday abroad on the grounds that he had not satisfied the immigration officer that he had established residence in Britain before 1968. According to Widgery

---

[41] *Re Bien & Cooke* (1943) 81 C.C.C. 316.

[42] See e.g. *Ex p. Shadeo Bhurosah* [1967] 3 All E.R. 831 (C.A.), where Denning M.R. noted that of eight original applicants: 'Two of them accepted the decision [of the Divisional Court] and have gone back to Mauritius. Now there are six left here who apply to this court.'

[43] The point was disposed of in two Australian cases: *Ex p. Lo Pak* (1888) 9 L.R.N.S.W. 221; *ex p. Leong Kum* (1888) 9 L.R.N.S.W. 250. In *Khawaja* v. *Secretary of State for the Home Department* [1984] A.C. 74, one of the applicants had been released after he applied for judicial review, but the appeal was dealt with as if it were a habeas corpus application and Lord Fraser of Tullybelton specifically noted (at 93): '... the appeal has been dealt with all along as if the appellant were still detained, and I think that is right because his personal liberty is undoubtedly restricted.'

[44] *R.* v. *Secretary of State for the Home Department, ex p. Mughal* [1973] 1 W.L.R. 1133.

C.J. '. . . this man is in custody not because he has been totally denied his freedom, but because he chose to remain in custody while this matter was being determined, rather than go back to Pakistan, as he could have done the very day that he arrived.'[45]

Admittedly, more is at stake in these cases than the applicant's immediate right to liberty. In effect, the habeas corpus proceedings are being used to determine the applicant's status in the law of immigration. It is submitted, however, that this incidental aspect of the proceedings should not obscure the fact that the applicant can only remain within the court's jurisdiction under restraint. It is difficult to see how, *vis-à-vis* that court, it can be said that there is no restraint. Habeas corpus has been used in a large number of similar cases, and it is submitted that the restriction suggested by the *Mughal* decision is unjustified.

The *Khawaja* decision makes it clear that there can be no distinction between British nationals and others with respect to the availability of habeas corpus and no basis upon which to deny non-patrials the benefit of the writ if they have been deprived of their liberty.[46] However, a distinction is drawn between those who are refused entry and those who are granted leave, but subsequently detained on grounds of alleged fraud or non-disclosure. In the former case, the scope of review will permit the court to ensure that prescribed procedures have been followed, but will be shaped by the deference due to an administrative decision reached under statutory authority. In the latter, the facts may be more fully explored.[47]

---

[45] [1973] 1 W.L.R. 1133 at 1136. In *R. v. Secretary of State for the Home Department, ex p. Thakrar* [1974] Q.B. 684 at 704, Lord Denning agreed with this dictum, but appears to have rejected the proposition in *R. v. Governor of Pentonville Prison, ex p. Azam* [1973] 2 W.L.R. 949 at 961. For a similar situation, see *R. v. Secretary of State for Foreign Affairs & Secretary of State for Colonies, ex p. Greenberg* [1947] 2 All E.R. 550 at 555–6, holding that a group of immigrants deported from Palestine, on board a British ship, could not question their imprisonment, *inter alia*, on the grounds that they had refused to disembark in France when given the opportunity. The court held that they had stayed on board of their own free will and there could therefore be no question of restraint. The case is further discussed *infra*, p. 197. See also *Re Rojas and The Queen* (1978) 41 C.C.C. (2d) 566 (Ont. C.A.). In *Ex p. Gilbreath* (1974) 20 C.C.C. (2d) 393 (Ont. H.C.) habeas corpus to review a committal for trial was refused on the ground that the applicant would have been released had he entered a recognizance pursuant to an order for judicial interim release.

[46] [1984] A.C. 74 at 111–12, per Lord Scarman.

[47] Ibid., at 122 per Lord Bridge of Harwich and at 127 per Lord Templeman. For a fuller discussion of the scope of review mandated by *Khawaja*, see *supra*, p. 74.

(i) *Restraint and Consent in Child Custody Cases*

Habeas corpus has long been used to gain the custody of infants.[48] The writ is issued on the application of the party seeking custody and it is directed against whoever has control of the infant. The writ notionally still rests on the idea of relieving a restraint, although it is quite clear that the ordinary rules of family law apply.[49] Habeas corpus was the common law remedy to decide questions of custody, and while it has been largely replaced by statutory procedures, it still may prove useful where those statutory remedies have been exhausted or are inappropriate.[50] Consideration of the factors which govern the question of child custody is not within the province of this book. There are, however, points to be noted with regard to the elements of restraint and consent in these cases.

That habeas corpus in custody cases differs fundamentally from its use to secure personal liberty has always been recognized. It is seen to involve 'not a question of liberty, but of nurture, control, and education',[51] it 'is being used not for the body, but for the soul of the child'.[52] Accordingly, the courts have consistently held that neither the allegation that the child is under no restraint, nor that the child consents to his situation, will prevent them from acting on habeas corpus.[53]

(j) *Conclusion*

On the basis of the authorities, there would seem to be little doubt that habeas corpus can be used in several situations where the applicant is not actually incarcerated. The courts have given little consideration to the principles at stake, but have allowed the writ to be used to question a variety of non-custodial restraints. A fictional restraint has

---

[48] The form of the writ is the same 'high prerogative writ' of habeas corpus ad subjiciendum: *Re Belson* (1850) 7 Moo. P.C.C. 114. As a result of the Judicature Act 1873, the courts of common law apply the principles of equity on habeas corpus to determine child custody: *R.* v. *Gyngall* [1893] 2 Q.B. 232 (C.A.).

[49] Habeas corpus cases which involve the issue of child custody are now heard only by the Family Division: Ord. 54, r.11.

[50] For recent examples, see *Re A.B.* [1954] 2 Q.B. 385; *Ex p. D.* [1971] 1 O.R. 311 (H.C.); *R.* v. *L., ex p. P.* (1967) 11 F.L.R. 25.

[51] *Barnardo* v. *McHugh* [1891] 1 Q.B. 194 at 204 per Lord Esher M.R. (aff'd [1891] A.C. 388).

[52] *Re Carroll* [1931] 1 K.B. 317 at 331, per Scrutton L.J.

[53] *R.* v. *Greenhill* (1836) 4 A. & E. 624; *R.* v. *Clarke, re Race* (1857) 7 E. & B. 186; *Ex p. M'Clellan* (1831) 1 Dowl. 81; *R.* v. *Howes* (1860) 3 E. & E. 332; *Stevenson* v. *Florant* [1925] S.C.R. 532.

been accepted in the cases dealing with bail. While the courts say that actual custody is required, in practice, individuals who have been bailed have been allowed to apply. There has, however, been virtually nothing in the cases to suggest a test which could be applied to determine whether a prospective applicant is sufficiently restrained to be entitled to relief on habeas corpus. Any suggested test is purely speculative, but an attempt should be made to define considerations which underlie the question.

The idea of personal liberty, that is, the physical freedom to come and go as one pleases, is considered to possess special value in the common law tradition. The importance which is attached to habeas corpus parallels this value. The writ is considered to provide an assurance that personal freedom will always be protected, and there may be a fear that if used in situations which do not plainly involve a significant curtailment of personal freedom, the force of the writ may be 'watered down'. On the other hand, many restraints which involve less than complete incarceration may still merit the weighty consideration which is symbolized by habeas corpus. It will not weaken the remedy to allow it to be used so long as that which is challenged palpably constitutes a restriction on personal liberty.

It is submitted that when the question is raised there should be an assessment of the nature of the control or restriction of rights which is challenged and a determination made as to whether that circumstance would ordinarily be seen as a significant curtailment of personal freedom.[54] If a restraint satisfies that test, the writ of habeas corpus should be available to question its legality.

2. TO WHOM THE WRIT SHOULD BE DIRECTED

The general rule is that the writ of habeas corpus should be directed to the person who has physical custody of the prisoner.[55] The writ may, however, be directed to several persons where there is some doubt as

[54] Cf. the test suggested by the American Supreme Court in *Jones* v. *Cunningham* 371 U.S. 236 at 243 (1963): '[Matters which] significantly restrain petitioners' liberty to do those things which in this country free men are entitled to do.'

[55] *Anon.* (1586) Godb. 44: 'the habeas corpus shall be alwayes directed to him who hath the custody of the body'. Cf. where the writ was used to remove a civil suit from an inferior court into the King's Bench when the writ was directed to the judges of the inferior court: Tidd, *Practice of the King's Bench and Common Pleas* (9th ed. 1828), vol. 1, 404.

to who has custody,[56] or, to some person other than the gaoler or actual custodian of the party detained. With respect to the latter possibility, problems may occur where it is doubted that the person to whom the writ is directed has sufficient custody or control of the prisoner.

This issue will usually arise where it is sought to make a minister of the crown respondent to the writ. This has been done in a large number of cases[57] without any argument or comment.

The cases which specifically deal with this point all present the situation of the prisoner being detained outside England, where the detention has been made on English authority, and the writ has been directed to someone in England.

In the leading case of this type, *R.* v. *Secretary of State for Home Affairs, ex p. O'Brien*,[58] an order had been made for the internment of the applicant by the Home Secretary, pursuant to the Restoration of Order in Ireland Act 1920, but after the Irish Free State had been established. The prisoner had been given over to the Irish, and it was impossible for the English courts to issue the writ to Ireland.[59] The writ was therefore directed to the Home Secretary, held by the Court of Appeal to be a proper respondent so long as he or she exercised *de facto* control over the applicant's detention. In fact, the nature of the Home Secretary's control was doubtful, and the court ordered the writ to issue so that the extent of his or her control could be tested. The decision makes it clear that the test is *de facto* rather than legal control,

---

[56] While Holt C.J. held in *R.* v. *Fowler* (1705) 1 Salk. 350 that the writ could not be addressed in the disjunctive to the sheriff or the gaoler, the writ has been directed to several persons on many occasions: see e.g. *Carus Wilson's Case* (1845) 7 Q.B. 984; *Re Douglas* (1842) 12 L.J.Q.B. 49; *Leonard Watson's Case* (1839) 9 A. & E. 731. See also s.6 of the Habeas Corpus Act 1640 which provides for the writ to be 'directed generally unto all and every sheriff, gaoler, minister, officer or other person in whose custody the party committed or restrained shall be' in the case of a committal by one of the Courts abolished by the Act.

[57] See e.g. *R.* v. *Home Secretary, ex p. Bressler* (1924) 131 L.T. 386; *Eshugbayi Eleko* v. *Officer Administering the Government of Nigeria* [1928] 1 A.C. 459 (P.C.); *R.* v. *Secretary of State for India in Council, ex p. Ezekiel* [1941] 2 K.B. 169; *Greene* v. *Secretary of State for Home Affairs* [1942] A.C. 284; *R.* v. *Governor of Brixton Prison & Secretary of State for Home Affairs, ex p. Pawel Sliwa* [1952] 1 K.B. 169; *De Demko* v. *Home Secretary* [1959] 1 All E.R. 341; *R.* v. *Secretary of State for Home Affairs, ex p. Soblen* [1962] 3 All E.R. 373.

[58] [1923] 2 K.B. 361 (C.A.) (appeal dismissed for want of jurisdiction [1923] A.C. 603).

[59] Habeas Corpus Act 1862, discussed *infra*, pp. 189–91. In *O'Brien*, Bankes L.J. was clear that the writ would not run: [1923] 2 K.B. 361 at 376; but Scrutton L.J. considered the problem to be one of some difficulty: ibid. at 391.

and that the crux of the matter is simply whether or not an order of the court can be made effective.

However, a more restrictive rule has been given in the protectorate cases where it was sought to make the Colonial Secretary respondent to the writ. The earlier cases tended to say that while '. . . the writ may be addressed to any person who has such control over the imprisonment that he could order the release of the prisoner',[60] the Colonial Secretary was not such a party since that official exercised a purely advisory capacity.[61] This was confirmed in the *Mwenya* case in 1960,[62] where the Divisional Court held that since the Colonial Secretary had taken no part in the decision to order the detention, and, at best, could only advise the sovereign to end the detention,[63] he could, therefore, not properly be made respondent to the writ. It is submitted that in failing to recognize the Colonial Secretary's power over the matter for what it was, the reasoning of the court was unsatisfactory. There can be little doubt about the Colonial Secretary's *de facto* control over the situation and the court could have made him respondent to the writ. In the end, the Court of Appeal held that the writ ran to the protectorate,[64] so that nothing turned on this issue in the result.

In any case, it is submitted that these cases may be distinguished from the situation which has usually arisen, namely, a challenge to the exercise of executive power which depends upon the interpretation of a statute rather than the royal prerogative. In these situations, there can usually be little doubt that the Minister exercises complete control over

---

[60] *R. v. Crewe (Earl), ex p. Sekgome* [1910] 2 K.B. 576 at 592 per Vaughan Williams L.J.

[61] Ibid. Cf. Farwell L.J.'s dictum, at 618, which goes the other way: 'Where a man who owes obedience to laws imposed by England is imprisoned and kept imprisoned without trial in a place maintained by England, and placed under the control of an officer of the Crown who acts under orders of the Colonial Office, and who has acted in the particular case with the assent and approval of and is supported by the Colonial Office, I should be slow to conclude that the Secretary of State could not be called on to make a return to the writ.' The more restrictive interpretation was followed in *Re Ning Yi-Ching* (1939) 56 T.L.R. 3.

[62] *Ex p. Mwenya* [1960] 1 Q.B. 241.

[63] The authority for the detention order in question in the *Mwenya* case was contained in an Order in Council passed pursuant to the Foreign Jurisdiction Act 1890. The Colonial Secretary explained his position in an affidavit: [1960] 1 Q.B. 241 at 244: 'As Her Majesty's Secretary of State for the Colonies I can only advise Her Majesty in regard to the exercise of Her power and jurisdiction in Northern Rhodesia and communicate Her Majesty's orders and instructions to His Excellency the Governor.'

[64] See *infra*, pp. 194–5 for a full discussion on this point.

the matter, and little doubt that he or she has the power to bring the detention to an end. The principle established in the *O'Brien* case is a sound one. It identifies the real issue as being that of control so that the court's order will be effective. The test may be stated as follows: if an order of discharge is made but not carried out, would it be reasonable to hold the prospective respondent to account for failure to implement the order?

3. CUSTODY LOST OR TRANSFERRED

As was seen in the *O'Brien* case,[65] the courts will issue the writ to determine whether the intended respondent does exercise sufficient control over the prisoner, and this procedure has been adopted in child custody cases where there is some doubt as to who has custody of the child as demonstrated by the decision of the House of Lords in *Barnardo* v. *Ford.*[66] A parent applied for the writ in respect of his child, but it appeared by affidavit that the respondent had parted with custody, and it was argued on that account that the respondent could no longer be called upon to produce the child. The House of Lords held that the writ should issue and that it could be determined on the return whether the respondent retained sufficient control over the child to be called upon to produce him. This is plainly a sensible and necessary rule as otherwise, the party having custody could deprive the person legally entitled to the infant by transferring physical custody, while retaining control.

It was also held by the House of Lords in *Barnardo* v. *Ford*, however, that habeas corpus cannot be used to inflict a penalty where the illegal detention by the respondent has in fact ceased. Their lordships were merely saying that the only concern on habeas corpus is to determine the legality of a restraint. This means that if the intended respondent does not exercise control over the prisoner or party sought at the time the application is made, that party cannot be made liable to the writ, even though he or she may at one time have held the party in unlawful custody. An earlier Court of Appeal decision[67] holding that it was no

---

[65] *Supra*, pp. 176–9.
[66] [1892] A.C. 326. See also *Re Agar; Agar* v. *Jones* (1956) 114 C.C.C. 311 (Ont. C.A.), and *Re Matthews* (1859) I.R. 12 C.L. (R.) 233.
[67] *R.* v. *Barnardo* (*Tye's Case*) (1889) 23 Q.B.D. 305.

answer to the writ to say that the custody of the party had been unlawfully given up was expressly disapproved. The decision in *Barnardo* v. *Ford* makes it clear, however, that the court will hold in contempt anyone who parts with custody after being served with the writ, or who evades service in order to get rid of the prisoner. At the same time, it would not constitute contempt should the party lawfully, or even unlawfully, part with custody and control from mere apprehension that habeas corpus proceedings might be taken so long as that party did not have knowledge that such proceedings were actually being taken.[68]

The rule is a good illustration of the purely remedial character of the writ. If the respondent could not actually carry out the court's order to discharge the prisoner, the proceedings fall without any declaration of respective rights. The writ will issue even where the respondent's control is doubtful, and the court will determine on the return whether or not the respondent has taken sufficient steps to produce the party. The respondent who evades or flouts the process risks being held in contempt. Where, however, the respondent actually no longer exercises control over the party, even though he or she held the party at one time in unlawful custody, the matter ends since the court cannot make an effective and enforceable order to get the party released.

4. PROBLEMS OF TIME

The remaining part of this chapter examines several issues which may be conveniently grouped under the heading 'problems of time'. It has been held consistently that the relevant time at which the detention of the prisoner must be justified is the time at which the court considers the return to the writ. This rule means that nothing which has happened before the present cause of detention took effect will be relevant to the issue before the court, unless by reason of some special consideration arising from the particular proceedings. It also means that the prisoner will have difficulty challenging a cause of restraint which will only take effect at some time in the future.

(a) *Prior Illegality*

The general rule is that unless prior illegality vitiates the present

---

[68] See also *Re Thompson* (1888) 5 T.L.R. 540, where it was held that so long as the party has knowledge of the preceedings (there by newspaper report and telegram) he cannot avoid the process by saying that he had not actually been served with the writ.

cause of detention, it will not matter what has happened to the prisoner, so long as the detention is now justified.[69] Whether past illegality does vitiate the present grounds for the detention is a question to be answered by the particular legal rules applicable to the matter in question, and not by any general principles of the law of habeas corpus. The principle often comes into play where the applicant has been illegally arrested. It also will usually allow the authorities to amend and correct informalities which are relied on as grounds for an application.

(i) The Effect of Illegal Arrest.   In its usual and traditional form, the writ of habeas corpus calls for an explanation of both the taking and the detaining of the prisoner: 'We command you that you have ... the body ... together with the day and cause of his being taken and detained...'[70] The form of the writ suggests that an illegal arrest will be grounds for redress on habeas corpus, but the requirement to give the cause of the taking has not been interpreted to extend the grounds for complaint beyond the prisoner's present situation.

A prisoner may apply for the writ from the very moment of arrest,[71] and in that sense, he may challenge the legality of his arrest.[72] However, where there have been valid proceedings subsequent to the arrest, which are offered in justification of the detention, the prisoner will not usually be able to get redress.[73] The reason for this is twofold.

---

[69] See e.g. *Athanassiadis* v. *Government of Greece* [1969] 3 All E.R. 293 at 297 (H.L.); *R.* v. *Smith* (1960) 128 C.C.C. 407 (Ont. S.C.); *Ex p. Leclerc* (1973) 21 C.C.C. (2d) 16 (Que. C.A.); *R.* v. *Plymouth Justices, ex p. Driver* [1986] Q.B. 95; and cases cited *infra*, nn. 78–80, p. 182. Cf. *R.* v. *Bow St. Magistrates, ex p. Mackeson* (1981) 75 Cr. App. R. 24; *R.* v. *Hartley* [1978] 2 N.Z.L.R. 199, holding that there is a discretion to be exercised in favour of the prisoner where continuation of the proceedings would constitute an abuse of process.

[70] 14 *Court Forms* (2nd ed.), 64. In *Darnel's Case* (1627) 3 St. Tr. 1 at 52, it was said that as a general rule the writ called for the cause of the caption as well as the cause of the detention, although the form which had been used in that case did not require it. See also *R.* v. *Bethel* (1702) 5 Mod. 19 at 21; *Warman* (1777) 2 W.Bl. 1204.

[71] 'A person may apply while in the custody of a constable, immediately upon being arrested, and need not wait until he is incarcerated' per Rinfret J., *Re Isbell* (1929) 52 C.C.C. 170 at 173 (S.C.C.).

[72] Examples of cases where habeas corpus was used to challenge a warrant of arrest are: *R.* v. *Downey* (1845) 15 L.J.M.C. 29; *Re Waters* (1888) 6 N.Z.L.R. 545; *Ex p. Archambault* (1910) 16 C.C.C. 433 (Que. K.B.).

[73] *Ex p. Scott* (1829) 9 B. & C. 446; *R.* v. *Weil* (1882) 9 Q.B.D. 701 (C.A.); *Re Parisot* (1888) 5 T.L.R. 344; *R.* v. *O./C. Depot Battalion, R.A.S.C. Colchester, ex p. Elliot* [1949] 1 All E.R. 373; *R.* v. *Whitesides* (1904) 8 C.C.C. 478 (Ont. C.A.); *R.* v. *Lee Chu* (1909) 14 C.C.C. 322 (N.S.S.C.); *Re Webber* (1912) 19 C.C.C. 515 (N.S.S.C.); *Re Gaudin* (1915) 34 N.Z.L.R. 401; *R.* v. *Gage* (1916) 26 C.C.C. 385 (Ont. H.C.); *R.* v. *Gigliotti* (1936) 65 C.C.C. 55 (Ont. S.C.); *R.* v. *Haagstrom* (1942) 78 C.C.C. 332 (B.C.S.C.).

First, there is the rule that habeas corpus only calls for justification of the detention at present. The second is to be found in the law of criminal procedure. It is a general principle that where an accused person has been illegally arrested and brought before a court for trial, the court will not lack jurisdiction over the person on account of the illegal arrest.[74] There may be grounds for appeal, or evidence may be rendered inadmissible, but the validity of the proceedings is not affected. It may be, of course, that the wording of a statute requires a proper arrest as a condition precedent to the valid exercise of jurisdiction. In such a case, relief will be afforded on habeas corpus,[75] but this is nothing more than the use of habeas corpus to achieve jurisdiction review. Apart from such an exceptional case, it has been consistently held that the applicant cannot complain of an irregular arrest when presently held on some other proper authority.

The law supposes that the right to maintain a civil action in trespass provides an adequate protection against illegal arrests. One may be sceptical of the effectiveness of actions for false imprisonment as a device to keep the authorities within proper legal bounds, but it may often be equally difficult to justify the discharge of persons accused of crime simply to control the police.

The treatment of illegal arrests was, however, markedly different in civil proceedings. In the law of detention under civil process, the validity of the detention was always regarded as being contingent on a proper arrest, and a valid process subsequent to an improper arrest did not support the detention.[76] The reason for this distinction between civil and criminal cases is not clear. Perhaps it is simply not seen to be in the public interest that persons accused of crime should go unpunished because of impropriety on the part of the authorities, while in civil cases, such considerations of public interest do not apply.

---

[74] *R. v. Hughes* (1879) 4 Q.B.D. 614 (Cr. Cas. Res'd). The Canadian cases, a few of which go the other way, are collected by Tremeaar, *Criminal Code* (6th ed. 1964), 709–11. See also *Leachinsky v. Christie* [1945] 2 All E.R. 395 at 403–4 per Scott L.J. (varied [1947] A.C. 573): 'Neither the committing magistrate nor the trial court will lose jurisdiction merely because ... the prisoner has been arrested in circumstances which, for any of the reasons I have stated, was unlawful, although the fact may well influence discretion as to bail; but the person so wronged will have his cause of action against the person who arrested him unlawfully; and in an action for false imprisonment every harm to the plaintiff casually [*sic*] resulting from the original wrong will be a matter for the jury to consider in assessing the quantum of general damages....'

[75] See e.g. *R. v. Wishart* (1910) 18 C.C.C. 146 (Ont. C.A.), a case under the Fugitive Offenders Act 1881 (Imp.).

[76] *Hooper v. Lane* (1857) 6 H.L.Cas. 443.

In any case, the law of habeas corpus reflects this difference and there are instances of a prisoner being discharged because of an improper arrest even though the detention rests on an otherwise valid civil process.[77]

(ii) Amending the Cause of the Detention. The rule that it is only the present circumstances of the restraint which are relevant has meant that the courts are always prepared to allow for a substituted warrant which corrects a defect in the first committal.[78] It will be permissible for there to be a substituted warrant even after the writ is issued and served.[79] Indeed, it has been held that it is possible to amend the return to the writ or to supply a new and better cause for the detention as the court commences the hearing.[80] It would seem that so long as material proffered tends to show present justification, it will be accepted by the court at any stage of the proceedings.[81]

[77] *Re Eggington* (1853) 2 E. & B. 717; *Ex p. Thomas* (1849) 13 J.P. 762. In *Re Hunt* [1959] 1 Q.B. 378, where a litigant committed for contempt argued (unsuccessfully) that he was improperly arrested, the court seemed to accept this as a possible ground.

[78] See e.g. *Ex p. Page* (1818) 1 B. & Ald. 568; *R. v. Richards* (1844) 5 Q.B. 926; *Re Terraz* (1878) 39 L.T. 502; *Ex p. Cross* (1857) 2 H. & N. 354; *Ex p. Karchesky* [1967] 3 C.C.C. 272 (S.C.C.); *Re Courlander* [1948] N.Z.L.R. 822.

[79] *Ex p. Dauncey* (1843) 12 M. & W. 271; *Ex p. Phipps* (1863) 27 J.P .503; *R. v. Barre* (1905) 11 C.C.C. 1 (Man. K.B.); but cf. *Re Joly and The Queen* (1978) 41 C.C.C. (2d) 538 (Ont. H.C.), holding that the Crown could not pre-empt habeas corpus to review a committal for trial by preferring an indictment: at 539 per Krever J.: 'In this situation, the race cannot be to the swifter', approved in *The Queen* v. *Chabot* [1980] 2 S.C.R. 985 at 997–8, where it was held that the indictment only became operative to preclude review on habeas corpus when it was lodged with the trial court at the opening of the accused's trial.

[80] *Anon.* (1673) 1 Mod. 103; *Leonard Watson's Case* (1839) 9 A. & E. 731 at 746; *Ex p. Fong Goey Jow* [1948] S.C.R. 37; *Ex p. Dearing* (1975) 64 D.L.R. (3d) 382 (B.C.S.C.). In Canada, s.775 of the Criminal Code, discussed *supra*, p. 56 allows the court to remand the prisoner to be dealt with further. In two cases falling outside the statute involving the revocation of parole, the court announced its decision that the applicants had the procedural right to a proper hearing, but postponed making a formal order for release to afford the authorities to convene the required hearing: *Re Swan and The Queen* (1983) 7 C.C.C. (3d) 130 (B.C.S.C.).; *Re Martens and The Queen* (1983) 8 C.C.C. (3d) 336 (B.C.S.C.). In *Re Evans and The Queen* (1986) 30 C.C.C. (3d) 1 (Ont. H.C.) the court went one step further and dismissed the application for habeas corpus, but ordered a proper hearing pursuant to s.24(1) of the Charter. Cf. *R. v. Catterall* (1730) Fitz-G. 266, holding that no amendment could be allowed after the return was filed. In *Anon.* (1711) Fort. 273, Parker C.J. suggested one reason for allowing amendments: 'otherwise the officer might on purpose make a defective return, and then the prisoner must be discharged.' To the same effect: *Re Power and Jackson* (1826) 2 Russ. 583.

[81] *R. v. Secretary of State for the Home Department, ex p. Iqbal* [1979] 1 All E.R. 675. In *R. v. Governor of Durham Prison, ex p. Hardial Singh* [1984] 1 W.L.R. 704 the respondent was given three days to support the detention, failing which the court said it would make an order for release.

(b) *Questioning Restraints Which Take Effect in the Future*

(i) *Applicant Presently in Custody.* A problem consequent on the principle that habeas corpus only tests the present legality of the detention is that which the American literature calls the 'prematurity' question.[82] This arises where the prisoner is held for two causes which either overlap in time or run consecutively. A strict application of the time rule would suggest that so long as there is a valid present cause for holding the prisoner, there is no standing to question the legality of a cause which is to take effect in the future. Viewed in another light, it means that unless the prisoner is seeking immediate release, habeas corpus will be of no avail.[83]

The problem will usually arise where a convicted prisoner is serving more than one sentence. For example, the prisoner may be serving a series of consecutive sentences, and seek to challenge the propriety of being held on one sentence, the time of which has not yet started to run. Perhaps on account of the infrequent use of habeas corpus to challenge the remanent of a sentence in England,[84] the problem does not appear to have arisen in the cases.

There are, however, several Canadian cases which hold that a prisoner is not entitled to question the legality of a sentence unless actually incarcerated at the time of the application by virtue of that very sentence.[85] In the cases in which this rule was enunciated, the prisoner had been sentenced to a term of imprisonment, and had been fined as well, with a further term of imprisonment to be added in case of default of payment of the fine. It was argued that the provision with respect of the fine was illegal, and it was contended that, therefore, the warrant on which the prisoner was held was bad, and that an order of discharge

---

[82] See e.g. 'Developments in the Law—Federal Habeas Corpus' (1970) 83 Harv. L. Rev. 1038, 1087–93.

[83] See also, *supra*, pp. 151–5 discussing the use of habeas corpus to test conditions of confinement where an analogous problem may arise.

[84] *Supra*, pp. 147–8. A somewhat analogous case is *Ex p. Garcia* (1836) 3 Bing. N.C. 299, where it was held that the prisoner could not gain release because of one bad warrant where he was held on several other good ones: per Tindal C.J.: 'The prisoner may question the legality of the warrant the moment he is in custody under it: here, he is not.'

[85] *R.* v. *Carlisle* (1903) 7 C.C.C. 470 (Ont. C.A.); *Collette* v. *R* (1909) 16 C.C.C 281 (Que. K.B.); *R.* v. *Wong Yuen* (1925) 44 C.C.C. 338 (B.C.S.C.); *Ex p. Henderson* (1929) 52 C.C.C. 95 (S.C.C.); Tremeaar, *Criminal Code* (6th ed. 1964), 1327; *Ex p. Hamilton* (1974) 23 C.C.C. (2d) 189 (Ont. H.C.). See also *Re Johnson and The Queen* (1977) 36 C.C.C. (2d) 403 (Ont. H.C.), refusing habeas corpus to review a committal for trial where the applicant was also detained by virtue of a conviction and sentence for a previous offence. Cf. the case cited *infra*, n. 89, p. 184.

should be made forthwith. In other words, the prisoner was claiming an entitlement to immediate release, even though the sentence being served was valid, on the grounds that the illegal provision for the fine tainted the whole process. In these cases, the courts had no difficulty in finding that the fine, however bad, was severable from the rest of the warrant. Moreover, it was held that as the prisoner was not serving a valid sentence, there was no right to immediate release simply because an illegal sentence would take effect in the future.

This is obviously a different matter from asking the court to decide that a sentence which is to be served at some future time is illegal. There was a reluctance in the cases to make any declaration with respect to the validity of the impugned portion of the sentence,[86] but all the court really decided was that the inclusion of an illegal sentence yet to be served did not entitle the prisoner to immediate release.

Ingenious techniques have been devised to get round the supposed rule, including suing for a declaration,[87] or claiming an order of mandamus to correct the prison records to show that the prisoner is entitled to be released on the day it is claimed the sentence will expire.[88] It is difficult to see why the court should not grant an order on habeas corpus which would be declaratory for the time being. There can be no justification in requiring the prisoner to serve part of the impugned sentence and re-apply on exactly the same grounds, especially as it appears relief may be available by using another remedy.

It is submitted that the 'prematurity' rule does not necessarily follow from the general 'time' rules. Whatever the reason for refusing to allow prior illegality to vitiate a present cause of detention it has nothing to do with the question of allowing for an order which can only take effect at a future time.[89]

---

[86] Cf. *R.* v. *Miller* (1913) 25 C.C.C. 151 (Alta. S.C.) where the court refused the application, but gave its opinion that the prisoner would be entitled to release at the end of a stated period.

[87] *Sedore* v. *Commissioner of Penitentiaries* [1972] F.C. 898 (T.D.); *Re Ellis & The Queen* (1973) 9 C.C.C. (2d) 149 (Fed. Ct. T.D.). Cf. *Re MacDonald and Commissioner of Penitentiaries* (1975) 24 C.C.C. (2d) 335 (Fed. Ct. T.D.), holding that a motion for such a declaration should be amended to proceed as a motion for certiorari.

[88] *Re Weston and Superintendent of Prison for Women* [1972] 1 O.R. 342 (H.C.) where, however, there was noted the problem of determining who was the proper respondent to such an application; *Re Ostello and Solicitor-General of Canada* (1975) 26 C.C.C. (2d) 261 (Ont. H.C.).

[89] For a case where such an order was made, apparently without consideration of the authorities, see *Ex p. Newfield* (1973) 9 C.C.C. (2d) 222 (Alta. S.C.). See also *R.* v. *Syrnyk* (1954) 110 C.C.C. 221 (Man. Q.B.) where the court followed the rule, but also decided the case on the merits.

(ii) Applicant at Liberty. While there is one case from the seventeenth century where habeas corpus was granted *de bene esse* to protect a litigant from interference,[90] it is perhaps unlikely that a court would grant the writ to provide a means of protection against some restraint anticipated in the future.[91] The difficulty in challenging a future restraint has been dealt with to some extent in the discussion of the problem of prematurity, and consideration of the discussion of the extent of restraint required to allow for habeas corpus is also of some relevance.

A strong case can be made, however, for extending a remedy to someone who faces a near certain restraint in the future. If the applicant can satisfy the court that there is a real likelihood of immediate detention, there can be little point in forcing such an individual to spend time in gaol before permitting a challenge to the legality of the imprisonment. It may be, however, that a more appropriate remedy would be injunction,[92] or in certain cases, prohibition.

(c) *Proceedings After the Detention has Ended*

There is little authority on the extent to which proceedings may be entertained after the detention has ended. It has been seen[93] that while the writ may be directed to someone even though it is uncertain whether or not he still exercises sufficient control over the prisoner, the writ will not be issued simply in order to inflict a penalty where it is shown that the illegal detention by the respondent has ceased. It is, then, extremely unlikely that the court would entertain an application simply to decide a point of law.[94]

Different considerations apply, however, where an application or an appeal is pending after the detention has ended. The Divisional Court

[90] *Blackwell's Case* (1626) Benloe 301, 307.
[91] *Brown* v. *Kalal* (1976) 7 N.S.W.L.R. 423. See *Ex p. Stanton* [1957] Crim. L.R. 249, where the court refused habeas corpus where the applicant, now free from restraint, sought to question a twelve-year-old order under the Mental Deficiency Act 1913, under which he had been again summoned to appear before the visiting justices.
[92] See *O'Boyle & Rodgers* v. *A.G. & General O'Duffy* [1929] I.R. 558, where an injunction was granted on the application of individuals who feared that they would be arrested and removed from Irish jurisdiction so as to be deprived of habeas corpus.
[93] *Supra,* pp. 178–9.
[94] Proceedings have been discontinued in several cases where the prisoner was discharged, but without any argument on this point: *R.* v. *Spencer* (1778) Gude, *Crown Practice,* 278; *Ex p. Cresswell* (1844) 4 L.T.O.S. 142; *Re Davidson* (1879) 2 S.C.R. (N.S.) (N.S.W) 303.

has proceeded to deal with costs in such a case,[95] and the Judicial Committee of the Privy Council has entertained appeals after the prisoner's release.[96] The Court of Appeal is apparently willing to entertain an appeal on the merits of the case where the only issue left between the parties is that of costs.[97] Finally, it should be noted that the Administration of Justice Act 1960 allows for an appeal from an order of release in certain cases, and that often this will take the form of a moot appeal.[98]

(d) *Conclusion*

On the present state of the law, in almost every instance, the relevant time at which the detention is to be justified is the time at which the court considers the case. Prior illegality will not be relevant unless by reason of some special rule derived from the particular nature of the proceedings involved.

With regard to illegality which has been corrected by the time the matter comes to court, it is submitted that there are two matters which should be taken into consideration. First, there is an important general value in maintaining compliance with legal standards. The countervailing factor is that it will usually be difficult to justify the release of an offender or anyone who should be imprisoned simply because of some prior misconduct on the part of the authorities.

In the cases, the courts have given full weight to the second con-

---

[95] *Ex p. Garrett* [1954] Crim. L.R. 621; *Ex p. Whitehead* [1957] Crim. L.R. 114; *Re Davidson* (1879) 2 S.C.R. (N.S.) (N.S.W.) 303.

[96] *U.S.* v. *Gaynor* [1905] A.C. 128; *King-Emperor* v. *Vimlabai Deshpande* (1946) 115 L.J.P.C. 71. Cf. *Hazlett* v. *Buttimore (No. 2)* [1931] N.Z.L.R. 32, refusing leave to appeal to the Privy Council on the grounds that the prisoner had been released. The Canadian courts have decided appeals after release to settle important points of law: see *Re Marshall and The Queen* (1984) 13 C.C.C. (3d) 73 (Ont. H.C.); *Cardinal* v. *Director of Kent Institution* [1985] 2 S.C.R. 643; *Morin* v. *National Special Handling Unit Review Committee* [1985] 2 S.C.R. 662. See also *Re Zwann* [1981] I.R. 395. Cf. however *Re Cadeddu and The Queen* (1983) 4 C.C.C. (3d) 112 (Ont. C.A.), holding that an appeal from an order for release abated with the death of the applicant, even though an important point of law was at issue. In *Re Desroches and The Queen* (1983) 6 C.C.C. (3d) 406 (Ont. H.C.) an application for habeas corpus proceeded as an application for judicial review and declaration after the applicant's release.

[97] *Ex p. Lees* [1941] 1 K.B. 72. Cf. *Fraser* v. *Tupper* (1880) Cassels S.C. 421 (S.C.C.). Note that in criminal cases in Canada there is no authority to award costs on habeas corpus, absent conduct justifying the court to invoke its inherent power to order costs for an abuse of process or to control its own proceedings: *Re Ange* [1970] 5 C.C.C. 371 (Ont. C.A.); *A.G. Quebec* v. *Cronier* (1981) 63 C.C.C. (2d) 437 (Que. C.A.); *Mayrand* v. *Cronier* (1981) 63 C.C.C. (2d) 561 (Que. C.A.).

[98] *Infra*, pp. 208–10.

sideration and have assumed, with respect to the first, that legal standards can be upheld in a civil action if the party affected feels aggrieved.

One wonders, however, whether the threat of civil action is always effective, and it is submitted that there is another approach which the courts could take. It will be seen in a subsequent chapter[99] that release on habeas corpus will only constitute a bar to further proceedings where those proceedings would involve the potential relitigation of the same point. This could help to solve those cases where the judge considers that the original proceedings are so tainted with illegality that the importance of maintaining compliance with legal standards requires that a remedy be given. In fact, a remedy can be given without necessarily precluding the authorities from taking further steps against the applicant after release.

It has also been seen that there may be difficulties where the applicant wishes to contest the legality of a restraint which is not in actual effect at the time of the application. In other words, the courts are reluctant to give declaratory judgments on habeas corpus. It has been argued that, especially where the applicant is already in custody and will continue in custody under the sentence or order he wishes to question, there should be no reason why the court could not give a judgment which would be, for the time being, merely declaratory.

[99] *Infra*, pp. 213–17.

8

Territorial Ambit of Habeas Corpus

(a) *Introduction*

The common law does not recognize the effectiveness of judicial process outside the territorial jurisdiction of the court and it is only by statute that a court has power to exercise jurisdiction over anyone found beyond its territorial limits.[1] As Coke pointed out, however, this rule applied only to 'remedial writs' or 'all writs real and personal, whereby the party wronged is to recover somewhat, and to be remedied for what wrong was offered unto him'. Other writs, deriving their authority and force from the crown, are 'mandatory' and 'are not tied to any place but do follow subjection and ligeance'.[2]

Habeas corpus is one of the prerogative writs, and rather than raise an issue between two parties which is to be decided by a court having jurisdiction over them both, it is supposed to issue on the part of the Queen so that she might have an account of any of her subjects who are imprisoned.[3] The writ is said to depend not on the ordinary jurisdiction of the court for its effectiveness, but upon the authority of the sovereign over all her subjects. While this does not make it possible to issue the writ to a foreign country, even where the respondent is a subject of the crown,[4] it does give the writ an extraordinary territorial ambit. At common law, all the prerogative writs had this broader ambit[5] and were said to run to all parts of the Queen's dominions.[6]

As a consequence of these rules, the old exempt jurisdictions, the

[1] *In re Busfield* (1886) 32 Ch. D. 123 at 131. Legislation permitting service outside the jurisdiction in the court's discretion was first enacted in 1852 (Common Law Procedure Act, s.18): *Lenders* v. *Anderson* (1883) 12 Q.B.D. 50. See now Ord. 11.

[2] *Calvin's Case* (1609) 7 Co. Rep. 1.

[3] *Wetherley* v. *Wetherley* (1608) 2 Rolle's Abridg. 69; *Bourn's Case* (1619) Cro. Jac. 543; *Alder* v. *Puisy* (1671) 1 Freem. K.B. 12; *R.* v. *Cowle* (1759) 2 Burr. 834.

[4] *R.* v. *Pinckney* [1904] 2 K.B. 84 (C.A.), holding that the writ could not even be issued and allowed to lie until the respondent returned. Cf. *Ex p. Wyatt* (1836) 3 Will. Woll. & Dav. 76, where the court hesitantly awarded a rule nisi for an attachment for disobedience to a writ of habeas corpus served in Calais.

[5] de Smith, *Judicial Review*, 517.

[6] *Wetherley* v. *Wetherley* (1608) 2 Rolle's Abridg. 69; *Anon.* (1671) Cart. 221; *R.* v. *Cowle* (1759) 2 Burr. 834; *Ex p. Anderson* (1861) 3 E. & E. 487; 3 Bl. *Comm.*, 131; Bentwich, 'Habeas Corpus in the Empire' (1911), 27 L.Q.R. 454. See also the cases

Cinque Ports, Counties Palatine, and Berwick-upon-Tweed, were not exempt from the writ of habeas corpus.[7] The privilege of these jurisdictions was merely to determine disputes between parties within their jurisdiction, and this, it was said, could not prevent the royal prerogative calling for an account of the imprisonment of a subject from having full force.

The power to send the writ outside England was based on the common law, but partially confirmed by the Habeas Corpus Acts 1679[8] and 1816.[9] It was, however, greatly curtailed by the Habeas Corpus Act 1862.[10]

(b) *The Decision in Ex p. Anderson and the Act of 1862*

The Act of 1862 was passed in response to the decision in *Ex p. Anderson*.[11] A writ of habeas corpus was sent by the Queen's Bench to the colony of Upper Canada, the court holding that writs of habeas corpus might be issued to all parts of the dominions of the crown wherever a subject was illegally imprisoned, notwithstanding the existence of a local, independent judicature with full power to grant the same relief. The inconvenience and impracticality of the result is obvious. Parliament was not slow to act, and it was explained that: 'The fact of a writ having been issued by the Court of Queen's Bench in this country to a colony in which a Court of Queen's Bench already existed, naturally created a great sensation in the colonies.'[12] Partly, then, to

cited *infra*, n. 7, on the exempt jurisdictions, and *Ex p. Mwenya*, discussed *infra*, pp. 194–5.

[7] *Bourn's Case* (1619) Cro. Jac. 543; *Jobson's Case* (1625) Latch 160; *Anon.* (1670) 1 Mod. 20; *Alder* v. *Puisy* (1671) 1 Freem. K.B. 12; *R.* v. *Pell and Offly* (1674) 3 Keb. 279; *Taylor* v. *Reignolds* (1706) 12 Mod. 666. Cf. habeas corpus ad faciendum et recipiendum and ad respondendum which were considered to be adjuncts of the ordinary civil suit and did not run to the exempt jurisdictions: *Anon.* (1669) 1 Sid. 431; *Anon.* (1705) 1 Salk. 354.

[8] s.10.

[9] s.5.

[10] The Act of 1862 was held not to apply in some Australian States, so that the extraordinary ambit of the writ still prevails: *Glasson* v. *Scott* [1973] 1 N.S.W.L.R. 689; *Zwillinger* v. *Schulof* [1963] V.R. 407. For further discussion of the ambit of the writ in Australia, see *infra*, p. 198.

[11] (1861) 3 E. & E. 487. For the background to this case, see Ryan, 'Ex parte John Anderson' (1981) 6 Queen's L.J. 382; Brode, *Sir John Beverly Robinson* (1984), 264–9; Reinders, 'The John Anderson Case, 1860–1: A Study in Anglo-Canadian Relations' (1975) 56 Can. Hist. Rev. 393.

[12] 165 *Parliamentary Debates*, col. 1708; 'The English Writ of Habeas Corpus' (1861) 7 U.C.L.J. 53. Before the English writ had arrived, Anderson had been liberated by order of the Upper Canada Court of Common Pleas on a subsequent application,

placate colonial feelings, and partly to avoid the obvious difficulty of summarily deciding the legality of a detention across the ocean, the Act of 1862 was passed. It provides as follows:

1. No writ of habeas corpus shall issue out of England, by authority of any judge or justice therein, into any colony or foreign dominion of the Crown where Her Majesty has a lawfully established court or courts of justice having authority to grant and issue the said writ, and to ensure the due execution thereof throughout such colony or dominion.

Section 2 of the Act preserves the right of appeal from the colonial courts to the Privy Council.

After the Act was passed, there were judicial attempts to qualify the *Anderson* decision,[13] but, presumably, the decision does confirm the extraordinary territorial ambit of habeas corpus, and a case not expressly covered by the Act will fall within the common law rule stated in the decision.[14]

The scope of the Act of 1862 has been limited in two ways. First, it has been held that the phrase 'foreign dominion' does not include those territories brought within the realm by virtue of feudal subjection rather than overseas conquest or cession.[15] This means that notwithstanding the Act, the writ does run to the Isle of Man and the Channel Islands.[16] Secondly, it has also been held that the word 'dominion' includes only territorial dominions and not protectorates or those areas where the Crown exercises dominion only in the sense of control and power.[17] The result is that the Act covers only overseas colonies and leaves untouched the common law as it applies to dominions within the British Isles on the one hand, and protectorates on the other.

As for the requirement that the colony have a court empowered to grant and issue the writ, it is not clear whether that court must grant

adding, no doubt, to the English embarrassment. See [1861] 11 U.C.C.P. 9 for the Canadian court's decision to release Anderson. Cf. the earlier unsuccessful application: (1860) 20 U.C.Q.B. 124.

[13] '... this court, in a case where life and death were depending, thought that there was sufficient doubt about the matter to issue the writ to Upper Canada, leaving the effect of it to be discussed afterwards. The facts there did not require that the question should be decided; and immediately after that case [the 1862 Act] was passed.' *Ex p. Brown* (1864) 5 B. & S. 280 at 294; see also *R. v. Mansergh* (1861) 1 B. & S. 400 at 411.

[14] *Ex p. Mwenya* [1960] 1 Q.B. 241 (C.A.), *infra*, pp. 194–5. See e.g. the Australian cases discussed *supra*, n. 10, p. 189.

[15] *Ex p. Brown* (1864) 5 B. & S. 280.

[16] Ibid., and see *infra*, pp. 191–2.

[17] *R. v. Crewe (Earl), Ex p. Sekgome* [1910] 2 K.B. 576 (C.A.); *Ex p. Mwenya* [1960] 1 Q.B. 241 (C.A.); *infra*, pp. 194–5.

the writ of habeas corpus itself, or whether some analogous relief will suffice. The Act speaks of the 'said writ' and in one case the question was treated as an open one.[18] It has also been suggested that where the local law temporarily does not permit the exercise of habeas corpus jurisdiction, the Act will not preclude the English writ running[19] since there is no court 'having authority to grant and issue the said writ.'[20] As there are only a few remaining colonies,[21] questions of the applicability of the Act are now less likely to arise.

(c) *British Isles*

(i) Scotland. The English writ of habeas corpus does not run to Scotland.[22] Before the union of the thrones in 1603 under the Stuarts, Scotland was regarded as a foreign country and was not a dominion of the crown of England. The union of the crowns meant that Scots were no longer regarded as aliens since they bore allegiance to a common sovereign,[23] but union did not extend the prerogative of the English crown to Scotland. Scotland remained a foreign dominion of the prince who succeeded to the English throne, and the union of crowns provided no basis on which habeas corpus could run. The Act of Union 1706, provided for a united Parliament and the continuation of a common King under the Hanovers and their successors, but still did not alter the distinction between England and Scotland for the purposes of the prerogative writs. Scots law was expressly preserved, and it was provided that no cause in Scotland was cognizable in the English courts.[24]

(ii) Isle of Man. The Isle of Man is part of the British Isles[25] but not part of the United Kingdom,[26] nor is it a colony. It is a self-governing

---

[18] *Ex p. Brown* (1864) 5 B. & S. 280. See also Palley, *The Constitutional History and Law of Southern Rhodesia, 1888–1965*, 733.

[19] *R. v. Crewe (Earl), Ex p. Sekgome* [1910] 2 K.B. 576 at 621–2, per Kennedy L.J.

[20] Cf. Roberts-Wray, *Commonwealth and Colonial Law* (1966), 612–13, suggesting that English control would properly be exercised through diplomatic channels or not at all.

[21] de Smith, *Constitutional and Administrative Law* (5th ed. 1985), 658.

[22] *R. v. Cowle* (1759) 2 Burr. 834; 'Note on the Power of the English Courts to Issue the Writ of Habeas Corpus out of England' (1896) 8 Jurid. Rev. 157; and generally, Smith, *The British Commonwealth—Scotland* (1962), 49–60; Mitchell, *Constitutional Law* (2nd ed. 1968), 92–8.

[23] *Calvin's Case* (1609) 7 Co. Rep. 1.

[24] 6 Anne, c.11, Art. 19.

[25] Interpretation Act 1978, Sched. I.

[26] *Davison v. Farmer* (1851) 6 Exch. 242.

dominion of the Crown of England.[27] It had long been held in feudal subjection by the English sovereign as overlord, and by the Isle of Man Purchase Act 1765, it was transferred to the King and his successors inalienably so that it is held by the English sovereign, not in his personal right, but in right of the Crown. As part of the Royal prerogative, the writ of habeas corpus runs to the Isle of Man.[28]

(iii) Channel Islands.   The Channel Islands do not form part of the United Kingdom, but maintain respectively independent internal legal orders.[29] They are the only part of the Duchy of Normandy still annexed to the English Crown. Consequently, the prerogative of the Crown does extend to these islands, and there are several reported cases of writs of habeas corpus being directed to them.[30]

(iv) Northern Ireland.   Surprisingly enough, the question of the possibility of the English courts directing a writ of habeas corpus to Northern Ireland was not presented until the *Keenan* case in 1971[31] when it was held that the writ did not run. There was some authority that the writ ran to Ireland in the seventeenth and eighteenth centuries.[32] There is no reason, in principle, why this should not have been, although there do not appear to have been any cases where the writ actually did run.[33] Ireland was acquired by conquest and for that reason did not share Scotland's status as a place outside the scope of the English prerogative. The English Habeas Corpus Act 1679 did not apply in Ireland until its terms were enacted by the Irish Parliament in 1782, but of course this relates only to the Irish courts and not to the issue of the availability of the English writ in Ireland. The Act of 1862,

---

[27] Keeton (ed.), *The British Commonwealth—United Kingdom* (1955), 485 *et seq.* describes the constitutional status of the Isle of Man.

[28] *Re Crawford* (1849) 13 Q.B. 613; *Ex p. Brown* (1864) 5 B. & S. 280.

[29] Keeton (ed.), op. cit. 1141 *et seq.*; Le Masurier, *Le Droit de l'Isle de Jersey* (1956), 337–40; De L. Bois, 'Parliamentary Supremacy in the Channel Islands' [1983] Public Law 385. See also *Navigators and General Insurance Co. Ltd.* v. *Ringrose* [1962] 1 All E.R. 97 (C.A.).

[30] *R.* v. *Overton* (1668) 1 Sid. 386; *R.* v. *Salmon* (1669) 2 Keb. 450; *Carus Wilson's Case* (1845) 7 Q.B. 984 (see (1844) 4 L.T. 164 for the initial refusal and reasons given by the Royal Court of Jersey to enforce the English writ); *Re Belson* (1850) 7 Moo. P.C.C. 114; *Dodd's Case* (1858) 2 De G. & J. 510.

[31] *Re Keenan* [1972] 1 Q.B. 533 (C.A.).

[32] *Anon.* (1681) 1 Vent. 357; *R.* v. *Cowle* (1759) 2 Burr. 834.

[33] For the argument that the writ never did run, see Yale, [1972] C.L.J. 4, commenting on the *Keenan* decision.

as has been noted,[34] does not apply to British dominions within the British Isles, and the fact that the Irish courts have long had jurisdiction themselves to grant the writ would not, of itself, preclude the possibility of the English writ running to Ireland.

In *Keenan*, the Court of Appeal accepted that the writ had run to Ireland before 1782 but it decided that the Act[35] of that year, providing for the judicial independence of Ireland, by implication, precluded further habeas corpus applications to the English court, even though the Act did not mention habeas corpus.[36] It is submitted that on strictly legal grounds this argument is beside the point. As noted above the Channel Islands, the Isle of Man, and the Province of Upper Canada in 1862, all present examples of places with judicial independence, yet the writ runs (or ran) to those places because of its extraordinary prerogative nature. It can readily be seen why the English courts do not wish to become involved with the problems of Northern Ireland,[37] and there is a sound argument to be made that the matter should be left with the local courts.[38] This same argument applies to other places outside England with judicial systems of their own, but it has always been rejected. The fact that Irish judicial independence had its source in a statute rather than by custom, made it possible for the court to imply an abrogation of the right to apply for the English writ.

---

[34] *Supra*, p. 190.

[35] 22 Geo. III, c.53, confirmed by 23 Geo. III, c.28.

[36] The Act simply repealed an act of 1719 (6 Geo. I, c.5) which had provided for the legislative supremacy of the English Parliament, and had taken away the competence of the Irish House of Lords to reverse decisions of the Irish courts.

[37] Especially in the circumstances of this case. The applicants were internees who alleged that they had been improperly arrested, and that the validity of their detention was contingent on a proper arrest. This argument later succeeded in the Northern Ireland courts: *Re McElduff* (1971) 23 N.I.L.Q. 112, discussed *supra*, p. 107, but did not prevent the authorities from re-arresting the applicants by taking the proper procedures. The application was initially made in England in the hope that the prisoners would be released in England where they would be free from further detention as the power of internment could not be exercised outside Northern Ireland. Moreover, a large number of internees had been arrested in the same way, and plans were made for further applications if the *Keenan* case proved successful: see Boyle (1972) 23 N.I.L.Q. 334, 335, n. 6. All this, of course, may have been unknown to the court. Cf. *Ex p. Mwenya* [1960] 1 Q.B. 241 at 308, per Sellers L.J.: 'There may come times in a country's history when it may appear highly inconvenient or politically hazardous that the law should pursue its course, but in a court of law such considerations are irrelevant and cannot serve to deprive a subject of a right which an English court could give and enforce.'

[38] It could be argued that as a matter of policy, Northern Ireland should enjoy the same immunity as that of Scotland, although this analogy was not made in the *Keenan* case.

(d) *Protectorates*

In *Ex p. Mwenya*, 1960[39] the Court of Appeal held that it is possible for the English writ of habeas corpus to run to a protectorate. The territory in question was Northern Rhodesia but the matter was put before the Court of Appeal on a number of agreed assumptions and the court was faced with what Lord Evershed described as

... a general and academic question, namely: Has the court here any jurisdiction to make an order of habeas corpus directed to any territory other than territories strictly described as colonies or foreign dominions (as that phrase is understood, for example, in the Habeas Corpus Act 1862)?[40]

The matter was not entirely one of first impression,[41] but it had never before been fully examined. The Divisional Court had accepted the argument that there could, in law, be only one sovereign over any territory, and that the British Crown could not be said to share sovereignty by reason simply of the exercise of control. If the Crown was not legally sovereign, the prerogative did not reach the protectorate, and habeas corpus could not run. The Court of Appeal rejected this Austinian theory of the indivisibility of sovereignty and taking a more realistic approach, focused upon the certainty of the effectiveness of the writ and the desirability of extending British justice to areas which are, in fact, under British control. The court held that where the nature of control is indistinguishable in effect from that exercised in a colony or in a territory acquired by conquest, the absence of a formal assumption of sovereignty does not preclude the exercise of the prerogative upon which the writ of habeas corpus depends. The obvious rider to the decision is that as the label 'protectorate' does not, in itself, define the extent of control exercised,[42] each case will have to depend upon its own facts.[43]

[39] [1960] 1 Q.B. 241.   [40] Ibid. at 292.

[41] In *R.* v. *Crewe (Earl), ex p. Sekgome* [1910] 2 K.B. 576, Vaughan Williams and Farwell L.JJ., both thought that the writ would run to a protectorate, but Kennedy L.J. did not, and all comments on this point were clearly obiter. In *Re Ning Yi-Ching* (1939) 56 T.L.R. 3, Cassels J. followed the dictum of Kennedy L.J. and held that the writ would not run.

[42] The legal authority for rule in a protectorate is found in the Foreign Jurisdiction Act 1890, s.1: 'It shall be lawful for Her Majesty the Queen to hold, exercise, and enjoy any jurisdiction which Her Majesty now has or may at any time hereafter have within a foreign country in the same and as ample a manner as if Her Majesty had acquired that jurisdiction by the cession or conquest of territory.' This does not, however, define the extent of control actually exercised, and the meaning of 'protectorate' in this sense is not defined in either English law (*Mwenya* [1960] 1 Q.B. at 298–9, 301) or in international law (*Oppenheim's International Law* (8th ed. 1967), vol. 1, 192–6).

[43] Cf. *Baker* v. *Alford* [1960] A.C. 786 (P.C.), where the court simply accepted the

One of the assumptions in the case was that the applicant was a British subject. This is a matter of considerable doubt in protectorate cases, and it may be asked whether the result would be the same had the applicant been non-British. It is submitted that the court would have reached the same result. The principle underlying the decision is that British rule should be, so far as possible, subject to English law. The theory is that habeas corpus runs outside England because the sovereign has the right to inquire into the legality of a restraint upon the subject. If formal sovereignty is not required, then there should be no difficulty in applying the proposition where subjection to the Crown is a matter of fact rather than law.

It is submitted that the *Mwenya* decision provides an excellent example of the creative use of the sometimes arid and ancient rules which make up the law of habeas corpus. The court adopted the seventeenth-century language of the old cases to meet a modern situation and derived a result very much in the spirit of the old rules. The practical importance of the decision has, of course, greatly diminished in recent years as there are no British protectorates left.[44]

(e) *Diplomatic Immunity*

The only known case illustrating the rule of diplomatic immunity as it relates to habeas corpus is one involving the Chinese leader, Sun Yat Sen in 1896.[45] It was alleged that he was being illegally held in the Chinese legation in London, probably with a view to being sent to China for trial as a revolutionary. It was sought to direct the writ to the Chinese minister, and Wright J. refused the application on the ground of diplomatic immunity.[46]

Immediately following these proceedings, however, the Chinese Minister was formally requested by the Foreign Office to release his prisoner, and this demand was complied with.[47] The result would

Secretary of State's certificate regarding British control in a protectorate: see Bowett, (1960) 36 B.Y.I.L. 406.

[44] de Smith, *Constitutional and Administrative Law* (5th ed. 1985), 659.

[45] Unreported but see Short and Mellor *Crown Practice* (2nd ed. 1908), 318; Mews Digest (1924), vol. xi, 306; 7 British Digest of International Law 898.

[46] Wright J. is reported (*supra*, n. 45) as saying that he hesitated to order the writ to issue 'against a foreign legation', but McNair, *International Law Opinion* (1956), vol. 1, 88, suggests that he meant 'against a foreign diplomatic representative'.

[47] McNair, *International Law Opinions*, vol. 1, 86–7, gives the draft Foreign Office Despatch which reads in part: '... in the absence of any Treaty stipulations giving the Chinese Representative in this country extra-territorial jurisdiction over Chinese subjects, the detention within the legation house of any person, even though such person

appear to be that, while the immunity of diplomatic representatives and premises preclude habeas corpus proceedings, the enforced detention of a person within the embassy is a breach of immunity which requires diplomatic proceedings to obtain the release of the person so detained.[48]

Diplomatic and consular immunity have now been the subject of international conventions, the terms of which have been implemented by legislation. The privileges are broadly worded, and would presumably make protected persons and premises as immune to habeas corpus as to any other judicial process.[49]

(f) *Territorial Waters and Ships at Sea*

The normal rules of jurisdiction with respect to territorial waters and ships on the high seas[50] probably apply to habeas corpus. There is little authority, but in the mid-nineteenth century it was thought that the immunity of a foreign warship deprived the California court of jurisdiction to direct a writ of habeas corpus to a British ship in San Francisco Bay.[51]

Even where the writ can issue, it is now provided by legislation that, subject to certain exceptions, a detention for a disciplinary offence on board the ships of certain designated states shall be deemed to be lawful.[52] It has been held that even where a prisoner is brought ashore,

should be an undoubted subject of China, is a serious abuse of the privileges and immunities which are granted to foreign representatives and which have for their sole object to secure for such representatives complete freedom and independence in the discharge of their mission.'

[48] Satow, *A Guide to Diplomatic Practice* (5th ed. 1979), 110.

[49] The Diplomatic Privileges Act 1964 gives effect to the Vienna Convention on Diplomatic Relations 1961. Diplomatic premises are inviolable (Art. 22), and diplomatic representatives enjoy immunity from the civil, criminal and administrative jurisdiction of the receiving state's courts (Art. 31). Members of staff also enjoy immunity with respect to acts performed in the course of their duties. The immunity of consular premises and consular offices for acts performed in the course of duty is granted by the Consular Relations Act 1968 Art. 31 and 43 (implementing the Vienna Convention on Consular Relations 1963). For a similar protection for international organizations and their officers, see International Organizations Act 1968, Sched. I, Pts. I and III. See also *Agbor* v. *Metropolitan Police Commissioners* [1969] 2 All E.R. 707 (C.A.). Cf. *R.* v. *Turnbull, ex p. Petroff* (1971) 17 F.L.R. 438 (Aust.), a habeas corpus case holding that an offence committed on the property of an embassy was subject to local law.

[50] See e.g. Colombos, *International Law of the Sea* (6th ed. 1967), 131–46 (territorial matters), 264–84 (war-ships), 298–310 (merchant vessels).

[51] *The Sitka* (1855) 7 Opinions of the Attorneys-General 122.

[52] Consular Relations Act 1968, s.6: 'Her Majesty may by order in Council designate any State for the purposes of this section; and where a state is so designated, a member of the crew of a ship belonging to that State who is detained in custody on board for a disciplinary offence shall not be deemed to be unlawfully detained unless—(a) his

the legality of the detention may be supported by a foreign conviction,[53] but the better view is probably that such a prisoner can only be held pursuant to ordinary extradition proceedings.

A problem in cases of this type is posed by the *Greenberg* case[54] in 1947, where habeas corpus was sought on behalf of a group of Palestinian deportees on board a British ship at sea. The writ was refused, but Jenkins J. suggested that it could not have been awarded in any case since the applicants would have been subject to immigration controls, and would not have been able to enter the country to be brought before the court. This, it is submitted, is wrong. Under the modern practice, the prisoners could be released without being brought before the court and, in any case, it is inconceivable that the court would have to refuse relief merely because the applicant was subject to immigration controls.[55] That is another question entirely, and such controls could be exercised after the release of the prisoner.

(g) *Federal Jurisdictions*

(i) Canada. In Canada, it has been held that one province has no power to send a writ of habeas corpus beyond its own territorial limits,[56] even where the prisoner is detained by order of a court of that province in a federal prison in another province.[57] In such a case, the courts of the province in which the prisoner is detained have habeas corpus jurisdiction.[58] It has also been held in child custody cases that

detention is unlawful under the laws of that State or the conditions of detention are inhumane or unjustifiably severe; or (b) there is reasonable cause for believing that his life or liberty will be endangered for reasons of race, nationality, political opinion or religion, in any country to which the ship is likely to go.'

[53] *Re Sutherland* (1922) 39 W.N. (N.S.W.) 108; Charteris, 'Habeas Corpus in Respect of Detention on a Foreign Merchantman' (1926) 8 Journal of Comp. Leg. (3rd) 246; Colombos, op. cit. 303.

[54] *R.* v. *Secretary of State for Foreign Affairs and Secretary of State for Colonies, ex p. Greenberg* [1947] 2 All E.R. 550 at 556.

[55] de Smith, *Judicial Review* (C.A.); Harvey, *The Law of Habeas Corpus in Canada* (1974), 66. In *Re Bell and Director of Springhill Medium Security Institution* (1977) 34 C.C.C. (2d) 303 (N.S.S.C.) the applicant, having been convicted in Newfoundland, successfully challenged in the Nova Scotia courts his transfer to a prison in that province and was returned to Newfoundland to serve his sentence according to law. Cf. *Kuchenmeister* v. *Home Office* [1958] 1 Q.B. 496, where an alien in transit and having been refused permission to enter, was prevented from getting his connecting flight by immigration officers and succeeded in an action for false imprisonment.

[56] *R.* v. *Riel (No. 1)* (1885) 2 Man. L.R. 302 (C.A.); *McGuire* v. *McGuire* (1953) 105 C.C.C. 335 (Ont. C.A.) (habeas corpus ad testificandum); *Ex p. Stather* (1886) 25 N.B.R. 374 (C.A.).   [57] *Ex p. Stather* (1886) 25 N.B.R. 374.

[58] *Gamble* v. *The Queen* [1988] 2 S.C.R. 595.

the writ can not issue where the child is in another province,[59] although it may be possible to continue proceedings if the child is removed after the application is made.[60]

While the Federal Court of Canada has jurisdiction throughout Canada, it has no jurisdiction to issue habeas corpus[61] except 'in relation to any member of the Canadian Forces serving outside Canada.'[62] In one case,[63] the court expressed doubt as to its ability to enforce such an order. It may be that by analogy to the common law doctrine discussed earlier in this chapter such an order could be enforced as against Canadian military authorities overseas.

(ii) Australia.   In Australia, it has been held[64] that the Act of 1862 does not apply, and that the writ therefore retains its extraordinary common law ambit. In child custody cases, the writ may be issued from the courts of one state naming a respondent beyond that state's borders.[65] However, it has also been held that there is a discretion in the nature of forum non conveniens to be exercised,[66] and that the writ should only issue if the respondent said to have control of the child is present within the jurisdiction, or if the child is ordinarily resident within the state.[67] It has also been held that where the respondent is presently outside the jurisdiction, the writ cannot be issued in anticipa-

---

[59]   *Re Hilker* (1914) 6 O.W.N. 82 (H.C.); *Re Dalgleish* (1968) 3 N.S.R. (1965–9) 472; *Re Berg and Young* (1982) 140 D.L.R. (3d) 451 (Alta. Q.B.); *Re Vadera and Vadera* [1972] 1 O.R. 441 (H.C.); *Kovacs* v. *Graham* (1981) 23 R.F.L. (2d) 201 (Alta. Q.B.); *Re Popperl and Popperl* (1982) 135 D.L.R. (3d) 153 (Man. C.A.).

[60]   *Re Harding* (1929) 63 O.L.R. 518. See also *Barnardo* v. *Ford* [1892] A.C. 326, discussed *infra*.

[61]   *Re Pannu and Minister of Employment and Immigration* (1982) 1 C.C.C. (3d) 328 (Fed. Ct. T.D.); *Ex p. Quevillon* (1974) 20 C.C.C. (2d) 555 (Fed. Ct. T.D.). The Federal Court does, however, have exclusive certiorari and judicial review jurisdiction in relation to the federal administration, and in many situations an applicant will have a choice between judicial review in the Federal Court and habeas corpus in the provincial superior court. Note also that the exclusive jurisdiction of the Federal Court in relation to certiorari does not preclude a provincial superior court from issuing certiorari in aid of habeas corpus even where the issue relates to the decision of a federal board or tribunal: see *supra*, n. 156, p. 52.

[62]   Federal Court Act, s.17(6).

[63]   *Re Publicover and The Queen* (1981) 120 D.L.R. (3d) 310 (Fed. Ct. T.D.).

[64]   *Supra*, n. 10, p. 189.

[65]   *Kelly* v. *Panayioutou* [1980] 1 N.S.W.L.R. 15n; Nygh, *Conflict of Laws in Australia* (5th ed. 1984), 392–4.

[66]   *Glasson* v. *Scott* [1973] 1 N.S.W.L.R. 689; *A.* v. *B.* [1979] 1 N.S.W.L.R. 57.

[67]   *A.* v. *B.*, *supra*; *McM.* v. *C. (No. 1)* [1980] 1 N.S.W.L.R. 1

tion on the basis that his or her return is expected and that at the restraint would likely be regarded as illegal at that time.[68]

(h) *Persons Held Beyond the Reach of Habeas Corpus*

One of the great abuses of practice which was remedied by the Habeas Corpus Act 1679 was that of taking prisoners outside the jurisdiction to deprive them of the benefit of habeas corpus.[69] The practice was made a serious offence and the section remains in force, the penalty being praemunire.[70]

However, the mere fact that the place where the prisoner is held is outside the ambit of the writ will not necessarily deprive the court of the power to act. The jurisdiction of the court seems not to depend upon the place of imprisonment, but on whether there is someone within the jurisdiction who can be made respondent to the writ. The test is whether the intended respondent exercises *de facto* control over the prisoner and whether he or she has the power to bring the detention to an end.[71] The leading example is the *O'Brien* case[72] where the Home Secretary had interned the applicant and delivered him to the Irish authorities. At the time of the application, O'Brien was imprisoned in Dublin and the Home Secretary had to rely on the good will of the Irish authorities to secure his release in obedience to the court's order. In *Barnardo* v. *Ford*,[73] where the applicant sought the custody of a child who had been sent out of England by the respondent, the House of Lords held that the writ should issue to determine whether or not the respondent did retain sufficient control over the child.

Presumably, however, the imprisonment must bear a real relation to English law before the courts would entertain an application with respect to someone outside the writ's ambit.[74] This has not been explored in the cases, but it is doubtful that the mere physical presence in the jurisdiction of a person with control over the prisoner would be enough to enable the court to act.

[68] *Brown* v. *Kalal* (1986) 7 N.S.W.L.R. 423.
[69] *Supra*, p. 18.
[70] In the *O'Brien* case in 1923 (*infra*, n. 72) it appeared that proceedings could have been taken against the Home Secretary under this section, and the Restoration of Order in Ireland (Indemnity) Act 1923 was passed to protect him: see Chandler, 'Praemunire and the Habeas Corpus Act' (1924) 24 Colum. L.R. 273.
[71] *Supra*, pp. 175–8.
[72] *R.* v. *Secretary of State for Home Affairs, ex p. O'Brien* [1923] 2 K.B. 361 (C.A.).
[73] [1892] A.C. 326. See also *Re Harding* (1929) 63 O.L.R. 518.
[74] de Smith, *Judicial Review*, 599, says that the writ will not, in general, issue in respect of detention on foreign soil, save in exceptional cases.

An injunction will be granted to prevent the removal of a prisoner pending determination of a habeas corpus application, and an attempt to thwart the jurisdiction of the court by removing a prisoner amounts to contempt.[75]

[75] *Re Pereira and Minister of Manpower and Immigration* (1978) 91 D.L.R. (3d) 706 (Ont. C.A.).

9

Appeals, Successive Applications, and Re-Arrest

1. APPEALS AND SUCCESSIVE APPLICATIONS

(a) *Introduction*

Discussion of this rather technical and intricate aspect of habeas corpus will be facilitated by a brief introductory statement of the salient points. At common law, no decision on habeas corpus could be questioned by way of appeal or by proceedings in error. An order of release was final in all respects and could never be questioned. Where, however, the court refused to grant the writ, or refused to make an order of release, a further or 'successive' application could be made on the same grounds. The previous decision was not considered to bind another judge or court. The law with respect to appeals was partially altered by the Judicature Act 1873, which gave a right of appeal in civil cases, and it was held in 1959 that the Judicature Act had also affected the right to make successive applications. Parliament clarified and altered the law on both counts in 1960 by eliminating successive applications, but allowing for appeals in all cases.

Before examining the law as it now stands, it will be useful to examine the common law background further. The rules were unusual and came to be regarded as being, in many ways, fundamental to the nature of the protection extended by habeas corpus. The legislation of 1960 had to be framed against this background. Certain aspects of habeas corpus had to be rationalized but care had to be taken not to derogate from the fundamental nature of the writ.

(b) *Common Law Rules*

Habeas corpus, like certiorari, mandamus and prohibition, is a 'prerogative' writ. One aspect of proceedings on a prerogative writ is that while the court makes an order or award disposing of the matter before it, there is no formal judgment, no *ideo consideratum est*, of the kind rendered in ordinary proceedings between parties on pleadings.[1] In other words, the proceedings are summary. At common law, the only way a decision of a superior court of first instance would be questioned was by writ of error, and it was held that where there was no formal judgment, there could be no writ of error.[2] There is, moreover, a dictum of Lord Coke to the effect that a judicial decision which was not reviewable by writ of error did not constitute *res judicata* and could not conclude the parties to it.[3] The correctness of this dictum is gravely suspect, and it was repudiated by Lord Holt.[4] It is generally accepted that even if a summary decision does not constitute *res judicata*, it does bind parties to it by the doctrine of estoppel by record.[5] In any case, however incorrect Lord Coke's statement may have been in theory, it did give birth to the idea that a habeas corpus decision is not binding in subsequent proceedings and, therefore, that successive applications on the same grounds are permissible.

There can be little doubt, however, that whatever the technical origin of the rule, the underlying reason for maintaining that neither *res judicata* nor estoppel by record applied and that successive applications should be allowed, was that there was no appeal against a refusal for the writ to issue or for an order of discharge. It was simply thought intolerable that a person should have the legality of a restraint finally determined by the first court or judge to hear the matter.

(c) *Successive Applications*

While it is not certain when the practice started,[6] it was always assumed, until the *Hastings* decisions in 1959,[7] that there existed the right to make successive applications for habeas corpus.[8] It was

---

[1] *R.* v. *Dean and Chapter of Dublin* (1722) 1 Str. 356; *Pender* v. *Herle* (1725) 3 Bro. Parl. Cas. 505; Goddard, 'A Note on Habeas Corpus' (1949) 65 L.Q.R. 30, 35. See also *Cox* v. *Hakes* (1890) 15 App. Cas. 506 at 525.

[2] Ibid.

[3] *Bonham's Case* (1609) 8 Co. Rep. 107.

[4] *Philips* v. *Bury* (1694) 1 Ld. Raym. 5; *Groenvelt* v. *Burwell* (1704) 1 Ld. Raym. 454; Gordon, 'The Unruly Writ of Habeas Corpus' (1963) 26 Mod. L.R. 520, 527.

[5] Gordon, op. cit.; see *Re Tarling* [1979] 1 All E.R. 981, discussed *infra*, p. 207.

[6] For an early statement of the rule, see *R.* v. *Suddis* (1801) 1 East 306 at 314; per Lord Kenyon C.J.: 'I feel no difficulty in delivering the opinion which I entertain; because the prisoner will not be concluded by it, but may if he is dissatisfied apply to the other Courts of Westminster-Hall.'

[7] [1959] 1 Q.B. 358; [1959] Ch. 368.

[8] Other cases supporting the rule are: *Re Leak* (1829) 3 Y. & J. 46; *R.* v. *Alves* (1839) 8 L.J.Ex. 229; *Re Cobbet* (1845) 5 L.T.O.S. 130; *Ex p. Partington* (1845) 13 M. & W. 679; *Secretary of State for Home Affairs* v. *O'Brien* [1923] A.C. 603 at 609. See also the Commonwealth cases cited *infra*, pp. 210–12 and the 'judge to judge' cases, *infra*, nn. 10–11, p. 203.

thought that there was a right to go to every judge in turn, and the right to go from judge to judge[9] (rather than just from court to court) was supported not only by Lord Halsbury's dictum in *Cox* v. *Hakes*,[10] but also by the decision of the Privy Council in the *Eshugbayi Eleko*[11] case in 1928.

The Privy Council held in that case that since each individual judge clearly had jurisdiction to grant the writ in vacation,[12] and as the courts did not sit in vacation, it followed that there must have been the right to go from judge to judge out of term. If there was not the right to go from judge to judge in term as well, then the applicant would be better off in vacation than in term, and, thought the Privy Council, such an anomalous result was to be avoided. Moreover the Privy Council was reluctant to find, in the absence of express language, that the Judicature Act 1873 should have the incidental effect of taking away what had come to be regarded as a fundamental right.[13] The argument that the fusion of the courts precluded successive applications was accordingly rejected.

In *Hastings*, the Queen's Bench Division was faced with an application which had been rejected on the merits by a differently constituted Queen's Bench Divisional Court. Perhaps with more concern for the technical legal rules than had been shown by the Privy Council, and certainly with the possibility of law reform very much in mind,[14] the court ended the practice. It was held that under the old practice, before the Judicature Acts, the writ was granted in term by the court and not by a single judge and that therefore, going from judge to judge was impossible in term. Clearly, an applicant could have gone from

---

[9] In *Hastings* [1959] 1 Q.B. 358 at 365, Lord Parker C.J. admitted that this was generally assumed to be the law.

[10] (1890) 15 App. Cas. 506 at 514. Cf. the formulation of the rule by Lords Bramwell, 523–4, Hershell, 527–8, and Field, 543, all putting it as the right to go from court to court. Lord Esher M.R. correctly analysed the effect of the Judicature Act 1873 on the rule in the Court of Appeal: 20 Q.B.D. 1 at 13. There is some doubt about what was said in *Ex p. Partington* (1845) 13 M. &. W. 679, the case cited by Lord Halsbury. Heuston, *Essays in Constitutional Law* (2nd ed. 1964), 120–2, examines the other reports of *Partington* (14 L.J.Ex. 122; 9 Jur. 92; 92 J.P. 443; 2 Dowl. & L. 650) and concludes that the case did not support Lord Halsbury's formulation.

[11] *Eshugbayi Eleko* v. *Officer Administering the Government of Nigeria* [1928] 1 A.C. 459. See also Denning L.J.'s dictum in *Ex p. Chapple* (1950) 66 T.L.R. (Pt. 2) 932, Goddard, (1949) 65 L.Q.R. 30.

[12] This was confirmed by the Habeas Corpus Act 1679 as well as by practice of the courts: see *supra*, pp. 17–18.

[13] On this same point in the context of appeals, see *Cox* v. *Hakes* (1890) 15 App. Cas. 506, discussed *infra*, pp. 205–6.

[14] [1959] 1 Q.B. 358 at 378.

court to court, but the application was heard by the full court and could not be renewed before that same court or before a judge of that court.[15] Lord Halsbury's dictum in *Cox* v. *Hakes* was found to be unsupported, and the Privy Council's reasoning was rejected.

Having got rid of the premise that the right was to go from judge to judge, the Divisional Court considered the effect of the Judicature Act 1873. As a result of this Act, the Queen's Bench Division exercises in the name of the High Court of Justice the jurisdiction of the three common law courts (King's Bench, Common Pleas, and Exchequer). While this jurisdiction can be exercised by Divisional Courts of varying composition, the pre-1873 courts are fused, and the decision of one Divisional Court is the decision of the whole court.[16] Consequently, the court held, there is no longer another court on the common law side to which an application can be made.

Lord Parker C.J. carefully avoided commenting on the jurisdiction of the Chancery Division, although his reasoning strongly suggested that an application to that side would be similarly precluded. An application was in fact made by Hastings, and the Chancery Division predictably held[17] that as the Judicature Act 1873 had fused all the courts into one High Court, the order of one Divisional Court was the order of the whole court and that the Chancery Division did not constitute a separate entity for this purpose.

An appeal to the Court of Appeal was dismissed for want of jurisdiction, being an appeal in a criminal cause or matter.[18] The decisions left vacation practice unclear, and it was suggested that the applicant could still have gone from judge to judge in vacation.[19] The result clearly did

---

[15] *Re Cobbett* (1845) 5 L.T.O.S. 130 is cited for this proposition although it was not, strictly speaking, a successive application, but a motion to rescind an order remanding the prisoner. See also *Cobbett* (1851) 15 Q.B. 182n., which does support what was said. It is submitted that Lord Parker C.J. was inaccurate in saying that this rested on a discretionary power to refuse the writ: [1959] 1 Q.B. at 371. The writ issues *ex debito justitiae*, upon proper grounds and there is no discretion to refuse it: *supra*, pp. 58–9. As a practical matter, it would have been difficult to convince the court, which had already decided that the grounds were insufficient, to change its mind, and this is probably the real explanation for the refusal to re-hear the case.

[16] A similar result had been reached in *The State (Dowling)* v. *Kingston (No. 2)* [1937] I.R. 699; and in a few Commonwealth cases: *infra*, pp. 210–12. See also Heuston, 'Habeas Corpus Procedure' (1950) 66 L.Q.R. 79.

[17] [1959] Ch. 368.

[18] [1959] 1 W.L.R. 807.

[19] de Smith, (1959) 2 Mod. L.R. 421; Thompson, [1959] Crim. L.R. 720; and Wilson, [1959] Camb. L.J. 3. See also Heuston, op. cit. 127, suggesting that there was still a possibility of successive application during short vacations, notwithstanding the

makc legislation imperative since apart from the vacations, an applicant in a criminal case was without recourse if refused relief on his initial application, because, as will be seen presently, before 1960 there was no appeal in a criminal case.

(d) *Appeals Before 1960*

It will be recalled that until 1873, there were no appeals or proceedings in error which could arise from habeas corpus.[20] The Judicature Act 1873 did give a right of appeal in all matters except a 'criminal cause or matter'.[21] A habeas corpus case was considered to be a criminal cause or matter where it arose from proceedings '. . . the direct outcome of which may be the trial of the applicant and his possible punishment for an alleged offence by a court claiming jurisdiction to do so . . .' whether or not the offence would be criminal by the law of England in the case where the applicant is to be dealt with outside the country.[22] While there was no appeal in criminal cases,[23] this meant that for the first time appeals could be had in habeas corpus cases of a non-criminal nature, but the seemingly all-encompassing language of the Judicature Act was restricted in the important case of *Cox* v. *Hakes* in 1890.[24] The applicant had been imprisoned as a result of ecclesiastical proceedings and had obtained an order of release from the Queen's Bench Division. The Court of Appeal reversed this order but on further appeal to the House of Lords, it was held that there could be no appeal from an order of release, that the Court of Appeal should not have heard the matter, and the applicant's right to liberty was reaffirmed. In Lord Halsbury's words, 'the essential and leading

1960 legislation (*infra*, p. 207) since only one judge is available and one judge cannot finally refuse applications in a criminal case. The anomaly in the rules has been removed, and there is now adequate provision for the constitution of a Divisional Court during each vacation: Ord. 64(3).

[20] *Supra*, p. 202.

[21] s.47.

[22] *Amand* v. *Home Secretary and Minister of Defence, Netherlands* [1943] A.C. 147 at 156. See also *Ex p. Woodhall* (1888) 20 Q.B.D. 832; *Re Clifford and O'Sullivan* [1921] 2 A.C. 570. See also *Re Storgoff* [1945] S.C.R. 526 for the adoption of the test in Canada. Cf. Qasem, 'Habeas Corpus Appeals' (1952) 15. Mod. L.R. 55, arguing that habeas corpus itself constituted a civil proceeding, and that it should not take its colour from the circumstances.

[23] The Court of Appeal also refused to hear criminal matters as a successive application on the basis that it had no original jurisdiction to grant the writ: *Ex p. Le Gros* (1914) 30 T.L.R. 249; *Re Carroll* [1931] 1 K.B. 104; *Ex p. Chapple* (1950) 66 T.L.R. (Pt. 2) 932.

[24] (1890) 15 App. Cas. 506.

theory of the whole procedure is the immediate determination of the right to the applicant's freedom'. Before it could be said that this 'policy of centuries' had been reversed, and the right of personal freedom made 'subject to the delay and uncertainty of ordinary litigation', there would have to be express statutory language.[25] This was extended by the *O'Brien* case in 1923,[26] where it was held that even if the applicant had not been released, there could be no appeal from an order that the writ be issued, where the decision on that order had in substance determined the applicant's right to freedom.[27] The *O'Brien* decision also makes it clear that it was possible to appeal a refusal for the writ to issue as well as a refusal for an order of discharge, a question left open in *Cox* v. *Hakes*. The scales were tipped in favour of the applicant on all counts and what started out as technical common law rules had become fundamental guarantees.

The only exceptions to the rule that an order of release could not be appealed were child custody cases and appeals to the Privy Council. In child custody cases, the issue is that of the child's interest rather than personal liberty and for this reason, an order transferring custody was appealable.[28] Colonial appeals to the Judicial Committee of the Privy Council are in the nature of a petition to the royal prerogative. They do not require legislative sanction and the decision in *Cox* v. *Hakes* does not prevent the Privy Council from hearing an appeal against an order of release on habeas corpus.[29]

Before the legislation in 1960, the law, then, stood as follows. There could never be an appeal in proceedings arising out of a criminal cause or matter. There was an appeal in all non-criminal cases, including an

---

[25] Ibid. 517. Cf. the Australian cases, *infra*, p. 212. For cases where the writ was quashed for having been improperly issued, see *Ex p. Brocke* (1805) 6 East 238; *R.* v. *Slipp, Ex p. Gardiner* (1934) 61 C.C.C. 401 (N.B.C.A.).

[26] *Secretary of State for Home Affairs* v. *O'Brien* [1923] A.C. 603.

[27] One of the technical arguments raised in *Cox* v. *Hakes* was that there was no means to have the applicant re-arrested once he had been released. This left the doubt, settled in *O'Brien*, about what should happen where the appeal was brought before the prisoner had actually been released.

[28] *Barnardo* v. *McHugh* [1891] A.C. 388.

[29] Bentwich, 'Habeas Corpus in the Empire' (1911) 27 L.Q.R. 454; *King-Emperor* v. *Vimlabai Deshpande* (1946) 115 L.J.P.C. 71, where, however, leave to appeal was granted on the condition that the applicant not be re-arrested whatever the result of the appeal. Cf. *King-Emperor* v. *Sibnath Banerji* (1945) L.R. 72 Ind. App. 241, where it was held that an order of release could be appealed because of legislation conferring a right of appeal. An order of release was appealed without argument on the competence of the Privy Council to entertain such an appeal in *A.G. for Canada* v. *Fedorenko* [1911] A.C. 735; and in *U.S.* v. *Gaynor* [1905] A.C. 128.

appeal against a refusal to order the writ to issue, but in no circumstances could there be an appeal from an order of release, subject to the exceptions noted for child custody cases and appeals to the Privy Council.

(e) *The Administration of Justice Act 1960*

The law with regard to successive applications and appeals was the subject of legislation in 1960, in response to the *Hastings* decisions.[30] The *Hastings* result was confirmed by the Act, with one small qualification noted below, and the Act provided for appeals to fill the gap left by the disappearance of successive applications.

In both civil and criminal cases,[31] it is specifically provided that no application can be made more than once on the same grounds,[32] unless some fresh evidence is adduced on the subsequent application.[33] A subsequent application must be based upon evidence which is not only different, but which also could not reasonably have been put forward on the earlier application.[34] An applicant is not permitted to proceed on one ground, reserving a separate ground for a renewed application, but must 'put forward on his initial application the whole of the case which is then fairly available to him.'[35] This rule applies whether the application is made to a single judge or to a Divisional Court, except that in a criminal case, the writ can only be refused by a Divisional Court.[36] In other words, a single judge must

---

[30] *Supra*, pp. 203–5.

[31] The meaning of 'criminal cause or matter' is extended by s.14(3) to include a case arising from '... an order or direction under Part V of the Mental Health Act 1959 (otherwise than by virtue of 73(2)(e) or (f) of that Act) ...' The courts have previously dealt with the meaning of 'criminal cause or matter:' see *supra*, p. 205.

[32] s.14(2). 'Notwithstanding anything in any enactment of rule of law, where a criminal or civil application for habeas corpus has been made by or in respect of any person, no such application shall again be made by or in respect of that person on the same grounds, whether to the same court or judge or to any other court or judge, unless fresh evidence is adduced in support of the application.' Note that s.15(1), *infra*, n. 37, p. 208, provides only for an appeal from a refusal of an order of release. *Quaere* whether the applicant has any recourse where his initial *ex parte* application for the writ is refused? It is submitted that an appeal should be heard, if it is not possible to make a further ex parte application.

[33] In *Ex p. Schtraks* [1964] 1 Q.B. 191, it was held that 'fresh evidence' must be relevant to the point in issue on habeas corpus, and that this was not the case where evidence was adduced to show that the magistrate had come to the wrong conclusion.

[34] *Re Tarling* [1979] 1 All E.R. 981.

[35] Ibid. at 987 per Gibson J.

[36] s.14(1). 'On a criminal application for habeas corpus an order for the release of the person restrained shall be refused only by a Divisional Court of the Queen's Bench Division, whether the application is made in the first instance to such court, or to a single judge in accordance with the rules of court.'

refer an application for the writ in a criminal case to the Divisional Court if not prepared to grant the application. The Act confers, for the first time, an appeal in criminal cases.[37] The right of appeal in civil cases is confirmed,[38] but there is an important change which allows for an appeal against an order of release as well as against a refusal to discharge.[39] In civil cases, the appeal against an order of discharge is purely moot, and it cannot affect the applicant's right to liberty gained on the initial application.[40] This was apparently intended to allow the authorities to obtain a higher ruling on a point of law in cases of general public importance.[41] However, in criminal cases, an order may be made for the continued detention or bailing of the applicant, in which case the applicant's right to liberty will depend upon the final determination on appeal.[42] In civil cases, the appeal is to the Court of Appeal, and then to the House of Lords.[43] In criminal cases, the appeal is directly to the House of Lords, and, unlike civil cases, leave to appeal is required.[44] The

---

[37] s.15(1). 'Subject to the provisions of this section, an appeal shall lie, in any proceedings upon an application for habeas corpus, whether civil or criminal, against an order for the release of the person restrained as well as against the refusal of such an order.' There is, however, no appeal from the order of a single judge: s.15(2), see further, *infra*, p. 209.

[38] s.15(1) *supra*, n. 37.

[39] Ibid.

[40] s.15(4). 'Except as provided by s.5 of this Act in the case of an appeal against an order of a Divisional Court on a criminal application, an appeal brought by virtue of this section shall not affect the right of the person restrained to be discharged in pursuance of the order under appeal and (unless an order under subsection (1) of that section is in force at the determination of the appeal) to remain at large regardless of the decision on appeal.'

[41] The courts are usually reluctant to entertain academic or moot points: see, e.g., de Smith, *Judicial Review*, 507–9. It is suggested by Street, *Freedom, the Individual and the Law* (5th ed. 1982), 46–7, that this was intended to solve the problem posed by the *Rutty* case in 1956 (discussed *supra*, pp. 32–4), whereby the authorities, not being able to appeal the point of law, felt constrained to release some three thousand mental patients from custody.

[42] s.15(4), *Supra*, n. 40; s.5(1). 'Where the defendant ... would, but for the decision of the court below, be liable to be detained, and immediately after that decision the prosecutor is granted, or gives notice that he intends to apply for leave to appeal, the court may not be released except on bail ... so long as any appeal under section 1 of this Act is pending.' Such an order was made in *R. v. Governor of Pentonville Prison, ex p. Sotiriadis* [1974] 2 W.L.R. 253 at 262. If the prisoner is released outright rather than on bail, no order for rearrest may be made, even if the appeal is successful: *United States Government* v. *McCaffery* [1984] 2 All E.R. 570 (H.L.).

[43] See *Supreme Court Practice* 773.

[44] s.1. In rebutting the argument that appeals should be allowed as of right in criminal cases as well, Lord Parker C.J. commented as follows in the House of Lords debate on the bill: 222 H.L. Deb. ser. 5, col. 269 (24 March 1960): 'that sounds all very well in

requirement of a certificate that the appeal involves a point of public importance, which applies to ordinary criminal appeals to the House of Lords, does not apply to appeals on habeas corpus.[45]

For the most part, the Act properly retains the common law bias in favour of the applicant,[46] while eliminating certain awkward aspects of the common law rules. The extension of the right of appeal to applicants in criminal cases as well as civil cases, is adequate compensation for the demise of successive applications. The provision for moot appeals achieves an appropriate balance between the right of the individual to maintain freedom once gained, and the public interest to have points of law settled by the appellate courts. It is unfortunate that in criminal cases there should be the power to order further detention and regrettable that no guidelines for the exercise of this discretion are offered. Putting the liberty of the successful applicant at risk does derogate from the accepted common law protection and the reasons which were offered for this new power are unconvincing.[47]

On the other hand, it is not immediately apparent why there should be no appeal from an order of release made by a single judge in a criminal case. Paradoxically, a single judge cannot refuse the writ in a criminal case, but must refer the application to the Divisional Court and it is difficult to see why a single judge's order of release should be more conclusive than that of the Divisional Court. One reason for this anomaly may be that applications to a single judge will ordinarily only

theory; but I would recommend anyone who is so minded to come to the Divisional Court on Tuesdays and Fridays. There he will see that by far the majority of these applications are, on the face of them, hopelessly misconceived. The vast majority are made by prisoners serving long terms of imprisonment, serving sentences imposed by a court of competent jurisdiction from which an appeal has led to the Court of Criminal Appeal which has been refused. Those applications are misconceived.'

[45] s.15(3). See also *Zacharia* v. *Republic of Cyprus* [1963] A.C. 634, holding that an appeal on habeas corpus together with s.10 relief under the Fugitive Offenders Act 1881 (see now Fugitive Offenders Act 1967) did not require the certificate.

[46] Cf. Gordon, 'The Unruly Writ of Habeas Corpus' (1963) 26 Mod.L.R. 520, arguing that the applicant is unduly favoured by there being no appeal from a single judge's order of release in a criminal matter, and that the system of justice could be brought into disrepute by allowing a man to go free after the highest court had said that he should be imprisoned under the moot appeals scheme. Other writers have deprecated the possibility of an appeal leading to further confinement. Street, op. cit. 33; Downey, (1961) 24 Mod. L.R. 261.

[47] In the Commons Debate on the bill, the Solicitor-General, Sir Jocelyn Simon, said that the government had in mind cases under the Mental Health Act where dangerous psychopaths might be improperly released, and extradition cases, where Britain's treaty obligations could be impaired: 625 H.C. Deb. ser. 5, col. 1756 (1 July 1960).

be made in vacation when the Court of Appeal is not sitting, and as appeals are now possible in such cases, the applicant could have been subjected to a prolonged detention notwithstanding his initial success.[48]

Finally, with regard to moot appeals, it is by no means apparent how they are to be argued. It is difficult to imagine the applicant bearing the costs of such an appeal as it will not affect his rights. It may be that counsel could be briefed by the Official Solicitor.

(f) *Canada—Appeals and Successive Applications*

(i) Criminal Cases under Dominion Legislation. In Canada, the question of successive applications was a matter of great controversy in criminal cases until Parliament acted in 1964. It is now provided[49] that there shall be no application again made on the same grounds unless fresh evidence is adduced, but that there shall be a right of appeal to the provincial court of appeal and then to the Supreme Court of Canada from the refusal of an application.[50] There may not, however, be an appeal from an order for the writ to issue, and the only parties permitted to appeal a judgment on the return to habeas corpus are the applicant or the Attorney-General of the province concerned or the Attorney-General of Canada. There would seem to be no doubt that an appeal from an order of release is possible.[51]

These provisions, however, will only affect criminal cases and only those criminal cases under Parliament's legislative competence. There are a number of minor quasi-criminal matters over which the provinces have legislative competence[52] (liquor offences and traffic violations for example), and the broad area of 'property and civil rights' is within provincial control.[53] Habeas corpus is deemed to take its nature

---

[48] Cf. 625 H.C. Deb. ser. 5, col. 1754 (1 July 1960), where the Solicitor-General gave the reason that an appeal was unnecessary since a single judge would only grant the writ on his own in the clearest cases.

[49] Criminal Code, s.784. This section confers a right of appeal from refusal to grant the writ in an extradition case: *Re Federal Republic of Germany and Rauca* (1983) 4 C.C.C. (3d) 385 (Ont. C.A.).

[50] Ibid., s.784(3). Where judgment is given dismissing the application after the writ has been issued, leave to appeal to the Supreme Court of Canada is necessary: s.784(5). This distinction is anomalous as the modern practice is to deal with the substance of the case on the motion for the writ to issue: see *infra*, pp. 218–20.

[51] See *Ex p. Simoneau* [1971] 2 O.R. 561 (Ont. C.A.), allowing an appeal and ordering the re-arrest of the applicant.

[52] British North America Act 1867, s.92(15).

[53] Ibid., s.92(13).

from the proceedings out of which it has arisen,[54] and legislation giving a right of appeal or affecting successive applications by one level of government will only affect cases arising from a matter over which that government has legislative competence.[55] It is, therefore, necessary to examine the provisions made by the various provinces with respect to habeas corpus.

(ii) Provincial Matters. Some provinces have legislation precluding successive applications,[56] but most do not, and in those latter provinces, the answer will have to depend upon the cases.[57] In several jurisdictions, the cases are in irreconcilable conflict and a reading of them is unedifying. It is submitted that the better view is that expressed in the *Hastings* case, and that this result should be followed, especially

---

[54] *Re Storgoff* [1945] S.C.R. 526   [55] Ibid.

[56] Nova Scotia: Liberty of the Subject Act R.S.N.S. 1967, c.164, s.13, Quebec: Code of Civil Procedure 1965, c.80, s.857, which allows an application to be renewed once before two judges of the Court of Appeal, and then it may be appealed. See also s.20 of the pre-Confederation Habeas Corpus Act C.S.L.C. 1860, c.95, which forbade successive applications.

[57] Most of the cases arose from criminal proceedings before s.784 was enacted in 1964. *Ontario*: the result in *Hastings* was followed in *Ex p. Shane* (1959) 124 C.C.C. 160 (Ont. H.C.) but in an earlier proceeding, *Ex p. Johnston, Re Johnston and Shane* (1959) 124 C.C.C. 23 (Ont. C.A.), the Court of Appeal suggested that successive application was possible. The result may depend on a series of old cases holding that when a pre-Confederation statute gave a right of appeal, there was no right to re-apply: *Re Hall* (1883) 8 O.A.R. 135 (C.A.); *Taylor* v. *Scott* (1899) 30 O.R. 475 (Div. Ct.) *R.* v. *Miller* (1909) 15 C.C.C. 87 (Ont. Div. Ct.); cf. *R.* v. *Graves (No. 2)* (1910) 16 C.C.C. 318 (Ont. Div. Ct.). In *Ex p. Johnston, supra*, it was held that this right of appeal no longer existed. In provincial cases, an appeal is clearly given, and this suggests that, on the reasoning in the old cases, there would be no successive application. See also *R.* v. *Jackson* (1917) 29 C.C.C. 352 (Ont. C.A.), saying that there is no right to re-apply.
Alberta: pro successive application; *R.* v. *Rombough (No. 2)* (1964) 41 C.R. 270 (Alta. S.C.); *contra Jackson* (1914) 22 C.C.C. 215 (Alta. C.A.).
British Columbia: *R.* v. *Loo Len* (1924) 41 C.C.C. 388 (B.C.C.A.) said that there was no right to re-apply but was not followed in *R.* v. *Gee Dew* (1924) 42 C.C.C. 188 (B.C.S.C.), and said to have been overruled by *Eshugbayi Eleko* [1928] 1 A.C. 459 (P.C.) by Farris C.J.S.C. in *Re Ciminelli (No. 2)* (1943) 79 C.C.C. 362 (B.C.S.C.). See also *State of N.Y.* v. *Wilby* (1944) 82 C.C.C. 1 (B.C.C.A.) and *R.* v. *Bowack* (1892) 2 B.C.R. 216 which favour the right to re-apply.
Manitoba: Pro successive application: *R.* v. *Helik* (1939) 72 C.C.C. 76 (Man. K.B.); *R.* v. *Barre* (1905) 11 C.C.C. 1 (Man. K.B.); *Re Royston* (1909) 15 C.C.C. 96 (Man. K.B.); *contra R.* v. *Romanchuk* (1924) 42 C.C.C. 231 (Man. K.B.).
New Brunswick: Pro successive application: *Ex p. Byrne* (1883) 22 N.B.R. 427 (N.B.C.A.).
Nova Scotia: Pro successive application: *R.* v. *Carter* (1902) 5 C.C.C. 401 (N.S.S.C.).
Before the 1964 legislation, the Supreme Court of Canada approved of *Hastings*: *Re Goldhar* [1960] S.C.R. 431 at 437–8, per Kerwin, C.J. (obiter); but cf. *Re Seeley* (1908) 41 S.C.R. 5 where it was said that there was a right to re-apply.

since an appeal will always be possible under provincial legislation.

Appeals in provincial cases will always be available, either under the general grant of a right of appeal, or under specific provision with respect to habeas corpus. In jurisdictions where it is not expressly provided that an appeal lies from *any* habeas corpus decision, the question of the propriety of appealing an order of release could still arise.[58]

(g) *Australia*

In Australia, there is some authority favouring the right of successive application.[59] It is unlikely that the Australian courts would follow the *Hastings* result in preference to the earlier decision of the Privy Council[60] favouring the right to re-apply.[61] A strong reason for allowing successive applications is that in most states there is no right of appeal in criminal cases to the state courts.[62] There is a right of appeal in civil cases to state courts and the High Court of Australia hears appeals in criminal cases. It has been held that the High Court may hear appeals against an order of release as well as against a refusal to discharge in cases over which it has appellate jurisdiction.[63]

(h) *New Zealand*

In New Zealand, it was held as early as 1900 that the fusion of the common law courts into one Supreme Court had ended any right to apply more than once on the same grounds for a writ of habeas corpus.[64]

[58] *Cox* v. *Hakes* (1890) 15 App. Cas. 506, discussed, *supra*, pp. 205–6.

[59] *Ex p. Rowlands* (1895) 16 L.R. (N.S.W.) 239; *Williamson* v. *Director of Penal Services* [1959] V.R. 205; *Ex p. Williams, re Poundall* (1931) 48 W.N. (N.S.W.) 228; *Trotter* v. *The Queen* [1977] Tas. S.R. 68 at 76–7; *Tobin* v. *Minister for Correctional Services* (1980) 24 S.A.S.R. 389.

[60] *Supra*, p. 203.

[61] Brett and Hogg, *Cases and Materials on Administrative Law* (3rd ed. 1975), 76; Campbell and Whitmore, *Freedom in Australia*, (1973), 54.

[62] *Williamson* v. *Director of Penal Services* [1959] V.R. 205; *Re Iles* [1968] V.R. 628 (Victoria).

[63] This is notwithstanding the decision in *Cox* v. *Hakes* because of the broad powers given the High Court by s.73 of the Constitution: *A.G. for Commonwealth* v. *Ah Sheung* (1906) 4 C.L.R. 949; *Collis* v. *Smith* (1909) 9 C.L.R. 490; *Lloyd* v. *Wallach* (1915) 20 C.L.R. 299. Cf. *Wall* v. *R.* (1927) 39 C.L.R. 245, where *Cox* v. *Hakes* was followed since the appeal depended upon an ordinance of the Supreme Court of the Northern Territory rather than the Constitution. See also *Ex p. Sampson, re Governor of H.M.'s Prison at Malabar* [1966] 1 N.S.W.R. 305 (C.A.), holding that an appeal lies from an order of release on the basis of s.254, Common Law Procedure Act 1899–1962.

[64] *Ex p. Bouvy (No. 2)* (1900) 18 N.Z.L.R. 601; cf. *Re Tamalese* [1929] N.Z.L.R. 209 at 211.

2. PROTECTION AGAINST RE-ARREST

(a) *Habeas Corpus Act 1679, s.5*

It has been seen that the rule of *res judicata* has not been considered to be applicable to habeas corpus matters.[65] While the most important consequence of this doctrine was to permit successive applications, it must also be considered in the context of re-arrest following release on habeas corpus. The matter is governed by s.5 of the Habeas Corpus Act 1679.[66]

The meaning of s.5 has never been entirely clear. It provides as follows:

5. And for the prevention of unjust vexation by reiterated committments for the same offence ... noe person or persons which shall be delivered or sett at large upon any habeas corpus shall at any time hereafter bee againe imprisoned or committed for the same offence by any person or persons whatsoever other then by the legall order and process of such court wherein he or they shall be bound by recognizance to appeare or other court haveing jurisdiction of the cause and if any other person or persons shall knowingly contrary to this Act recommitt or imprison or knowingly procure or cause to be recommitted or imprisoned for the same offence or pretended offence any person or persons delivered or sett at large as aforesaid or be knowingly aiding or assisting therein then he or they shall forfeite to the prisoner or party grieved the summe of five hundred pounds any colourable pretence or variation in the warrant or warrants of committment notwithstanding to be recovered as aforesaid.

On its face, it appears to have a very broad scope, seemingly forbidding any re-arrest for the same matter following a successful habeas corpus application, but it has never been so interpreted, and was probably intended to meet a much narrower class of case. It has been suggested, probably correctly, that the section was never intended to do more than prevent the re-arrest and imprisonment of someone who had been bailed on habeas corpus.[67] The proviso that allows re-arrest by 'the legall order and process of such court wherein he or they shall be bound by recognizance to appear' is said to demonstrate that the

---

[65] *Supra*, pp. 201–2.

[66] There is some Canadian authority to the effect that the ordinary rule of *res judicata* should apply here: *Ex p. Seitz (No. 2)* (1899) 3 C.C.C. 127 (Que. Q.B.); *R. v. Thompson (No. 2)* (1946) 86 C.C.C. 206 (Ont. C.A.).

[67] *Attorney-General for Hong Kong* v. *Kwok-a-Sing* (1873) L.R. 5 P.C. 179 at 201; *Ex p. Stallman* [1912] 3 K.B. 424 at 449; Friedland, *Double Jeopardy* (1969), 268.

framers of the section were contemplating release on bail prior to trial. The added words 'or other court haveing jurisdiction of the cause' were inserted to cover the case of an indictment having been removed by certiorari.[68]

The cases do give the section a somewhat broader interpretation than may have been originally intended, however, and the test suggested by the *Kwok-a-Sing* decision of the Privy Council in 1873[69] seems to be the accepted interpretation. In that case, it was held that a previous order of release from an extradition committal did not bar further proceedings on a fresh warrant and for another offence, but Mellish L.J., delivering the decision of the Board, added:

[Their Lordships] do not say, however, that the section may not also apply to cases where a prisoner is discharged unconditionally upon the ground that the warrant, on which he is detained, shews no valid cause for his detention. They think, however, it can only apply when the second arrest is substantially for the same cause as the first, so that the return to the second writ of habeas corpus raises for the opinion of the court the same question with reference to the validity of the grounds of detention as the first.[70]

There appears to be no reported case in which the section, as interpreted by the *Kwok-a-Sing* case, has been applied to the benefit of the prisoner, although the courts have consistently held that this is the proper interpretation.[71] Simply put, the test seems to be that where re-arrest would involve the potential re-litigation of the same point, then the section operates as a bar. In one case, it was said that s.5 would operate, for example, to bar further proceedings on the same charge in an extradition matter once it had been held that the offence was not extraditable.[72] On the other hand, it has been held repeatedly

---

[68] *Attorney-General for Hong Kong* v. *Kwok-a-Sing* (1873) L.R. 5 P.C. 179 at 202.
[69] Ibid.   [70] Ibid.
[71] There are authorities which suggest that an order or release always bars re-committal. *Ex p. Eno* (1884) 10 Q.L.R. 165, 173 (Que. Q.B.); *Ex p. Duvernay* (1875) 19 L.C.J. 248 (Que. Q.B.). See also broad statements in Spencer-Bower and Turner, *Res Judicata* (2nd ed. 1969), 215; 11 Hals. (4th) 797; Paley, *Summary Convictions* (9th ed. 1926), 793. These statements are all too sweeping: see Friedland, op. cit. 267, 270. On the other side, see the decision of the Australian High Court in *Wall* v. *R.* (*No. 2*) (1927) 39 C.L.R. 266, where it was said that the *Kwok-a-Sing* test was the proper one. Yet on the facts, the court flatly refused to apply it to the prisoner's benefit. On the initial application, (1927) 39 C.L.R. 245, it had been held that the applicant was not a person subject to deportation, yet the High Court allowed a re-arrest and further deportation proceedings.
[72] *R.* v. *Governor of Brixton Prison, ex p. Stallman* [1912] 3 K.B. 424. In two instances, the courts have been faced with successive habeas corpus applications by prisoners who

that where the grounds for release in the first case were that there had been some jurisdictional or procedural defect which could be avoided the second time, the first decision will not bar a re-arrest.[73] For example, in a war-time case,[74] an internee was not given the proper document giving the reason for the detention, and an order of release was made on habeas corpus. The internee was re-arrested and given the proper document and the court held, on a second application for habeas corpus, that the re-arrest was not barred as the justification then offered for the imprisonment was sufficient and did not suffer from the same infirmity.

Similarly, a discharge on the ground of insufficient evidence in committal proceedings will not bar further proceedings based on more complete evidence.[75] It has also been held in Canada that where an accused person obtains release because of a defective committal, there is nothing to prevent the prosecution from directly preferring an indictment and ignoring the impugned proceedings.[76]

Neither will the section prevent recommittal to prison where the applicant has been released due to a defective warrant of committal following conviction.[77] So long as the conviction itself remains unimpeached, an amended warrant in execution will always provide fresh justification for the imprisonment and s.5 is not a bar.[78]

It is submitted that strictly applied, the section does leave a gap which allows for the possibility of harassment. It does appear to allow the authorities to re-arrest for the same substantive cause, and to

lost the first round, were extradited, escaped and then were arrested again. *Re Guerin*, discussed *supra*, n. 115, p. 85; *R. v. Governor of Winson Green Prison, Birmingham, ex p. Littlejohn* [1975] 1 W.L.R. 893.

[73] Ibid.; *Ex p. Seitz (No. 2)* (1899) 3 C.C.C. 127 (Que. Q.B.); *R. v. Frejd* (1910) 18 C.C.C. 110 (Ont. C.A.); *Ex p. Mohamet Ali* (1919) 32 C.C.C. 65 (N.S.S.C.); *Re Royston* (1909) 15 C.C.C. 96 (Man. Q.B.); *Ex p. Malatsky* (1925) 43 C.C.C. 306 (P.E.I.S.C.); *R. v. Young Kee* (1917) 28 C.C.C. 236 (Alta. S.C.); *Re Ley and Ley* (1883) 17 S.A.L.R. 125; *Ex p. Chung* (1975) 26 C.C.C. (2d) 497 (B.C.C.A.); *In Re Rees* [1986] 1 A.C. 937; *Re Singer (No. 2)* (1964) 98 I.L.T.R. 112; *The People (D.P.P.) v. Walsh* [1980] I.R. 294; Walker, 'Arrest and Rearrest' (1984) 35 N.I.L.Q. 1 at 24–6.

[74] *Ex p. Budd* [1942] 2 K.B. 14 (C.A.), discussed further *infra*, n. 79, p. 216.

[75] *Harsha v. U.S.* (1906) 42 Can. L.J. 754 (P.C.); *Re Royston* (1909) 15 C.C.C. 96 (Man. K.B.). The same rule applies to a discharge given by the magistrate; the rule of autrefois acquit does not apply: see Friedland, op. cit. 270–2.

[76] *Re Carmichael* (1865) 1 C.L.J. 243; *R. v. Dick* (1913) 22 C.C.C. 188. Cf. the cases cited *supra*, n. 79, p. 182.

[77] *Ex p. David* (1928) 49 C.C.C. 381 (N.B.S.C.); *Re Banniti* (1925) 45 C.C.C. 75 (Ont. S.C.); *R. v. Ransome* (1932) 57 C.C.C. 282 (N.S.S.C.); *Arscott v. Lilley* (1886) 11 O.R. 153 (aff'd 14 O.A.R. 297).

[78] See *supra*, pp. 56–7.

support the second detention by filing a little more material.[79] The danger in permitting re-arrest must always be that there will be a violation of what Lord Halsbury called 'the essential and leading theory of the whole procedure' of habeas corpus, namely, that there be 'the immediate determination of the right to the applicant's freedom'.[80] The problem is to strike a balance between protecting the subject from protracted and expensive proceedings once he or she has been released, and at the same time, to ensure that final success does not depend on trivial grounds. Apart from giving s.5 a broader interpretation, there is the possibility of the courts exercising their power to prevent an abuse of the process in a case of real harassment.[81]

(b) *Action for the Penalty under s.5*

S.5 provides for a penalty and forfeiture of £500 to the party aggrieved. There are two reported cases of actions for this penalty, both unsuccessful.[82] It is clear from the language of the section that to be liable, the defendant must have 'knowingly' acted contrary to its provisions. A gaoler or other officer will have a complete defence where he or she has innocently acted upon a warrant which is in the usual form.[83]

(c) *Non-Criminal Cases*

It will be remembered that the Habeas Corpus Act 1679 applies only to criminal cases. In at least one case,[84] however, the court seems to have ignored this, and dealt with the argument as if s.5 could apply to a non-criminal matter. In principle, such a case falls to be decided without the benefit of the Act.

---

[79] See e.g. *Ex p. Budd* [1941] 2 All E.R. 749, a war-time internment case, where the Home Secretary was allowed to support the validity of a re-arrest on the grounds, *inter alia*, that more material had been filed to support his belief that the applicant was a person who should be interned. Stable J., dissenting, points out the danger of harassment where the prisoner is re-arrested for the same substantive cause. The Court of Appeal ([1942] 2 K.B. 14) upheld the decision on other grounds, pointing out that the Home Secretary was not required to support his belief, and that the applicant should never have been released on those grounds on the first application: see *supra*, pp. 100–6.

[80] *Cox* v. *Hakes* (1890) 15 App. Cas. 506 at 517.

[81] *Ex p. Malatsky* (1925) 43 C.C.C. 306, 310 (P.E.I.S.C.); *Re Gerhard* (1901) 27 V.L.R. 655.

[82] *Arscott* v. *Lilley* (1886) 11 O.R. 153 (aff'd 14 O.A.R. 297); *Smith* v. *Collis* (1910) 10 S.R. (N.S.W.) 800.

[83] *Smith* v. *Collis* (1910) 10 S.R. (N.S.W.) 800.

[84] *Ex p. Budd* [1942] 2 K.B. 14 (C.A.).

Before the Act was passed, there was some protection against re-arrest as the court would issue an attachment against anyone who ignored its order that the application was to remain at large.[85] This is perhaps not as broad as the protection given by s.5, but the courts have really only interpreted that section so as to give the kind of protection which would apply if the ordinary rules of *res judicata* or estoppel were to apply.[86] If, therefore, a court has to decide a case without the benefit of s.5, it can reach a satisfactory result by simply applying the concept of estoppel by record, if not *res judicata*. There is now no reason at all why these principles could not be applied in habeas corpus cases. Their exclusion from habeas corpus may well have been wrong in the first place,[87] and now, the technical reasons for their exclusion have disappeared.

[85] *Searche's Case* (1588) 1 Leon. 70.
[86] See Friedland, op. cit. 269.
[87] *Supra*, p. 202.

10

Aspects of Practice

1. BRINGING THE APPLICATION BEFORE THE COURT[1]

(a) Ex Parte *Application*

The first step in making application for habeas corpus is to apply *ex parte* to the Divisional Court of the Queen's Bench, or to a single judge in court if no Divisional Court is sitting.[2] If no judge is sitting in court, the application may be made in chambers.[3] All cases involving the custody of infants must he heard by the Family Division.[4]

The purpose of the initial *ex parte* application is to enable the court or judge to determine whether the matter has sufficient merit to warrant a full hearing.

The application should be supported by an affidavit of the prisoner, or, if the prisoner is unable to give one because of the restraint, from someone else, explaining the circumstances.[5] A copy of the warrant or other order, which the gaoler is bound by the 1679 Act to provide,[6] should be annexed to the affidavit.[7] The affidavit should set out the nature of the restraint suffered by the prisoner and should give the factual grounds for the application.

The strength of the case which is to be made out to take the applicant beyond the first stage of the proceedings has never been defined with precision. The issue has already been discussed in so far as issues of fact are concerned, in the section on burden of proof.[8] There, it was suggested that the prisoner had, as a practical matter, to satisfy an initial burden of adducing evidence so as to raise an issue of fact which would be determined on the full hearing. Clearly the

---

[1] For the practice in Canada, see Harvey, *Habeas Corpus in Canada* (1974), and for discussion of Irish practice, see Kenny, 'Informality in Modern Irish Habeas Corpus Practice' (1974) 9 Irish Jur. 67.

[2] Ord. 54, r.1(1). [3] r.1(a).

[4] r.11; Supreme Court Act 1981, s.61, Sched. 1, para. 3. [5] r.1(2), (3).

[6] s.4. For cases enforcing the section see *Ward* v. *Snell* (1788) 1 H. Bl, 10; *Sedley* v. *Arbourin* (1800) 3 Esp. 173; *Huntley* v. *Luscombe* (1801) 2 Bos. & P. 530; *Cobbett* v. *Morish* (1875) 39 J.P. 103; *Re West* (1874) 8 S.A.L.R. 84; *Gunning* v. *Dwyer* (1887) 16 Aust. Dig. 901; cf. *Hudson* v. *Ash* (1718) 1 Str. 167.

[7] r.1(2). [8] *Supra*, pp. 85–91.

applicant should not have to bear the burden of convincing the judge or the court at this point. Often the application will be made on short notice with little time to prepare the legal argument and the factual material. It is probably enough that a doubt be raised in the mind of the judge regarding the validity of the detention and an arguable case be shown which deserves further consideration.

(b) *Determination of Matters in Issue*

If the court or judge is satisfied that there is an arguable case for the writ, the matter is adjourned so that proper notice may be given to the respondent and to other necessary parties.[9] It is possible, however, for the court or judge to order that the writ issue forthwith on the *ex parte* application.[10] This is a somewhat extraordinary step, and would be taken in cases of special urgency, for example, a danger that the respondent will flee from the jurisdiction and deprive the prisoner of the remedy.[11] In such a case, a formal return to the writ is required, and the substance of the matter is argued on the return.

In the ordinary case, however, the hearing on the summons or notice of motion for the writ becomes almost invariably the substantive hearing,[12] the respondent producing the alleged justification for the restraint by affidavit and full argument from all sides being presented. This is the modern version of the old rule nisi procedure which was evolved to avoid having to deal with formal returns.[13] The court comes to a determination and either orders that the prisoner be remanded or discharged.[14] The court may order the writ to issue so that the prisoner is brought up and formally discharged, but this seems unnecessary and is not usually done.[15] If this does happen, it is quite clear that the order for the writ to issue must be treated as a final determination in favour of the prisoner, and proceedings after an order for the writ are purely formal.[16]

[9] r.2(2) requires that 8 clear days notice be given unless otherwise ordered. The same rule permits the judge or court to order that persons other than the custodian of the applicant be served, and this is used, for example, to bring in foreign governments seeking extradition: *R.* v. *Governor of Brixton Prison, ex p. Minervini* [1959] 1 Q.B. 155.
[10] r.2(1).
[11] *Ex p. Witte* (1853) 13 C.B. 680; *Re Prezewloski, ex p. Zytominski* (1947) unreported, referred to in Griffiths, *Guide to Crown Office Practice* (1947), Supp. 41. In *Re B* [1972] N.Z.L.R. 897, the court ordered the prisoner's discharge on the *ex parte* motion on the grounds that the application was bound to succeed.
[12] r.4; *Supreme Court Practice* (1988), 813. The practice is similar in Canada, see Hart [1961] *Law Society of Upper Canada Special Lectures* 313, 319.
[13] *Infra*, p. 220.   [14] r.4.   [15] *Supreme Court Practice* (1988), 813–14.
[16] *R.* v. *De Portugal* (1885) 55 L.J.Q.B. 567; *Secretary of State for Home Affairs* v. *O'Brien* [1923] A.C. 603

It is still possible, however, for the court or judge to make an order that the writ actually issue, and in such a case, a formal return is required.[17] The writ must be personally served upon the person to whom it is directed together with notice stating the directions as to time and place for the return as ordered by the court.[18] The original writ is left with the party served,[19] and that party is required to endorse upon the writ or annex to it all causes for the detainer of the prisoner.[20] On the hearing, the return is read and then the court entertains the motion for discharge, remand, or amending or quashing the return, as the case may be.[21] It is difficult to see why it should be necessary to follow the formal procedure of having the writ issue in any but the exceptional case.

(c) *Former Practice*

It has been observed earlier on that in certain respects, the practice followed on habeas corpus may shape the substantive relief afforded by the writ.[22] Understanding the earlier cases requires an awareness of the procedural changes which have been adopted through the years.

Before 1938, when the modern practice was adopted, and from about 1780,[23] the practice was as follows. The initial *ex parte* application was framed as a request for a rule nisi requiring the respondent to show cause, on a certain day, why the writ should not issue. If the court was satisfied that the applicant had an arguable case, the rule would issue. The applicant would serve the respondent with notice of the rule nisi, and it was then incumbent upon the respondent to make out a case for the detention on the return of the rule. The argument at this stage usually became the substantive hearing.[24] While the court could still order the writ to actually issue, the matter could readily be determined at this stage. The requirement to show cause or justification for the detention was cast upon the respondent just as if the writ had issued, but the rule nisi procedure allowed the court to try the matter

---

[17] r.5–8.   [18] r.5, 6(4).
[19] *Re Agar* (1956) 114 C.C.C. 311 (Ont. C.A.). R.6(2) permits service on a servant or agent in certain cases.
[20] r.7(1).   [21] r.8.   [22] *Supra*, p. 23.
[23] The practice is believed by Short and Mellor, op. cit. 320, to have started with *Wade's Case* (1784), referred to in *Blake* (1814) 2 M. & S. 428, but for an earlier example, see *R.* v. *Evered* (1777) Cald. 26.
[24] See *R.* v. *Governor of Brixton Prison, ex p. Savarkar* [1910] 2 K.B. 1056 at 1074, where the early practice is discussed; see also *Cox* v. *Hakes* (1896) 15 App. Cas. 506 at 536–7.

without a formal return and without the expense of having the prisoner brought physically before the court.[25]

The practice before 1780 was simply to have an *ex parte* motion for the writ, and if on that application the prisoner made out an arguable case, the writ issued.[26] The case was determined on the return of the body of the prisoner and the cause of detention. The gaoler's return was endorsed on the writ and the case turned on its sufficiency.

As noted above, it is still possible to try a habeas corpus case on a formal return to the writ, but this is rarely done. Indeed, for almost 200 years it has been possible to try a habeas corpus matter without a formal return, although, as has been seen, the law is sometimes still thought to be riddled with technical problems relating to the return.

2. LOCUS STANDI AND CAPACITY

Any person restrained may apply for the writ. There are no restrictions based on lack of capacity to sue. The technical reason for this is the prerogative nature of the writ. This was explained in a Canadian case where it was objected that a minor could not bring proceedings: 'As the writ issues in the King's name, the status of the petitioner is immaterial, and his detention may be inquired into even if legal disabilities would prevent his taking an action for the enforcement of civil rights.'[27] It is rarely suggested, for example, that mentally ill patients lack capacity to have the legality of their detention tested.[28] It is often supposed that alien enemies lack *locus standi* for the purposes of habeas corpus, but, as has been seen in another chapter, this is a misconception.[29] The courts have, in fact, entertained applications from alien enemy prisoners, although it is clear that if the applicant truly does fall within that class, the imprisonment will be justified.

There is, then, no restriction of the remedy on the grounds of *locus standi*, and any person restrained may apply for the writ.

---

[25] *R.* v. *Evered* (1777) Cald. 26.

[26] See e.g. Wilmot *Opinion* Wilm. 81–94.

[27] *Re A.B.* (1905) 9 C.C.C. 390 at 391 (Que.).

[28] Cf. *supra*, p. 162, where the possibility of a solicitor being liable for costs of an application made on behalf of an incompetent person is discussed.

[29] *Supra*, pp. 115–17, for a detailed discussion.

3. THIRD PARTY APPLICATIONS

Circumstances may arise where a prisoner is unable to instruct a legal adviser or a friend to take steps to bring habeas corpus proceedings. In such a case, it may be possible for some independent third party to initiate proceedings, even though that person acts neither as the agent of the prisoner nor on the prisoner's instructions.

It is obviously desirable to have flexible rules governing applications in this regard. If third parties were not allowed to initiate proceedings, a captor acting unlawfully would only have to hold his prisoner in especially close custody to prevent any possibility of recourse to the courts. To a certain extent, the technical nature of habeas corpus reflects this need. The writ issues in the name of the sovereign and represents the prerogative power to have an account of any subjects who are imprisoned.[30] The applicant, whether the prisoner or simply a concerned third party, is, strictly speaking, not so much a party to the proceedings as an informant.

Every case in which habeas corpus is used by one party to gain custody of a child or other person from the respondent may be taken as an example of a third party application.[31] The more significant cases are, however, those where a prisoner is being held in circumstances which do not allow for recourse to the courts. In such a case, an application from a third party will be entertained where it is shown (by affidavit) that the prisoner is so confined as to be unable to initiate proceedings.[32] There have been several cases of this sort, including applications made by charitable or philanthropic societies,[33] by concerned individuals,[34] and even one by the Home Secretary, on behalf of a Polish seaman seeking political asylum who was being held on board a ship in the Thames.[35] While there is little recent authority in support, it is likely that the court would entertain such an application

---

[30] *Supra*, p. 188.

[31] See e.g. *Re Price* (1860) 2 F. & F. 263; *Re Carroll* [1931] 1 K.B. 317 at 352 (C.A.).

[32] For an unusual case see *Ex p. John Doe* (1974) 46 D.L.R. (3d) 547 (B.C.C.A.), where an application was brought by counsel who alleged he could not even determine the name of the detainee.

[33] *Hotenttot Venus* (1810) 13 East 195; *Re Gootoo & Inyakwana* (1891) 35 Sol. Jo. 481; *Re Ning Yi-Ching* (1939) 56 T.L.R. 3.

[34] *Sommersett* (1772) 20 St. Tr. 1 seems to have been such a case. See also *Ex p. West* (1861) 2 Legge 1475 (N.S.W.).

[35] *Re Klimowicz* (1954) unreported, cited in 11 Hals. (4th), 787.

where the impediment preventing the prisoner from acting was ignorance or disability rather than close physical custody.[36]

Where there is an element of consent on the part of the person allegedly in fetters, a third party cannot initiate proceedings. For example, in several old cases, masters brought habeas corpus proceedings to recover their apprentices who had been conscripted into military service, but it appeared that the apprentice was quite content and habeas corpus was refused on the grounds of consent.[37] The court will consider whether the third party is genuinely concerned, and ordinarily the party applying must clearly make out a case on the facts showing why the court should be moved by a stranger rather than the prisoner, or the application will be refused.[38] An application for the writ usually is supported by an affidavit from the prisoner, and the court requires an explanation of the circumstances if such an affidavit is not filed [39]

(a) *Third Party Audience in Court*

While the courts have been willing to entertain applications launched by third parties in the circumstances outlined above, it has always been preferred to have the formal court application made on motion by counsel.[40]

Spouses[41] and parents[42] of prisoners have, on occasion, been allowed to appear in court to ask for habeas corpus, but on each occasion it has been stated that this will be allowed only in 'exceptional circumstances'. A similar rule has been made against prisoners appearing on their own behalf, which is discussed subsequently.[43] While it may be harsh to forbid a prisoner from arguing his or her own case, there is good reason to discourage third parties without legal training from appearing. Unless there is no time to seek legal advice (which would,

---

[36] See *Hotenttot Venus* (1810) 13 East 195, where an application of this nature was entertained.

[37] *Ex p. Lansdown* (1804) 5 East 38; *R.* v. *Reynolds* (1795) 6 T.R. 497; *R.* v. *Edwards* (1798) 7 T.R. 745. Cf. however *Re Thaw (No. 2)* (1913) 22 C.C.C. 3 (Que. S.C.)

[38] *R.* v. *Clarke* (1762) 3 Burr. 1362; *Ex p. Child* (1854) 15 C.B. 238; *Re Carter* (1893) 95 L.T.O.S. 37; *Clarkson* v. *R.* [1986] V.R. 464.

[39] For a case where the court refused to dispense with the prisoner's affidavit, see *Ex p. O'Brien* (1923) *The Times*, 24 Mar.; 16 Dig. 292.

[40] *Re Greene* [1941] W.N. 110; Short & Mellor, op. cit. 321; *Clarkson* v. *R.* [1986] V.R. 464. Cf. *Practice Note* [1947] W.N. 218, in which Lord Goddard said that litigants in person could move for the prerogative writs. In view of what was said to discourage such applications in habeas corpus in *Ex p. Hinds* [1961] 1 All E.R. 707, it seems that the note was not intended to include habeas corpus.

[41] *Ex p. Cobbett* (1851) 15 Q.B. 182n; *Ex p. Hinds* [1961] 1 All E.R. 707.

[42] *Re Newton* (1855) 16 C.B. 97.   [43] *Infra*, pp. 224–7.

undoubtedly, constitute an 'exceptional circumstance') it is preferable that legal skills be brought to bear in this rather technical area of the law. If a layperson represented the prisoner's interest, then this would be a departure from the normal rules restricting the right of audience in the courts to legally qualified people.[44] Legal aid is available, failing which an approach can probably be made to the Official Solicitor.

4. PRISONER APPLICATIONS

(a) *English Practice*[45]

The practice of the English courts with respect to informal applications made by prisoners on their own behalf was explained by Lord Parker C.J. in 1960.[46] While there is no right of access to the Divisional Court other than by counsel's application and according to the rules, as a concession, the court does consider a prisoner's written statement sent by letter to the Master of the Crown Office setting out the grounds of complaint. If the court finds that there is an arguable point, the Official Solicitor is asked to instruct counsel to make a formal application. If the court considers that there are no grounds, the prisoner is told that there will be no departure from the formal rules, so that if the matter is to proceed, it will have to be on formal application and according to the rules.[47] Successive applications are discouraged.

In these cases, the prisoner does not have the opportunity to be present or to present oral argument. Indeed, the practice of the court is to refuse to hear applications for habeas corpus *in personam* and to require applications to be made by counsel unless there are exceptional

---

[44] 3 Hals. (4th), 635, where a few exceptions to the rule are given.

[45] For a detailed examination and analysis of the practice in this area, see Drewry, Hughes and Shaw, 'Informal Applications for the Writ of Habeas Corpus' [1977] P.L. 149.

[46] *Re Wring, Re Cooke* [1960] 1 All E.R. 536. The application was made by a convicted prisoner serving a sentence, and the Court made it clear that it would not allow habeas corpus to be used as a means of appeal, the only possible place for habeas corpus in such a case being where the prisoner had been held beyond the period of his sentence; see *supra*, pp. 147–8. The Appeal Committee of the House of Lords has adopted a practice similar to that outlined in the text with respect to applications for leave to appeal: [1962] Crim. L.R. 382.

[47] For a case where the court has refused such an informal application see *Ex p. Askew* [1963] Crim. L.R. 507. The text of the form letter sent to prisoners to explain the procedure is given in Drewry, Hughes and Shaw, op. cit., at 166–7.

circumstances.[48] In the situation of informal written applications, the court does not decide the case at all, but simply determines whether the prisoner's letter indicates grounds for an application to be made.

(b) *Practice in other Jurisdictions*

Courts in other jurisdictions have not spelled out their procedures with equal clarity, but it does appear that in Canada, prisoner applications are entertained.[49] In these cases, the English rule, requiring counsel, is not always followed, but on the other hand, the courts have said that they have a discretion to refuse to have the prisoner brought up for oral argument where the application is considered to be without merit.[50] This may be compared with the situation in the case of a criminal appeal where the prisoner may be given a statutory right to be present.[51] The Canadian courts do appear to treat all these applications as if formally made, and either grant or dismiss them on the merits just as if presented in strict accordance with the rules.

(c) *The Problems of Prisoner Applications*

It is submitted that the importance of maintaining means for prisoners to present habeas corpus applications is self-evident. It would be contradictory to proclaim the efficacy of the remedy of habeas corpus and at the same time to curtail access to it by people who are imprisoned. On the other hand there must be some way of limiting abuses by

[48] *Re Greene* [1941] W.N. 110. See further, *supra* pp. 222–4, where third party applications are discussed. See also *Practice Direction* [1962] Crim. L.R. 382, for a similar rule with regard to appeals to the House of Lords in habeas corpus matters.

[49] Although not always with great sympathy: see *Huculak* v. *Aitkens* (1969) 68 W.W.R. 82 at 83 (Sask. Q.B.): 'There is a large number of applications for prerogative writs originating in our penitentiaries and perhaps it should be pointed out that the law is not such a technical ass as many partially informed persons may think.'

[50] *Ex p. Durocher* [1966] 3 C.C.C. 397 (Ont. H.C.). *Ex p. Johnson* [1968] 4 C.C.C. 225 (B.C.C.A.) and *R.* v. *Olson* (1968) 63 W.W.R. 46 (B.C.S.C.) both held that the prisoner was entitled to notice of the day the application is to be considered so that he might apply through the court register for a judge's order that he be brought up for hearing if the judge considers this to be appropriate. In *Ex p. Karchesky* [1967] 3 C.C.C. 272 (S.C.C.) a prisoner's application was entertained without oral argument from the prisoner, he having consented to have the application determined on the basis of the written material, but in *Morrison* v. *R.* [1966] S.C.R. 356, the prisoner's application was dismissed and his request to be allowed to present oral argument was refused as the material filed clearly disclosed no ground for relief. In *R.* v. *Olson* (1987) 38 C.C.C. (3d) 534 (Ont. C.A.) it was held that where the written material disclosed a serious legal issue to be determined, the prisoner should be given the right to appear in court to argue the case.

[51] *R.* v. *Dunleavey* [1901] 1 K.B. 200; *Smith* v. *R.* [1966] 1 C.C.C. 162 (S.C.C.); *Frederick* v. *R.* [1966] 4 C.C.C. 146 (S.C.C.).

litigious prisoners, or prisoners who are bored and simply hope to obtain relief from the monotony of prison life.

The English practice probably works very well in cases where the prisoner's own material discloses an arguable case. In such a case, the prisoner will have the benefit of a proper application and the advice of counsel. However, not all prisoners will be able to phrase their applications clearly in writing, and there may well be deserving cases which appear to be without merit on the basis of the prisoner's written material. In an analogous situation, the Widgery Commission on Legal Aid in 1966 found that the inability of prisoners to frame their own notices of appeal properly was a source of some injustice.[52]

Moreover, the rule that a formal application may only be made by counsel is open to criticism. It is difficult to see why a prisoner capable of setting out the written material in a legally satisfactory way should be forced to have counsel for the oral argument. Ordinarily, litigants are permitted to appear and to represent themselves in judicial proceedings.[53] It has been held in one case, however, that the 'mere fact that an applicant prefers to act as his own advocate should not be regarded as good ground' to depart from the normal practice.[54] The courts undoubtedly fear getting into the position of having to hear a large number of prisoners present frivolous applications, but this seems unlikely to happen if the written applications are properly screened.

The maintenance of a channel for prisoner applications may, however, be more important in principle than in practice. Any conceivable system to have prisoner applications judicially considered must involve screening at some level on the basis of written material, and the difficulty of some prisoners in this regard has already been noted. The more important issue is perhaps the accessibility of legal advice to prisoners. Following a series of challenges to the European Court of Human Rights, the Prison Rules were amended to remove certain restrictions on prisoners' access to legal advice.[55] The English courts have also strictly limited the powers of prison authorities to interfere

[52] *Report of the Departmental Committee on Legal Aid in Criminal Proceedings* (1966: Cmnd. 2934), pp. 64–5.

[53] 3 Hals. (4th), 635.

[54] *Re Greene* [1941] W.N. 110.

[55] *Knechtl* v. *United Kingdom* [1970] 13 Yearbook 730; *Golder* v. *United Kingdom* (1975) 1 E.H.R.R. 524; *Silver* v. *The United Kingdom* (1983) 5 E.H.R.R. 347; *Reed* v. *United Kingdom* (1981) 5 E.H.R.R. 165; *Campbell and Fell* v. *United Kingdom* (1984) 7 E.H.R.R. 165.

with communication between prisoners and solicitors,[56] although the
Prison Rules and Standing Orders still confer a discretion on prison
authorities to interfere with solicitor–client communications which is
unduly restrictive.[57]

5. WHEN APPLICATIONS MAY BE MADE

If circumstances require, an application for habeas corpus may be
made to a judge at any time of the day or night,[58] or on Sunday.[59] In
such cases, there has usually been the fear that the prisoner is to be
taken outside the jurisdiction. By bringing the question of the legality
of the detention before the courts, the prisoner is able to forestall
further action.

In court, habeas corpus matters enjoy precedence over all other
business.[60] This is designed to ensure a speedy determination of the
question, but in this context it should be noted that the rules of court
require, in the ordinary course, at least eight days notice to parties
concerned.[61]

[56] *Raymond* v. *Honey* [1983] 1 A.C. 1; *R.* v. *Secretary of State for the Home Department,
ex p. Anderson* [1984] 1 All E.R. 920. See also *Solosky* v. *The Queen* [1980] 1 S.C.R. 821;
but cf. *Guilfoyle* v. *the Home Office* [1981] 1 Q.B. 309 (C.A.).

[57] See Zellick, 'Legal Services for Convicted Prisoners' (1977–8) 16 Howard J. of
Pen. 65; 'Prisoner's Complaints and Access to Lawyers' [1984] P.L. 341; 37 Hals. (4th),
776–7.

[58] See e.g. *R.* v. *Secretary of State for Home Affairs, ex p. Soblen* [1962] 3 All E.R. 373,
where Mocatta J. said that he had made an order for the issue of the writ 'in the very
early hours of the morning'.

[59] In *Re N.* [1967] 1 All E.R. 161, Stamp J. granted an interim injunction on a
Sunday, taking as authority the idea that habeas corpus could be issued at any time:
Crowley's Case (1818) 2 Swanst. 1 at 48.

[60] *Supreme Court Practice* (1988), 811.   [61] r.2(2).

Table of Statutes

STATUTORY INSTRUMENTS

RULES OF THE SUPREME COURT

Table of Cases

Index